Best RECIPES Ever

TRANSCONTINENTAL BOOKS

1100 René-Lévesque Boulevard West
24th Floor
Montreal, Que. H3B 4X9
Tel: 514-340-3587
Toll-free: 1-866-800-2500
canadianliving.com

Bibliothèque et Archives nationales
du Québec and Library and Archives
Canada cataloguing in publication

Main entry under title :
Canadian living best recipes ever : fresh, fun and
tasty tested-till-perfect recipes from the hit show
Includes index.
ISBN 978-0-9813938-4-1
1. Quick and easy cookery. 2. Low budget cookery.
I. Canadian Living Test Kitchen.

TX833.5.C36 2011   641.5'55   C2010-942529-4
Project editor: Christina Anson Mine
Content editor: Alison Kent
Copy editor: Austen Gilliland
Indexer: Gillian Watts
Art direction and design: Chris Bond
Content coordinator: Patrick Flynn

Printed in Canada
© Transcontinental Books and
Canadian Broadcasting Corporation, 2011
Legal deposit – 1st quarter 2011
National Library of Quebec
National Library of Canada
ISBN 978-0-9813938-4-1

We acknowledge the financial support of
our publishing activity by the Government
of Canada through the Canada Book Fund.

For information on special rates for
corporate libraries and wholesale purchases,
please call 1-866-800-2500.

Canadian Living

CBC

Best RECIPES Ever

FRESH, FUN & TASTY TESTED-TILL-PERFECT RECIPES FROM THE HIT SHOW

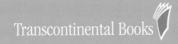

Transcontinental Books

Hey, *Best Recipes Ever* fans!

I have so much fun cooking with you every afternoon on our TV show. It's a thrill to teach you how to make great food that is fresh, fast and easy to prepare. But there wouldn't be a *Best Recipes Ever* without the delicious Tested-Till-Perfect recipes from our friends in The Canadian Living Test Kitchen.

Growing up, I can remember *Canadian Living*'s recipes being made in our kitchen – whenever we needed a quick dish to save us at dinnertime or a menu for a special occasion, the magazine was our go-to source for food ideas. And it's been inspiring Canadians for 35 years, so it's an honour to bring the pages of the magazine to life every day on our show.

Keeping you inspired in the kitchen is our job on *Best Recipes Ever.* We all want to eat more healthily and serve delicious food to our families and friends, but with our busy lives, this can be tricky to juggle. We love to help you find meal solutions that get food on the table fast, leaving you time to enjoy meals with your guests.

In each episode of *Best Recipes Ever,* I choose my favourite Tested-Till-Perfect recipes from the *Canadian Living* library and provide meal and menu options that solve everyday food challenges. This cookbook brings together the best-of-the-best recipes we've made on the show so far.

From weeknight dinners to weekend entertaining, you'll find a recipe in these pages to fit every occasion. If you need a quick meal before hockey practice, check out the "Beat the Clock" chapter (page 8). Need a holiday dinner with all the trimmings? Just refer to the "Party Fare" chapter (page 204). There are mouth-watering recipes for finger foods, main dishes, entertaining menus, everyday favourites and even some indulgent desserts for when you deserve a sweet treat.

Along with the incredible selection of recipes in this book, you'll also find loads of great tips that will save you time, energy and money in the kitchen. Who doesn't want that? Plus, *Canadian Living* has included plenty of ingredient substitutions that will give you options for how to use last night's leftovers and show you how to create a meal from what's in your pantry.

Enjoy the best recipes ever – from our kitchen to yours!

All the *Best,*
Kary Osmond

a note from Kary

beat the clock

meat-lover mains

around the world

lighten up!

contents

beat the clock

Grilled Chicken Niçoise Salad

Although Nice is in France, its namesake ingredients (olives, tomatoes and olive oil) are familiar in salads the world over. You can also broil or use a grill pan to cook the chicken.

4 **boneless skinless chicken breasts**

8 oz (250 g) **green beans,** trimmed

2 **tomatoes,** cut into 8 wedges each

4 cups (1 L) torn **Boston lettuce** or Bibb lettuce

⅓ cup (75 mL) **pitted black olives**

FRENCH DRESSING:

¼ cup (60 mL) **extra-virgin olive oil**

2 tbsp (30 mL) **white wine vinegar**

2 tsp (10 mL) **lemon juice**

1 tsp (5 mL) **granulated sugar**

½ tsp (2 mL) **herbes de Provence** or dried thyme

½ tsp (2 mL) **paprika**

¼ tsp (1 mL) each **salt** and **pepper**

French Dressing: In jar with lid, shake together oil, vinegar, lemon juice, sugar, herbes de Provence, paprika, salt and pepper. Pour 3 tbsp (45 mL) into bowl; add chicken and turn to coat. Marinate for 10 minutes.

Place chicken on greased grill over medium-high heat; close cover and grill, turning once, until no longer pink inside, about 12 minutes. Slice thinly.

Meanwhile, in saucepan of boiling salted water, cover and blanch green beans until tender-crisp, about 2 minutes. Drain and chill in cold water; drain well.

In large bowl, toss together green beans, tomato wedges, lettuce, olives and remaining dressing; divide salad among plates. Arrange chicken alongside.

Makes 4 servings.

PER SERVING: about 301 cal, 28 g pro, 17 g total fat (3 g sat. fat), 11 g carb, 3 g fibre, 67 mg chol, 425 mg sodium. % RDI: 6% calcium, 16% iron, 15% vit A, 37% vit C, 32% folate.

dinner on the run

Ham and Egg Pasta

Based on classic Italian spaghetti alla carbonara, this simple and satisfying dish is a delicious way to use up leftover ham, and it's the perfect dinner option for busy nights when time is tight.

1 tsp (5 mL) **vegetable oil**

1¾ cups (425 mL) **diced ham** (about 8 oz/250 g)

1 **onion,** chopped

4 cloves **garlic,** minced

3 **eggs**

½ tsp (2 mL) **salt**

1 lb (500 g) **spaghetti**

2 cups (500 mL) packed trimmed **fresh spinach**

½ cup (125 mL) grated **Parmesan cheese**

2 tbsp (30 mL) chopped **fresh parsley**

In skillet, heat oil over medium-high heat; fry ham, stirring occasionally, until golden, about 5 minutes.

Add onion and garlic; cook over medium heat, stirring occasionally, until softened, about 5 minutes. Set aside.

Lightly beat eggs with salt; set aside.

Meanwhile, in large pot of boiling salted water, cook spaghetti until al dente, 8 to 10 minutes. Add spinach. Reserving ½ cup (125 mL) of the cooking liquid, drain and return to pot over medium heat.

Immediately stir in Parmesan cheese, parsley, ham mixture and reserved cooking liquid. Stir in egg mixture; toss until sauce is opaque and pasta is coated, about 30 seconds.

Makes 4 to 6 servings.

PER EACH OF 6 SERVINGS: about 443 cal, 26 g pro, 10 g total fat (4 g sat. fat), 60 g carb, 4 g fibre, 123 mg chol, 1,227 mg sodium. % RDI: 16% calcium, 2% iron, 20% vit A, 8% vit C, 68% folate.

Easy Pita Pizzas

2 slices **bacon,** chopped

½ cup (125 mL) small **broccoli florets**

4 **Greek-style pitas** (pocketless) or pocket-style pita breads

¾ cup (175 mL) **pasta sauce** or pizza sauce

16 thin slices **pepperoni** (about 1 oz/30 g), optional

8 **pimiento-stuffed green olives,** sliced

4 **mushrooms,** sliced

Half **sweet red pepper,** chopped

1½ cups (375 mL) shredded **part-skim mozzarella cheese**

In small skillet over medium-high heat, fry bacon, stirring, until almost crisp, about 3 minutes. Drain on paper towel-lined plate, patting off fat on top.

Meanwhile, in small saucepan of boiling water, cook broccoli for 2 minutes. Drain.

Arrange pitas on large baking sheet. Spread each with sauce almost to edge. Top each with one-quarter each of the bacon, broccoli, pepperoni (if using), olives, mushrooms, red pepper and cheese.

Bake in bottom third of 450°F (230°C) oven until bottoms are golden and cheese is melted, 10 to 12 minutes.

Makes 4 servings.

PER SERVING: about 372 cal, 20 g pro, 13 g total fat (6 g sat. fat), 44 g carb, 3 g fibre, 26 mg chol, 1,205 mg sodium. % RDI: 35% calcium, 19% iron, 20% vit A, 57% vit C, 27% folate.

best tips:

Cook extra bacon, then crumble and freeze it in an airtight container or resealable bag. Simply thaw and sprinkle on salads, pizzas or pasta, or add to omelettes or frittatas.

Beef and Broccoli Stir-Fry Serve over hot cooked rice noodles or steamed rice.

12 oz (375 g) **flank marinating steak** or top sirloin grilling
   steak, thinly sliced across the grain

3 tbsp (45 mL) **oyster sauce**

4 cups (1 L) **broccoli florets** (about 2 stalks)

2 cloves **garlic,** minced

1 tbsp (15 mL) minced **gingerroot**

Sprinkle steak with ¼ tsp (1 mL) pepper; set aside.

In small bowl, whisk together ¾ cup (175 mL) water, oyster
sauce and 1 tbsp (15 mL) cornstarch; set aside.

In wok or skillet, heat 1 tbsp (15 mL) vegetable oil over
medium-high heat; stir-fry steak until browned but still pink
inside, about 3 minutes. Transfer to plate.

Add 1 tbsp (15 mL) vegetable oil to wok; stir-fry broccoli
florets, garlic and ginger for 1 minute. Cover and steam for
2 minutes.

Return beef and any accumulated juices to wok. Add
oyster sauce mixture; stir-fry until slightly thickened, about
3 minutes.

Makes 4 servings.

PER SERVING: about 253 cal, 21 g pro, 15 g total fat (4 g sat. fat),
8 g carb, trace fibre, 36 mg chol, 436 mg sodium. % RDI: 4% calcium,
16% iron, 20% vit A, 67% vit C, 19% folate.

Vaguely Coq au Vin

Serve this browned then wine-simmered chicken with sautéed mushrooms and boiled new potatoes.

8 **chicken thighs** (2 lb/1 kg total)

¼ cup (60 mL) **all-purpose flour**

2¼ tsp (11 mL) **dried thyme**

6 small **onions,** quartered

1 cup (250 mL) **dry white wine**

Pull skin off chicken and discard. In bag, shake together flour, 2 tsp (10 mL) of the thyme and ½ tsp (2 mL) each salt and pepper. Add chicken, in batches, and shake to coat.

In large skillet or Dutch oven, heat 1 tbsp (15 mL) olive oil over medium-high heat; brown chicken on both sides, adding more oil if necessary. Transfer to plate.

Drain off fat in pan; reduce heat to medium. Cook onions, stirring occasionally and adding more oil if necessary, until golden and softened, about 5 minutes.

Return chicken to skillet; pour wine over top. Cover and simmer, turning once, until juices run clear when chicken is pierced, about 20 minutes. Transfer to platter and keep warm.

Add remaining thyme and ¼ tsp (1 mL) each salt and pepper to pan juices; boil until thickened, about 5 minutes. Pour over chicken.

Makes 4 servings.

PER SERVING: about 262 cal, 24 g pro, 10 g total fat (2 g sat. fat), 16 g carb, 2 g fibre, 95 mg chol, 534 mg sodium. % RDI: 5% calcium, 20% iron, 2% vit A, 13% vit C, 17% folate.

best tips:

Use whatever bone-in chicken pieces you like. If you prefer to leave the skin on while cooking, then by all means do so. If you have fresh thyme, use 4 tsp (20 mL) in place of the dried.

Pork Chops With Balsamic Sauce and Mashed Sweet Potatoes

2 tbsp (30 mL) **extra-virgin olive oil**

2 tsp (10 mL) **dried Italian herb seasoning**

4 **pork loin centre chops**

2 tbsp (30 mL) **balsamic vinegar**

¾ cup (175 mL) **sodium-reduced chicken broth**

Mix together oil, Italian herb seasoning and pinch salt; brush over chops. In skillet, fry chops over medium-high heat until browned and just a hint of pink remains inside, about 4 minutes per side. Transfer to plate; keep warm.

Drain off any fat in pan; add balsamic vinegar. Simmer over medium heat for 30 seconds. Whisk 1 tsp (5 mL) cornstarch into broth; add to pan and bring to boil, stirring and scraping up any browned bits. Reduce heat and simmer until thickened, about 1 minute. Return chops and any juices to pan; heat through, turning to coat. Serve with Mashed Sweet Potatoes (below).

Makes 4 servings.

PER SERVING (WITH MASHED SWEET POTATOES): about 385 cal, 24 g pro, 16 g total fat (4 g sat. fat), 35 g carb, 3 g fibre, 66 mg chol, 231 mg sodium. % RDI: 6% calcium, 14% iron, 223% vit A, 42% vit C, 10% folate.

Mashed Sweet Potatoes: In large saucepan of boiling salted water, cover and cook 4 sweet potatoes, peeled and cubed, until tender, about 10 minutes. Drain and return to pot. Add ¼ cup (60 mL) sodium-reduced chicken broth and ½ tsp (2 mL) pepper; mash until smooth. Serve sprinkled with 2 green onions, sliced.

Makes 4 servings.

Bok Choy and Pork Stir-Fry

Five-spice powder is an aromatic Chinese spice blend. It is a combination of cinnamon, cloves, fennel, star anise and Szechuan peppercorns.

1 **pork tenderloin** (about 12 oz/375 g)

1 tbsp (15 mL) **cornstarch**

1 tbsp (15 mL) each **soy sauce** and **hoisin sauce**

2 tbsp (30 mL) **vegetable oil**

6 **baby bok choy,** halved lengthwise

3 **green onions,** sliced

½ tsp (2 mL) **five-spice powder**

1 clove **garlic,** minced

2 tsp (10 mL) grated **gingerroot**

Pinch **hot pepper flakes**

4 cups (1 L) hot **cooked rice**

Thinly slice pork tenderloin crosswise; set aside.

Whisk together ¾ cup (175 mL) water, cornstarch, soy sauce and hoisin sauce; set aside.

In wok or large skillet, heat half of the oil over high heat; stir-fry pork, in batches, until browned, about 3 minutes. Transfer to bowl.

Add remaining oil to wok. Stir-fry bok choy, green onions, five-spice powder, garlic, ginger and hot pepper flakes until greens are wilted, about 3 minutes.

Return pork and any accumulated juices to pan. Add soy sauce mixture; stir-fry until sauce is thickened, about 1 minute. Serve over rice.

Makes 4 servings.

PER SERVING: about 473 cal, 28 g pro, 10 g total fat (1 g sat. fat), 66 g carb, 3 g fibre, 50 mg chol, 410 mg sodium. % RDI: 14% calcium, 22% iron, 31% vit A, 55% vit C, 30% folate.

20-minute mains

Roasted Salmon With Prosciutto

¼ cup (60 mL) **Dijon mustard**

2 tbsp (30 mL) chopped **fresh chives** or green onions

¼ tsp (1 mL) **pepper**

4 **skinless salmon fillets** (each 6 oz/175 g)

4 thin slices **prosciutto** (about 2 oz/60 g)

Mix together mustard, chives and pepper; spread over both sides of salmon.

Place each fish fillet, bottom side down, on prosciutto slice; wrap around fish. Secure with toothpicks.

Place fish fillets, prosciutto seam side up, on parchment paper-lined baking sheet; roast in 425°F (220°C) oven until fish flakes easily when tested, 10 to 15 minutes. Remove toothpicks.

Makes 4 servings.

PER SERVING: about 311 cal, 33 g pro, 19 g total fat (4 g sat. fat), 1 g carb, 0 g fibre, 91 mg chol, 463 mg sodium. % RDI: 4% calcium, 6% iron, 3% vit A, 8% vit C, 21% folate.

best tips: You can use another firm-fleshed fish, such as halibut or trout, in place of the salmon. Choose thicker, centre-cut fillets, if available, and wide slices of prosciutto for maximum coverage.

Turkey Piccata

Traditionally, piccata consists of seasoned and floured veal that's sautéed and served with a quick lemony sauce. It's equally delicious made with turkey.

1 **egg**

½ cup (125 mL) **all-purpose flour**

2 tsp (10 mL) grated **lemon rind**

½ tsp (2 mL) **salt**

½ tsp (2 mL) **dried thyme**

¼ tsp (1 mL) **pepper**

4 pieces **turkey scaloppine** (1 lb/500 g)

2 tsp (10 mL) **butter**

2 tsp (10 mL) **olive oil**

2 tsp (10 mL) chopped **fresh parsley**

Lemon wedges

In shallow dish, beat egg. In separate shallow dish, combine flour, lemon rind, salt, thyme and pepper. One piece at a time, dip turkey into egg to coat; press into flour mixture, turning to coat and shaking off any excess.

In nonstick skillet, heat half each of the butter and oil over medium heat; cook half of the turkey, turning once, until no longer pink inside, about 6 minutes.

Drain any fat from pan; repeat with remaining butter, oil and turkey. Garnish with parsley; serve with lemon wedges.

Makes 4 servings.

PER SERVING: about 232 cal, 28 g pro, 8 g total fat (3 g sat. fat), 11 g carb, 1 g fibre, 110 mg chol, 356 mg sodium, 394 mg potassium. % RDI: 2% calcium, 16% iron, 4% vit A, 3% vit C, 19% folate.

best tips:

• Scaloppine is a thin, flattened cut of meat. If unavailable, turn 1 lb (500 g) turkey cutlets into thin pieces by pounding between waxed paper with a mallet to ¼-inch (5 mm) thickness.

• Because it's so thin, scaloppine cooks up in a flash, which saves time on busy nights. Look for veal, pork, chicken or turkey scaloppine at the meat counter.

Chicken, Snow Peas and Cashew Stir-Fry

Stir-fries are quick, healthy and popular with kids and adults alike. Serve with quick-cooking Asian noodles, such as chow mein or rice vermicelli, or over hot cooked rice.

3 tbsp (45 mL) **soy sauce**

4 tsp (20 mL) **cornstarch**

1 tbsp (15 mL) **granulated sugar**

1 tbsp (15 mL) **dry sherry** or chicken broth

1 tsp (5 mL) **sesame oil**

Dash **hot pepper sauce**

1 lb (500 g) **boneless skinless chicken thighs** or breasts

1 cup (250 mL) **snow peas** (4 oz/125 g)

1 **sweet red pepper**

1 tbsp (15 mL) **vegetable oil** or peanut oil

⅓ cup (75 mL) **roasted cashews**

1 clove **garlic,** sliced

1 piece (2 inches/5 cm) **gingerroot,** sliced

Whisk together soy sauce, cornstarch, sugar, sherry, sesame oil and hot pepper sauce. Cut chicken into bite-size pieces.

Trim and remove strings from snow peas; cut diagonally in half. Seed, core and cut red pepper into bite-size chunks.

In wok or large skillet, heat vegetable oil over high heat; stir-fry chicken, in batches, until browned, about 3 minutes. Transfer to plate.

Add snow peas, red pepper, cashews, garlic and ginger to wok; cover and steam until red pepper is tender-crisp, about 2 minutes.

Return chicken and any accumulated juices to pan; toss to combine. Stir in soy sauce mixture; simmer until glossy, about 1 minute.

Makes 4 servings.

PER SERVING: about 303 cal, 25 g pro, 16 g total fat (3 g sat. fat), 15 g carb, 2 g fibre, 94 mg chol, 876 mg sodium. % RDI: 3% calcium, 18% iron, 13% vit A, 102% vit C, 12% folate.

more 20-minute mains

Spaghetti Carbonara

This dish is a super-quick one-pot dinner made with staples you probably have on hand already.

4 slices **bacon,** chopped

1 small **onion,** chopped

2 cloves **garlic,** minced

4 **eggs**

¼ cup (60 mL) grated **Parmesan cheese**

2 tbsp (30 mL) chopped **fresh parsley**

¼ tsp (1 mL) each **salt** and **pepper**

12 oz (375 g) **spaghetti**

In large skillet, fry bacon over medium heat until crisp, about 5 minutes. Drain off fat. Add onion and garlic to pan; fry until softened, about 4 minutes. Meanwhile, whisk together eggs, cheese, parsley, salt and pepper; set aside.

Meanwhile in large pot of boiling salted water, cook pasta until al dente, 8 to 10 minutes. Drain; return to pot over low heat. Immediately stir in bacon and egg mixtures; heat, stirring, until sauce is opaque and pasta is coated, 30 seconds.

Makes 4 servings.

PER SERVING: about 482 cal, 22 g pro, 14 g total fat (5 g sat. fat), 66 g carb, 4 g fibre, 200 mg chol, 628 mg sodium. % RDI: 11% calcium, 29% iron, 9% vit A, 5% vit C, 92% folate.

best tips:

If you want to omit the first step of cooking the bacon, you can substitute 6 oz (175 g) prosciutto, chopped. Add to the egg mixture.

Rosemary Lamb Chops With Lentil Salad

3 cloves **garlic,** minced

1 tbsp (15 mL) chopped **fresh rosemary**
  (or 1 tsp/5 mL dried)

1 tsp (5 mL) coarsely ground **pepper**

½ tsp (2 mL) **salt**

8 **lamb loin chops** or 4 lamb shoulder chops
  (about 1½ lb/750 g)

Lemon wedges

LENTIL SALAD:

1 can (19 oz/540 mL) **lentils**

½ cup (125 mL) chopped **tomatoes**

¼ cup (60 mL) chopped **fresh parsley**

2 tbsp (30 mL) **sherry vinegar** or wine vinegar

1 tbsp (15 mL) **extra-virgin olive oil**

Lentil Salad: Drain and rinse lentils. Toss together lentils, tomatoes, parsley, vinegar and oil; set aside.

Mix together garlic, rosemary, pepper and salt; rub all over chops. Place on greased grill or in grill pan over medium-high heat or under broiler; close lid and grill or broil until desired doneness, about 4 minutes per side for medium-rare. Serve with lentil salad and lemon wedges.

Makes 4 servings.

PER SERVING: about 277 cal, 27 g pro, 9 g total fat (3 g sat. fat), 23 g carb, 5 g fibre, 68 mg chol, 562 mg sodium. % RDI: 4% calcium, 38% iron, 4% vit A, 18% vit C, 86% folate.

best tips:

• Choose your chop: lamb loin is thicker and more tender than the chewy, steak-flavoured shoulder. Either one cooks quickly and has lots of flavour.

• If you have fresh mint, replace half of the parsley with 2 tbsp (30 mL) chopped fresh mint leaves.

Braised Beef in Wine

Known as *boeuf en daube*, this traditional Provençale dish of beef marinated in wine is braised in a sealed casserole. The optional – but highly recommended – pig's foot (trotter) gives the sauce extra body; ask the butcher to halve it lengthwise for you.

3 lb (1.5 kg) **beef blade boneless pot roast**

1 **pig's foot,** halved (optional)

1¼ cups (300 mL) **dry red wine** or dry white wine

2 tsp (10 mL) **dried thyme**

½ tsp (2 mL) each **salt** and **pepper**

8 slices lean **thick-cut bacon,** coarsely chopped

1 can (28 oz/796 mL) **whole tomatoes**

2 cups (500 mL) halved **mushrooms**

2 cups (500 mL) thickly sliced **carrots**

½ cup (125 mL) chopped **fresh parsley**

2 **onions,** chopped

4 cloves **garlic,** minced

2 **bay leaves**

2 strips (each 3 x 1 inches/8 x 2.5 cm) **orange rind**

¼ cup (60 mL) **tomato paste**

1 cup (250 mL) **all-purpose flour**

Cut beef into 8 chunks; place in nonmetallic bowl. Add pig's foot (if using), wine, thyme, salt and pepper; mix well. Cover and marinate in refrigerator for 24 hours, turning occasionally.

Sprinkle half of the bacon in large Dutch oven or tall covered casserole. Place remaining bacon in large bowl. Drain and halve tomatoes; squeeze out seeds. Add seeded tomatoes to bowl along with mushrooms, carrots, parsley, onions and garlic; mix well.

With slotted spoon, arrange pig's foot (if using) and half of the beef over bacon in Dutch oven; cover with half of the tomato mixture. Add bay leaves and orange rind. Repeat layers of beef and tomato mixture. Whisk tomato paste into marinade; pour into Dutch oven.

In bowl, mix flour with ½ cup (125 mL) water to make stiff paste. Cover Dutch oven with lid; with floured hands, press paste onto edge of lid and Dutch oven to seal. Bake in 400°F (200°C) oven for 20 minutes. Reduce heat to 250°F (120°C); bake for 4 hours.

Remove seal from pot. Skim off fat; discard bay leaves and orange rind.

Makes 6 to 8 servings.

PER EACH OF 8 SERVINGS: about 447 cal, 40 g pro, 20 g total fat (10 g sat. fat), 24 g carb, 3 g fibre, 105 mg chol, 552 mg sodium. % RDI: 7% calcium, 44% iron, 76% vit A, 33% vit C, 21% folate.

one-pot wonders

Upside-Down Nacho Bake This quick, tasty, kid-friendly meal starts out on the stove then finishes baking in the oven.

1 lb (500 g) **lean ground beef** or turkey

½ cup (125 mL) chopped **onion**

2 cloves **garlic,** minced

1 **jalapeño pepper,** seeded and minced

1 **sweet green pepper** or sweet red pepper, chopped

1 tsp (5 mL) **ground cumin**

½ tsp (2 mL) each **salt** and **pepper**

½ tsp (2 mL) **dried oregano**

1 can (19 oz/540 mL) **black beans,** drained and rinsed

1 can (28 oz/796 mL) **diced tomatoes**

⅓ cup (75 mL) **tomato paste**

1 cup (250 mL) **corn kernels**

1 cup (250 mL) crumbled **baked tortilla chips** or corn chips

¾ cup (175 mL) shredded **Cheddar cheese**

1 **green onion,** thinly sliced

In large ovenproof nonstick skillet, sauté beef over medium-high heat, breaking up with spoon, until no longer pink, about 5 minutes.

Drain fat from pan; cook chopped onion, garlic, jalapeño pepper, green pepper, cumin, salt, pepper and oregano over medium heat until onion is softened, about 3 minutes. Add black beans, tomatoes and tomato paste; bring to boil. Reduce heat and simmer, stirring occasionally, until slightly thickened, about 10 minutes. Stir in corn.

Sprinkle with tortilla chips and Cheddar cheese; bake in 375°F (190°C) oven until cheese is melted, about 15 minutes. Sprinkle with green onion.

Makes 4 servings.

PER SERVING: about 628 cal, 40 g pro, 26 g total fat (12 g sat. fat), 62 g carb, 13 g fibre, 86 mg chol, 1,412 mg sodium. % RDI: 30% calcium, 51% iron, 29% vit A, 115% vit C, 47% folate.

best tips:
• To make a skillet ovenproof, wrap the handle with foil.
• Baked tortilla chips are lower in fat than fried, but you can use the fried ones (or even broken tostadas or taco shells) if you prefer.

Potato Fish Chowder

2 tbsp (30 mL) **butter**

1 small **leek** (white and light green parts only), diced

1 each **onion** and rib **celery,** diced

1 **bay leaf**

1 clove **garlic,** minced

Half **sweet red pepper,** diced

¼ tsp (1 mL) **salt**

¼ tsp (1 mL) **paprika**

3 tbsp (45 mL) **all-purpose flour**

2 bottles (each 240 mL) **clam juice**

1 **Yukon Gold potato,** peeled, quartered and cut in
     ¼-inch (5 mm) thick slices

1½ cups (375 mL) **milk**

12 oz (375 g) **halibut fillet** or other firm-fleshed fish, cut into
     1-inch (2.5 cm) chunks

2 tbsp (30 mL) chopped **fresh parsley**

In Dutch oven, melt butter over medium-high heat; cook
leek, onion, celery, bay leaf, garlic, red pepper and salt,
stirring often, until leek and onion are softened, about
5 minutes. Stir in paprika.

Add flour; cook, stirring, for 2 minutes. Stir in clam juice;
bring to boil. Add potato; cover and simmer over medium
heat until tender, about 10 minutes.

Add milk; return to simmer. Add fish; simmer until fish flakes
easily when tested, about 5 minutes. Discard bay leaf.
Sprinkle with parsley, and bacon (if using).

Makes 6 to 8 servings.

PER EACH OF 8 SERVINGS: about 126 cal, 10 g pro, 4 g total fat
(2 g sat. fat), 12 g carb, 1 g fibre, 31 mg chol, 272 mg sodium. % RDI:
7% calcium, 6% iron, 10% vit A, 28% vit C, 10% folate.

**best
tips:**

For added flavour and
texture, garnish with cooked
and crumbled bacon,
prosciutto or pancetta.

Chicken Noodle Stir-Fry

Broccoli florets can replace bok choy, and sodium-reduced chicken broth can replace water, in this quick and tasty dish.

6 **boneless skinless chicken thighs** or breasts

1 tbsp (15 mL) **sodium-reduced soy sauce**

1 tbsp (15 mL) **sesame oil**

¼ tsp (1 mL) **pepper**

2 cloves **garlic,** minced

1 lb (500 g) **baby bok choy**

2 tbsp (30 mL) **vegetable oil**

1 **sweet red pepper,** thinly sliced

1 tsp (5 mL) minced **gingerroot**

2 pkg (each 3½ oz/100 g) **dried ramen noodles**

¼ cup (60 mL) **hoisin sauce**

1 **green onion,** thinly sliced

Cut chicken into cubes. Toss together chicken, soy sauce, sesame oil, pepper and half of the garlic; marinate for 10 minutes.

Cut baby bok choy in half lengthwise; set aside.

In wok or large skillet, heat 1 tbsp (15 mL) of the vegetable oil over high heat; stir-fry chicken until browned and juices run clear when chicken is pierced, about 3 minutes.

Add bok choy, red pepper, ginger and remaining garlic; stir-fry until tender-crisp, about 2 minutes. Transfer to plate.

Add 1½ cups (375 mL) water and remaining vegetable oil to wok; bring to boil. Discarding spice packets in packages, add noodles to wok; cover and steam until softened and loose, about 3 minutes. Break noodles apart with spoon.

Return chicken mixture to wok. Add hoisin sauce and green onion; toss together until hot and combined.

Makes 4 servings.

PER SERVING: about 508 cal, 25 g pro, 25 g total fat (7 g sat. fat), 46 g carb, 5 g fibre, 72 mg chol, 534 mg sodium. % RDI: 14% calcium, 24% iron, 64% vit A, 140% vit C, 34% folate.

one-pot mains

Broccoli and Cheddar Frittata

This one-pan dish is prepped, cooked and on the table in about 20 minutes – perfect for weeknights.

1 tbsp (15 mL) **butter**

2 cups (500 mL) chopped **broccoli florets** and **stems**

1 **onion,** chopped

1 **sweet red pepper,** chopped

2 cloves **garlic,** minced

½ tsp (2 mL) each **salt** and **pepper**

8 **eggs**

¼ cup (60 mL) **milk**

½ cup (125 mL) shredded **Cheddar cheese**

2 tbsp (30 mL) minced **fresh parsley**

In 9- or 10-inch (23 or 25 cm) nonstick skillet, melt butter over medium heat; cook broccoli, onion, red pepper, garlic, salt and pepper, stirring occasionally, until broccoli is tender-crisp, about 5 minutes.

Whisk eggs with milk; pour over broccoli mixture. Cover and cook over medium-low heat until bottom and side are firm but top is still slightly runny, about 7 minutes.

Sprinkle with cheese; cover and cook until centre is set and cheese is melted, about 3 minutes. Sprinkle with parsley.

Makes 4 to 6 servings.

PER EACH OF 6 SERVINGS: about 179 cal, 12 g pro, 12 g total fat (5 g sat. fat), 6 g carb, 1 g fibre, 265 mg chol, 365 mg sodium. % RDI: 12% calcium, 9% iron, 28% vit A, 95% vit C, 25% folate.

best tips:

Versatile frittatas are the ideal way to use up leftover veggies, bits of cheese and cooked meat. Experiment to find your favourite frittata flavour combination.

Peel-and-Eat Shrimp Boil

Serve with crusty bread or dinner rolls, and a leafy green salad.

3 **bay leaves**

1 **onion,** quartered

1 **lemon,** cut in 6 wedges

4 cloves **garlic,** smashed

½ tsp (2 mL) each **salt** and **black peppercorns**

6 small **red potatoes** (1 lb/500 g), halved

4 cobs **corn,** shucked and halved crosswise

6 oz (175 g) **narrow kielbasa sausage,** cut into 1-inch (2.5 cm) thick slices (optional)

1 lb (500 g) large or jumbo **shrimp** (with shells)

2 tbsp (30 mL) minced **fresh parsley**

GARLIC BUTTER:

⅓ cup (75 mL) **butter,** melted

1 clove **garlic,** minced

Pour enough water into large Dutch oven to come three-quarters up side. Add bay leaves, onion, 2 of the lemon wedges, garlic, salt and peppercorns; cover and bring to boil.

Add potatoes, corn, and kielbasa (if using); return to boil. Reduce heat and simmer, covered, until vegetables are almost tender, about 8 minutes.

Add shrimp; cook until pink, about 3 minutes. Drain well. Arrange on platter. Sprinkle with parsley. Garnish with remaining lemon wedges.

Garlic Butter: In small bowl, mix butter with garlic; serve warm alongside for dipping.

Makes 4 servings.

PER SERVING: about 458 cal, 24 g pro, 19 g total fat (10 g sat. fat), 54 g carb, 7 g fibre, 170 mg chol, 552 mg sodium. % RDI: 7% calcium, 28% iron, 21% vit A, 58% vit C, 39% folate.

best tips:

If available, choose "zipperback" shrimp, which are deveined but still in their shells.

Salmon Cakes

Serve these golden, crispy patties with lemon wedges to squeeze over top, or stir up a batch of Lemon Aïoli (below).

2 large **potatoes** (1 lb/500 g), peeled and quartered

3 **green onions,** thinly sliced

¼ cup (60 mL) chopped **fresh coriander** or parsley

1 tbsp (15 mL) **Dijon mustard**

½ tsp (2 mL) **salt**

¼ tsp (1 mL) grated **lemon rind**

¼ tsp (1 mL) **pepper**

¼ tsp (1 mL) **hot pepper sauce**

1 **egg,** beaten

2 cans (each 7½ oz/213 g) **salmon,** drained and flaked

2 tbsp (30 mL) **vegetable oil**

In saucepan of boiling salted water, cover and cook potatoes until tender, 15 to 20 minutes. Drain.

In large bowl, mash potatoes until smooth; stir in onions, coriander, mustard, salt, lemon rind, pepper and hot pepper sauce. Blend in egg. Fold in salmon. Let cool for 5 minutes. Using hands, shape into eight ¾-inch (2 cm) thick patties.

In large nonstick skillet, heat half of the oil over medium heat; cook half of the patties until golden, about 5 minutes per side. Repeat with remaining oil and patties.

Makes 4 servings.

PER SERVING: about 280 cal, 21 g pro, 14 g total fat (2 g sat. fat), 18 g carb, 2 g fibre, 78 mg chol, 709 mg sodium. % RDI: 23% calcium, 11% iron, 5% vit A, 17% vit C, 12% folate.

Lemon Aïoli: Whisk together ½ cup (125 mL) light mayonnaise; 1 clove garlic, minced; 1 tbsp (15 mL) each extra-virgin olive oil and lemon juice; 1 tbsp (15 mL) each minced dill pickle and sweet red pepper (optional); ¼ tsp (1 mL) salt; and dash hot pepper sauce.

Makes about ½ cup (125 mL).

Pantry Raid Three-Bean Salad

Use whatever canned beans you have on hand, including black beans, romano beans or lentils. Toss in cubed Cheddar cheese for additional protein.

3 cups (750 mL) cut (1 inch/2.5 cm) **green beans**

1 can (19 oz/540 mL) **chickpeas,** drained and rinsed

1 can (19 oz/540 mL) **kidney beans,** drained and rinsed

2 **green onions,** thinly sliced

¼ cup (60 mL) chopped **fresh parsley**

1 tbsp (15 mL) minced **jalapeño pepper**

VINAIGRETTE:

3 tbsp (45 mL) **vegetable oil**

3 tbsp (45 mL) **wine vinegar**

1 clove **garlic,** minced

1 tsp (5 mL) **dried oregano**

¼ tsp (1 mL) **salt**

¼ tsp (1 mL) **pepper**

Vinaigrette: In large bowl, whisk together oil, vinegar, garlic, oregano, salt and pepper; set aside.

In saucepan of boiling water, cover and cook green beans until tender-crisp, about 5 minutes. Drain; add to vinaigrette.

Add chickpeas, kidney beans, green onions, parsley and jalapeño pepper; toss to coat. Refrigerate until chilled, about 30 minutes, or cover and refrigerate for up to 24 hours.

Makes 6 to 8 servings.

PER EACH OF 8 SERVINGS: about 177 cal, 7 g pro, 6 g total fat (1 g sat. fat), 25 g carb, 8 g fibre, 0 mg chol, 389 mg sodium. % RDI: 5% calcium, 13% iron, 5% vit A, 17% vit C, 35% folate.

best tips:

**Our Top 5 Pantry Must-Haves:
1. Canned tomatoes.** Italian San Marzano tomatoes are the ultimate canned variety for authentic pasta sauces. You can also use canned tomatoes in soups and stews.

2. Canned kidney beans and chickpeas. Beans are great on a green salad as an easy protein source, or in curries to make them go further. Our best fast chickpea solution: hummus.

3. Garlic and onions. They are the start to almost every meal. Store them in a cool, dark place, such as the bottom shelf of the pantry (not under the sink, where temperatures fluctuate).

Puttanesca Sauce

This quick, robust tomato sauce makes enough for four servings of pasta. Cook about 1 lb (500 g) spaghetti or other pasta; drain and toss with sauce.

1 tbsp (15 mL) **extra-virgin olive oil**

4 cloves **garlic,** minced

½ tsp (2 mL) **dried oregano**

¼ tsp (1 mL) **hot pepper flakes**

4 **anchovy fillets,** chopped (or 2 tsp/10 mL anchovy paste)

1 can (28 oz/796 mL) **whole tomatoes**

½ cup (125 mL) **oil-cured olives,** halved and pitted

2 tbsp (30 mL) drained rinsed **capers**

¼ cup (60 mL) chopped **fresh parsley**

In large skillet, heat oil over medium heat; cook garlic, oregano, hot pepper flakes and anchovies, stirring occasionally, until garlic starts to colour, about 3 minutes.

Add tomatoes, breaking up with spoon. Add olives and capers; bring to boil. Reduce heat and simmer until thickened to consistency of salsa, about 10 minutes. Stir in parsley.

Makes 4 servings.

PER SERVING: about 141 cal, 4 g pro, 10 g total fat (1 g sat. fat), 12 g carb, 3 g fibre, 3 mg chol, 1,132 mg sodium. % RDI: 9% calcium, 14% iron, 14% vit A, 53% vit C, 8% folate.

4. Pasta or rice. These staples are truly versatile: pasta can be a main or side dish, and rice serves as a side dish or as an ingredient in soups, stir-fries, stews or chilies.

5. Tuna. If you've got a can of tuna, you've got sandwiches, a healthy salad or the base for a tuna casserole.

Vegetarian Chili Fries
Just about everyone loves fries and chili, and this appetizer-size vegetarian version lends a quick comfort note to any gathering.

2 lb (1 kg) **baking potatoes** (about 4), scrubbed

2 tbsp (30 mL) **olive oil**

½ tsp (2 mL) **salt**

¼ tsp (1 mL) **pepper**

CHILI:

2 tbsp (30 mL) **olive oil**

¼ cup (60 mL) each diced **onion, celery** and **carrot**

2 cloves **garlic,** minced

1 tsp (5 mL) each **chili powder** and **paprika**

¼ tsp (1 mL) each **hot pepper flakes, salt** and **pepper**

1 can (28 oz/796 mL) **diced tomatoes**

1 can (19 oz/540 mL) **red kidney beans,** drained and rinsed

GARNISH:

¾ cup (175 mL) shredded **Cheddar cheese**

½ cup (125 mL) **sour cream**

¼ cup (60 mL) thinly sliced **green onions** (green parts only)

Chili: In saucepan, heat oil over medium heat; cook onion, celery and carrot until softened, about 5 minutes.

Add garlic, chili powder, paprika, hot pepper flakes, salt and pepper; cook for 2 minutes. Add tomatoes; bring to boil and cook, stirring often, for 12 minutes.

Add beans; simmer over medium-low heat until slightly thickened, about 12 minutes.

Cut potatoes lengthwise into ½-inch (1 cm) thick slices. Cut lengthwise into ½-inch (1 cm) wide sticks. Soak in cold water for 5 minutes. Drain and pat dry.

In bowl, toss together potatoes, oil, salt and pepper; spread on 2 parchment paper–lined baking sheets. Bake in 425°F (220°C) oven, turning once, until crisp and golden, about 50 minutes. Divide among 12 small dishes.

Garnish: Top each dish with heaping 2 tbsp (30 mL) chili; sprinkle with 1 tbsp (15 mL) cheese. Dollop with sour cream; sprinkle with green onions.

Makes 12 appetizer-size servings.

PER SERVING: about 190 cal, 6 g pro, 9 g total fat (3 g sat. fat), 23 g carb, 5 g fibre, 11 mg chol, 403 mg sodium, 594 mg potassium. % RDI: 10% calcium, 14% iron, 10% vit A, 27% vit C, 20% folate.

recipes from the pantry

Mediterranean Tuna Patties

Couscous adds unique texture to these delicious patties. Serve with Lemon Yogurt Sauce (below), chopped tomato salad and wedges of Greek-style pita bread.

½ cup (125 mL) **whole wheat couscous**

1 tbsp (15 mL) **lemon juice**

1 tsp (5 mL) **ground cumin**

2 cans (each 6 oz/170 g) **water-packed flaked tuna,** drained

¼ cup (60 mL) chopped **Kalamata olives**

¼ cup (60 mL) chopped drained **oil-packed sun-dried tomatoes**

¼ cup (60 mL) **light mayonnaise**

2 cloves **garlic,** minced

2 **eggs,** lightly beaten

2 tbsp (30 mL) chopped **fresh parsley**

½ tsp (2 mL) each **salt** and **pepper**

2 tbsp (30 mL) **vegetable oil**

In large bowl, combine couscous, lemon juice and cumin; pour in ½ cup (125 mL) boiling water. Cover and let stand until water is absorbed, about 5 minutes. Fluff with fork. Let cool.

Add tuna, olives, tomatoes, mayonnaise, garlic, eggs, parsley, salt and pepper; toss with fork to combine.

With wet hands, form into six ¾-inch (2 cm) thick patties, pressing firmly. Cover and refrigerate until firm, about 30 minutes, or up to 24 hours.

In large nonstick skillet, heat oil over medium heat; fry patties, turning once, until golden, about 8 minutes.

Makes 6 servings.

PER SERVING: about 238 cal, 16 g pro, 13 g total fat (2 g sat. fat), 16 g carb, 3 g fibre, 79 mg chol, 635 mg sodium. % RDI: 3% calcium, 14% iron, 5% vit A, 12% vit C, 6% folate.

Lemon Yogurt Sauce: Stir together ⅓ cup (75 mL) Balkan-style plain yogurt, 3 tbsp (45 mL) light mayonnaise, 2 tbsp (30 mL) lemon juice and pinch salt.

Makes about ½ cup (125 mL).

Chocolate Coconut Mounds

2 **egg whites,** at room temperature

Pinch **salt**

1 tsp (5 mL) **vanilla**

¾ cup (175 mL) **granulated sugar**

3½ cups (875 mL) **sweetened shredded coconut**

4 oz (125 g) **bittersweet chocolate,** melted

In bowl, beat egg whites with salt until foamy; beat in vanilla. Beat in sugar, 2 tbsp (30 mL) at a time, until stiff peaks form.

Fold in coconut. Drop by 1 tbsp (15 mL), 1 inch (2.5 cm) apart, onto parchment paper–lined rimless baking sheet. Bake in 325°F (160°C) oven until edges are golden, about 18 minutes. Let cool on pan for 5 minutes; transfer to racks and let cool completely.

Line rimless baking sheet with parchment paper. Drizzle tops of cookies with chocolate or dip bottoms of cookies into chocolate; place on pan. Refrigerate until hardened, about 10 minutes.

Makes about 36 cookies.

PER COOKIE: about 80 cal, 1 g pro, 4 g total fat (4 g sat. fat), 10 g carb, 1 g fibre, 0 mg chol, 27 mg sodium. % RDI: 2% iron.

Chef's Salad

Everyone knows that a chef's salad is tasty, but it's very handy to know how to make one that's even more delicious than any restaurant version.

5 oz (150 g) thinly sliced **Black Forest ham**

6 cups (1.5 L) torn **mixed salad greens**

1 cup (250 mL) thinly sliced **cucumber**

1 cup (250 mL) grated **carrot**

4 **hard-cooked eggs** (see Best Tips, page 45), cut into wedges

½ cup (125 mL) shredded **Swiss cheese**

CHIVE DRESSING:

⅓ cup (75 mL) **extra-virgin olive oil**

¼ cup (60 mL) **red wine vinegar**

2 tbsp (30 mL) minced **fresh chives** or green onions

1 tbsp (15 mL) **Dijon mustard**

¼ tsp (1 mL) each **salt** and **pepper**

Chive Dressing: In large bowl, whisk together oil, vinegar, chives, mustard, salt and pepper.

Roll up ham slices; cut into matchstick-size strips.

Add ham strips, greens, cucumber and carrot to dressing; toss to coat. Garnish with eggs. Sprinkle with cheese.

Makes 4 servings.

PER SERVING: about 365 cal, 19 g pro, 29 g total fat (7 g sat. fat), 8 g carb, 2 g fibre, 216 mg chol, 828 mg sodium. % RDI: 21% calcium, 14% iron, 108% vit A, 27% vit C, 47% folate.

fridge clean-out dinner

Clean-Out-the-Crisper Creamy Soup
Leftover croutons, crumbled crackers or even popcorn make great soup garnishes.

1 tsp (5 mL) **vegetable oil**

1 **onion,** chopped

2 **carrots,** chopped

2 cloves **garlic,** minced

½ tsp (2 mL) **dried thyme**

½ tsp (2 mL) **dried oregano**

3 cups (750 mL) **chicken broth** or vegetable broth

1 **potato,** peeled and chopped

2 cups (500 mL) chopped **broccoli**

1 cup (250 mL) **frozen peas**

1 cup (250 mL) **milk** or 10% cream

½ tsp (2 mL) **salt**

Pinch **pepper**

In large saucepan, heat oil over medium heat; cook onion, carrots, garlic, thyme and oregano, stirring occasionally, until onion is softened, about 5 minutes.

Add broth, potato and broccoli; bring to boil. Reduce heat, cover and simmer until potato is very tender, about 15 minutes. Add peas; cook for 5 minutes.

Pour half into blender; purée until smooth. Return to saucepan. Stir in milk, salt and pepper; heat until steaming.

Makes 4 servings.

PER SERVING: about 165 cal, 10 g pro, 4 g total fat (1 g sat. fat), 24 g carb, 4 g fibre, 5 mg chol, 966 mg sodium. % RDI: 12% calcium, 14% iron, 102% vit A, 68% vit C, 26% folate.

best tips:

Make your own stock by freezing chicken bones and/ or any aromatic vegetable trimmings, including onions, celery, garlic, carrots, tomatoes, and mushroom and herb stems. Once you have around 10 cups (2.5 L) of ingredients, place them in a stock pot, add just enough water to cover and bring to a boil. Reduce heat and simmer, skimming occasionally, for about 2 hours. Strain and use stock in place of commercial broth in any recipe.

Chicken Vegetable Stir-Fry

1 lb (500 g) **boneless skinless chicken breasts** or thighs

2 tbsp (30 mL) **vegetable oil**

1 tsp (5 mL) minced **gingerroot**

3 cloves **garlic,** minced

2 large **carrots,** thinly sliced

1 **sweet green pepper,** thinly sliced

2 cups (500 mL) thinly sliced **mushrooms**

¼ tsp (1 mL) **pepper**

2 cups (500 mL) **bean sprouts,** rinsed

2 **green onions,** thinly sliced

SAUCE:

½ cup (125 mL) **chicken broth**

2 tbsp (30 mL) **soy sauce**

1 tbsp (15 mL) **unseasoned rice vinegar**

2 tsp (10 mL) **cornstarch**

2 tsp (10 mL) **sesame oil**

¼ tsp (1 mL) **hot pepper sauce** or Asian chili paste

Cut chicken crosswise into thin strips. In wok or large deep skillet, heat half of the oil over high heat; stir-fry chicken, in 2 batches, until no longer pink inside, about 4 minutes. Transfer to plate.

Add remaining oil to wok; stir-fry ginger and garlic until fragrant, about 1 minute. Add carrots, green pepper, mushrooms and pepper; stir-fry for 1 minute. Add ¼ cup (60 mL) water; cover and steam until vegetables are tender-crisp, about 4 minutes.

Sauce: Meanwhile, in bowl, whisk together chicken broth, soy sauce, vinegar, cornstarch, sesame oil and hot pepper sauce; pour into centre of wok and boil, stirring, until thickened, about 2 minutes.

Return chicken to pan; stir-fry until sauce is thickened and glossy. Spread bean sprouts over platter; top with chicken mixture. Sprinkle with green onions.

Makes 4 servings.

PER SERVING: about 280 cal, 30 g pro, 11 g total fat (1 g sat. fat), 15 g carb, 3 g fibre, 66 mg chol, 714 mg sodium. % RDI: 4% calcium, 16% iron, 116% vit A, 52% vit C, 21% folate.

best tips:

•For perfect hard-cooked eggs, arrange eggs in single layer in saucepan; pour in enough cold water to cover eggs by 1 inch (2.5 cm). Bring to boil over high heat. Immediately remove from heat; cover and let stand for 20 minutes. Drain and run cold water over eggs until cooled.

•To peel, tap shell all over to crack. Start peeling from wide end of egg, where air cell is located. Hold under cold running water to help ease off shell.

Endive Salad With Herbed Goat Cheese

Goat cheese rolled in herbs and served with croûtes (toasted sliced bread) is tastier by far than just plain croutons. You can prepare the cheese, wash the greens, make the vinaigrette and bake the croûtes ahead so assembly takes just minutes.

2 tbsp (30 mL) each chopped **fresh chives** and **parsley**

½ tsp (2 mL) **herbes de Provence** or dried thyme

1 log (113 g) **goat cheese**

6 cups (1.5 L) torn **mixed salad greens**

18 leaves **Belgian endive** (about 1 large head)

LEMON VINAIGRETTE:

3 tbsp (45 mL) **vegetable oil** or olive oil

2 tsp (10 mL) **lemon juice**

½ tsp (2 mL) **Dijon mustard**

¼ tsp (1 mL) **granulated sugar**

Pinch each **salt** and **pepper**

CROÛTES:

1 **baguette**

Half clove **garlic**

2 tsp (10 mL) **extra-virgin olive oil**

¼ tsp (1 mL) **sea salt** or table salt

¼ tsp (1 mL) **pepper**

Croûtes: Cut baguette into twelve ½-inch (1 cm) thick slices; rub 1 side of each with cut side of garlic. Brush with oil; sprinkle with salt and pepper. Bake on baking sheet in 350°F (180°C) oven until crisp and light golden, about 8 minutes. Let cool.

Lemon Vinaigrette: Whisk together oil, lemon juice, mustard, sugar, salt and pepper.

On waxed paper, combine chives, parsley and herbes de Provence; roll goat cheese in herb mixture to coat. Wrap in plastic wrap and refrigerate for 2 hours or up to 24 hours.

In bowl, toss mixed greens with vinaigrette; arrange on 6 plates. Top each with 3 Belgian endive leaves. Cut goat cheese into 6 slices; place 1 slice on each salad. Add 2 croûtes to each plate.

Makes 6 servings.

PER SERVING: about 292 cal, 9 g pro, 17 g total fat (4 g sat. fat), 27 g carb, 3 g fibre, 9 mg chol, 438 mg sodium. % RDI: 10% calcium, 16% iron, 19% vit A, 18% vit C, 41% folate.

make-ahead meal

Roasted Carrot and Thyme Purée

Fresh thyme complements the earthiness of carrots. Roast them ahead so the purée needs only minutes to reheat on the stove top or in the microwave.

2 lb (1 kg) **carrots** (about 9)

1 **onion,** cut into chunks

2 tbsp (30 mL) **extra-virgin olive oil**

1 tbsp (15 mL) chopped **fresh thyme** (or 1 tsp/5 mL dried)

½ tsp (2 mL) **salt**

¼ tsp (1 mL) **pepper**

½ cup (125 mL) **sodium-reduced chicken broth**

Cut carrots into 1-inch (2.5 cm) chunks. In roasting pan, toss together carrots, onion, oil, thyme, salt and pepper. Roast in 425°F (220°C) oven until tender, about 45 minutes.

In food processor, purée carrot mixture with broth until smooth.

Makes 6 servings.

PER SERVING: about 87 cal, 1 g pro, 5 g total fat (1 g sat. fat), 11 g carb, 3 g fibre, 0 mg chol, 307 mg sodium. % RDI: 4% calcium, 4% iron, 191% vit A, 8% vit C, 8% folate.

Roasted Hazelnut-Stuffed Chicken Breasts

Hazelnut oil can withstand roasting, but the flavour diminishes slightly. Drizzle a bit more over the chicken before serving to restore the uniquely nutty flavour.

4 **boneless skin-on chicken breasts** (about 6 oz/175 g each)

2 tbsp (30 mL) **hazelnut oil**

¼ tsp (1 mL) each **salt** and **pepper**

HAZELNUT STUFFING:

1 tbsp (15 mL) **hazelnut oil**

1 **shallot,** minced

1 clove **garlic,** minced

¼ tsp (1 mL) **dried fines herbes** or dried thyme

¼ tsp (1 mL) each **salt** and **pepper**

⅓ cup (75 mL) **fresh bread crumbs**

2 tbsp (30 mL) chopped toasted **hazelnuts**

1 tbsp (15 mL) minced **fresh parsley**

Hazelnut Stuffing: In small skillet, heat oil over medium heat; fry shallot, garlic, fines herbes, salt and pepper, stirring occasionally, until softened, about 3 minutes. Transfer to bowl; mix in bread crumbs, hazelnuts and parsley.

Cut each chicken breast in half horizontally, almost but not all the way through; open like book. Spoon 2 tbsp (30 mL) stuffing over 1 side, leaving ½-inch (1 cm) border uncovered. Fold uncovered side over; secure with toothpicks.

Brush chicken all over with 1 tbsp (15 mL) of the oil; sprinkle with salt and pepper. Roast, skin side up, in small roasting pan in 425°F (220°C) oven until no longer pink inside and skin is crispy, about 25 minutes. Remove toothpicks; cut each diagonally into 6 slices. Drizzle with remaining oil.

Makes 4 servings.

PER SERVING: about 345 cal, 31 g pro, 23 g total fat (4 g sat. fat), 3 g carb, 1 g fibre, 97 mg chol, 375 mg sodium. % RDI: 2% calcium, 8% iron, 4% vit A, 2% vit C, 5% folate.

best tips:

• No hazelnut oil? Try olive oil or lemon-infused olive oil (the flavour will be slightly different). The hazelnuts can also be replaced with chopped toasted walnuts or pine nuts.

• If your butcher has boneless skin-on chicken breasts, all the better. Otherwise, purchase bone-in, skin-on breasts and use a sharp boning or carving knife to remove the bones.

Cheese-Stuffed Shells

To freeze, make up to point of sprinkling stuffed shells with cheese; let cool. Wrap in plastic and overwrap with foil; freeze for up to 2 weeks. Thaw in refrigerator. Unwrap and re-cover with foil; bake as directed.

2 tbsp (30 mL) **extra-virgin olive oil** or vegetable oil

1 lb (500 g) **lean ground beef**

2 **onions,** finely chopped

4 cloves **garlic,** minced

1½ tsp (7 mL) each **dried basil** and **oregano**

Pinch **hot pepper flakes**

Pinch each **salt** and **pepper**

1 can (28 oz/796 mL) **whole tomatoes,** puréed

1 can (14 oz/398 mL) **tomato sauce**

1 box (340 g) **jumbo pasta shells**

1 cup (250 mL) shredded **mozzarella cheese**

¼ cup (60 mL) grated **Parmesan cheese**

FILLING:

1 pkg (10 oz/300 g) **frozen chopped spinach,** thawed and squeezed dry

1 tub (475 g) **ricotta cheese**

1 cup (250 mL) grated **Parmesan cheese**

1 cup (250 mL) shredded **mozzarella cheese**

¼ cup (60 mL) chopped **fresh parsley**

2 **green onions,** chopped

2 **eggs,** beaten

1 tsp (5 mL) **dried basil**

¼ tsp (1 mL) **ground nutmeg**

¼ tsp (1 mL) **pepper**

In shallow Dutch oven, heat half of the oil over medium-high heat; cook beef, breaking up with spoon, until no longer pink, about 5 minutes. With slotted spoon, transfer to bowl.

Drain any fat from pan; add remaining oil. Sauté onions and garlic for 5 minutes. Add basil, oregano, hot pepper flakes, salt, pepper, tomatoes and tomato sauce. Return beef to pan; bring to boil. Reduce heat and simmer, stirring often, until thickened, 20 to 25 minutes.

Meanwhile, in large pot of boiling salted water, cook shells according to package directions until al dente. Drain and rinse under cold water; drain well. Place on damp tea towel.

Filling: Meanwhile, in bowl, combine spinach, ricotta, Parmesan, mozzarella, parsley, onions, eggs, basil, nutmeg and pepper.

Pour half of the tomato sauce into 13- x 9-inch (3 L) baking dish. Spoon heaping 1 tbsp (15 mL) filling into each pasta shell. Arrange snugly, stuffed side up, in dish. Spoon remaining sauce over top; sprinkle with mozzarella and Parmesan cheeses. Cover with foil.

Bake in 350°F (180°C) oven for 30 minutes. Uncover and bake until bubbly and cheese is golden, about 20 minutes.

Makes 8 servings.

PER SERVING: about 621 cal, 39 g pro, 30 g total fat (16 g sat. fat), 48 g carb, 5 g fibre, 146 mg chol, 1,001 mg sodium. % RDI: 52% calcium, 40% iron, 41% vit A, 38% vit C, 67% folate.

best freezable mains

Jerk Pork Stew

To freeze, let cool, then freeze in airtight containers for up to 1 month. Thaw in refrigerator. Reheat and serve with mashed potatoes or rice.

3 **green onions**

¼ cup (60 mL) **all-purpose flour**

1 tsp (5 mL) **dried thyme**

½ tsp (2 mL) **ground allspice**

¼ tsp (1 mL) **cayenne pepper**

1 lb (500 g) **pork shoulder,** trimmed and cubed, or pork stewing cubes

3 tbsp (45 mL) **vegetable oil**

6 cloves **garlic,** minced

1 tbsp (15 mL) minced **gingerroot**

2 cups (500 mL) **chicken broth**

2 tbsp (30 mL) **soy sauce**

1 tbsp (15 mL) packed **brown sugar**

Chop green onions, setting aside white and green parts separately.

In plastic bag, combine flour, thyme, allspice and cayenne pepper; add pork and shake to coat, reserving remaining flour mixture.

In Dutch oven, heat 2 tbsp (30 mL) of the oil over medium heat; fry pork, in 2 batches, until browned, about 5 minutes. Remove to plate. Add remaining oil to pan; fry white parts of onions, garlic and ginger until fragrant, about 2 minutes. Add reserved flour mixture; stir for 1 minute. Add broth and 1 cup (250 mL) water; bring to boil, scraping up browned bits.

Return pork and any accumulated juices to pan; stir in soy sauce and brown sugar. Reduce heat, cover and simmer, stirring occasionally, until pork is tender, about 45 minutes. Add green parts of green onions; simmer for 5 minutes.

Makes 4 servings.

PER SERVING: about 337 cal, 27 g pro, 19 g total fat (4 g sat. fat), 14 g carb, 1 g fibre, 76 mg chol, 995 mg sodium. % RDI: 4% calcium, 20% iron, 1% vit A, 5% vit C, 10% folate.

best tips:

Buy a couple of pork shoulders, then trim, cube and freeze them in 1-lb (500 g) portions to keep on hand for this spicy Jamaican stew.

Chicken and Black Bean Burritos

To freeze, after sprinkling with cheese, refrigerate burritos until cold. Wrap in plastic and overwrap with foil; freeze for up to 1 month. Unwrap and re-cover with foil; bake as directed, adding 10 minutes to baking time.

1 tbsp (15 mL) **vegetable oil**

1 **onion,** chopped

2 cloves **garlic,** minced

¼ tsp (1 mL) each **salt** and **pepper**

4 **boneless skinless chicken breasts,** cubed

1 **jalapeño pepper,** seeded and minced

1 **sweet red pepper,** chopped

1 can (19 oz/540 mL) **black beans,** drained and rinsed

1 cup (250 mL) **salsa**

8 large **whole wheat tortillas** (10 inches/25 cm)

2½ cups (625 mL) shredded **Cheddar cheese**

½ cup (125 mL) **light sour cream**

In skillet, heat oil over medium-high heat; fry onion, garlic, salt and pepper until softened, about 3 minutes. Add chicken, jalapeño and red peppers, beans and salsa; cook, stirring, until chicken is no longer pink inside, about 10 minutes. Let cool.

Spoon about ¾ cup (175 mL) of the filling down centre of each tortilla; sprinkle each with ¼ cup (60 mL) of the cheese. Fold in bottom edge, then sides; roll up. Place, seam side down, in greased 13- x 9-inch (3 L) baking dish. Sprinkle remaining cheese over top.

Bake in 400°F (200°C) oven until golden and hot, and cheese is melted, about 15 minutes. Serve with sour cream.

Makes 8 servings.

PER SERVING: about 436 cal, 34 g pro, 16 g total fat (9 g sat. fat), 48 g carb, 8 g fibre, 78 mg chol, 938 mg sodium. % RDI: 31% calcium, 21% iron, 19% vit A, 57% vit C, 27% folate.

best tips:

You can pack and freeze these burritos in one dish or wrap them separately for individual portions.

Turkey Potato Patties

This recipe is quick if you have leftover mashed potatoes. If you don't, boil 2 potatoes, cubed and peeled, in salted water until tender, about 12 minutes, then drain and mash. Serve with poached eggs (see Best Tips, page 56) and gravy, salsa or chili sauce.

1 **egg**

1½ cups (375 mL) diced **cooked turkey**

1 cup (250 mL) **mashed potatoes**

¼ cup (60 mL) **dry bread crumbs**

1 **green onion,** finely chopped

2 tbsp (30 mL) finely chopped **fresh parsley**

2 tsp (10 mL) **Dijon mustard**

¼ tsp (1 mL) each **dried thyme** and **sage**

¼ tsp (1 mL) each **salt** and **pepper**

1 tbsp (15 mL) **vegetable oil**

In bowl, beat egg; mix in turkey, potatoes, bread crumbs, green onion, parsley, mustard, thyme, sage, salt and pepper. Form into eight ½-inch (1 cm) thick patties.

In large nonstick skillet, heat oil over medium heat; fry patties, turning once and reducing temperature if browning too quickly, until crusty and golden, about 6 minutes.

Makes 4 servings.

PER SERVING: about 184 cal, 14 g pro, 7 g total fat (1 g sat. fat), 16 g carb, 1 g fibre, 73 mg chol, 401 mg sodium. % RDI: 4% calcium, 11% iron, 3% vit A, 8% vit C, 8% folate.

best leftover mains

Spaghetti Frittata

Enjoy this frittata with toast for breakfast or with warmed pasta sauce and salad for dinner. It's also great in a sandwich with sliced cheese and tomato.

2 tbsp (30 mL) **vegetable oil** or butter

1 cup (250 mL) cubed **ham** or kielbasa (about 4 oz/125 g)

2 **green onions,** thinly sliced

Half **sweet green pepper,** thinly sliced

½ tsp (2 mL) **dried thyme**

½ tsp (2 mL) each **salt** and **pepper**

3 cups (750 mL) **cooked spaghetti** (about 6 oz/ 175 g uncooked)

8 **eggs**

3 tbsp (45 mL) **water**

In 10-inch (25 cm) ovenproof skillet, heat oil over medium heat; fry ham, green onions, green pepper, thyme and half each of the salt and pepper until vegetables are tender, about 5 minutes. Add spaghetti and toss until heated through, about 3 minutes.

Meanwhile, in large bowl, whisk together eggs, water and remaining salt and pepper; pour over pasta in pan (do not stir). Transfer pan to 350°F (180°C) oven; bake until puffy and eggs are set, about 25 minutes. Let stand for 5 minutes.

Using flexible spatula, loosen edge and bottom of frittata. Slide out onto plate or cutting board; cut into wedges.

Makes 4 servings.

PER SERVING: about 415 cal, 26 g pro, 19 g total fat (4 g sat. fat), 32 g carb, 2 g fibre, 391 mg chol, 980 mg sodium. % RDI: 6% calcium, 19% iron, 18% vit A, 20% vit C, 50% folate.

best tips:

To perfectly poach eggs, pour enough water into large saucepan or Dutch oven to come 3 inches (8 cm) up side; bring to boil. Add 1 tsp (5 mL) vinegar; reduce heat to simmer. Break each egg into small dish; gently slip egg into water and cook to desired doneness (about 5 minutes for soft yolks and firm whites). Remove with slotted spoon, patting bottom of spoon on towel to dry.

Thai-Style Beef Salad

Not only is this a great way to use up leftovers, but it is also packed with healthful vegetables, such as cabbage and carrots.

Half **English cucumber**

6 cups (1.5 L) shredded **cabbage** (about one-quarter head)

1 large **carrot,** shredded

2 cups (500 mL) **bean sprouts**

6 **radishes,** sliced

3 cups (750 mL) cooked **roast beef strips** (12 oz/375 g)

¼ cup (60 mL) chopped **fresh basil** or parsley

¼ cup (60 mL) chopped **fresh coriander**

DRESSING:

3 tbsp (45 mL) **soy sauce**

2 tbsp (30 mL) **vegetable oil**

2 tbsp (30 mL) **lime juice**

2 tbsp (30 mL) **unseasoned rice vinegar**

2 tsp (10 mL) minced **gingerroot**

1 tsp (5 mL) **sesame oil**

1 small clove **garlic,** minced

½ tsp (2 mL) **Asian chili paste** or hot pepper sauce

Cut cucumber in half lengthwise; thinly slice crosswise. In bowl, combine cucumber, cabbage, carrot, bean sprouts and radishes.

Dressing: In small saucepan, heat together soy sauce, vegetable oil, lime juice, rice vinegar, ginger, sesame oil, garlic and chili paste until hot.

Pour dressing over cabbage mixture; toss to coat. Add beef, basil and coriander; toss to combine.

Makes 4 servings.

PER SERVING: about 308 cal, 30 g pro, 14 g total fat (3 g sat. fat), 16 g carb, 4 g fibre, 57 mg chol, 861 mg sodium. % RDI: 8% calcium, 27% iron, 74% vit A, 110% vit C, 55% folate.

best tips:

For variety, replace roast beef with cooked pork, chicken or shrimp. Or toss in cubed firm tofu that has been marinated in additional dressing for at least an hour.

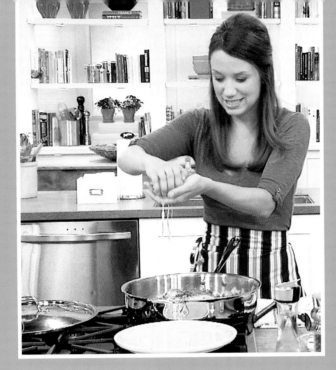

meat-lover mains

Family-Size T-Bone Steaks

Smoked sea salt delivers a woody aroma and unbeatable flavour. Look for it in specialty stores, or use your favourite sea salt.

2 **beef T-bone grilling steaks** (about 2 lb/1 kg total), each 1½ inches (4 cm) thick

2 tsp (10 mL) **smoked sea salt,** plain sea salt or table salt

2 tsp (10 mL) coarsely ground **pepper**

2 tbsp (30 mL) **extra-virgin olive oil**

1 **lemon,** cut in wedges

Sprinkle both sides of steaks with salt and pepper. Place on greased grill over medium-high heat; close lid and grill, turning once, until desired doneness, about 16 minutes for medium-rare.

Transfer to cutting board; tent with foil and let stand for 5 minutes before slicing. Arrange on platter; drizzle with oil. Serve with lemon wedges.

Makes 8 servings.

PER SERVING: about 355 cal, 38 g pro, 22 g total fat (8 g sat. fat), 1 g carb, trace fibre, 86 mg chol, 471 mg sodium. % RDI: 3% calcium, 27% iron, 5% vit C, 4% folate.

best meat-and-potatoes meal

The Ultimate Caesar Salad If desired, top salad with a sprinkle of crumbled cooked bacon.

1 head **romaine lettuce**

2 cups (500 mL) **croutons**

¼ cup (60 mL) grated **Parmesan cheese**

DRESSING:

¼ cup (60 mL) **vegetable oil** or extra-virgin olive oil

2 tbsp (30 mL) grated **Parmesan cheese**

1 tbsp (15 mL) **white wine vinegar**

2 tsp (10 mL) **Dijon mustard**

2 tsp (10 mL) **anchovy paste**

2 cloves **garlic,** minced

½ tsp (2 mL) each **salt** and **pepper**

½ tsp (2 mL) **Worcestershire sauce**

3 tbsp (45 mL) **light mayonnaise**

Dressing: In large bowl, whisk together oil, cheese, vinegar, mustard, anchovy paste, garlic, salt, pepper and Worcestershire sauce. Whisk in mayonnaise until smooth.

Tear lettuce into bite-size pieces; add to dressing along with croutons and cheese. Toss to combine.

Makes 12 servings.

PER SERVING: about 124 cal, 4 g pro, 9 g total fat (1 g sat. fat), 8 g carb, 1 g fibre, 4 mg chol, 298 mg sodium. % RDI: 7% calcium, 8% iron, 15% vit A, 23% vit C, 35% folate.

best tips:

There's a huge range of steaks to choose from. Here are the top cuts that are easy to grill and that you don't need to marinate. Any of these steaks would be great for pan-frying or broiling, too

•The **T-bone steak** is the perfect grilling steak for a crowd. It's flavourful and tender, so you can keep the seasoning simple, as we did in our Family-Size T-Bone Steaks recipe (page 61).

•The **New York steak** (a.k.a. striploin, shell steak, strip steak, Delmonico or Kansas City steak) is cut from the short loin, like the T-bone. It is boneless and tender, and has great beefy flavour.

Cheesy Broccoli Baked Potatoes

For a meatless variation, omit the bacon and fry onion in 1 tbsp (15 mL) butter or vegetable oil.

4 **baking potatoes**

CHEESY BROCCOLI SAUCE:

6 slices **bacon**

3 cups (750 mL) **broccoli florets**

1 large **onion,** chopped

3 tbsp (45 mL) **all-purpose flour**

2 cups (500 mL) **milk**

1 tsp (5 mL) **salt**

½ tsp (2 mL) **pepper**

1¾ cups (425 mL) shredded **old Cheddar cheese**

Scrub and prick potatoes; bake in 400°F (200°C) oven until tender, about 1 hour. (Or microwave on high for 8 minutes.)

Cheesy Broccoli Sauce: Meanwhile, in large skillet, cook bacon over medium-high heat until crisp, about 5 minutes. Drain on paper towel–lined plate. Reserving 1 tbsp (15 mL), drain fat from pan. Chop bacon and set aside.

In saucepan of boiling salted water, cook broccoli until tender, about 5 minutes. Drain and chill in cold water. Drain and pat dry; chop.

In same saucepan, heat reserved fat over medium heat; fry onion, stirring occasionally, until softened, 5 minutes. Stir in flour; cook for 30 seconds. Whisk in milk, salt and pepper; bring to boil. Reduce heat and simmer, whisking, until thickened,
1 minute. Remove from heat. Stir in 1 cup (250 mL) of the cheese until melted. Stir in bacon and broccoli.

Cut potatoes in half lengthwise. Leaving ¼-inch (5 mm) thick shell, scoop out flesh into bowl. Mash potato flesh; fold into sauce. Mound filling in shells; sprinkle with remaining cheese.

Broil on foil-lined rimmed baking sheet until cheese is bubbly and golden, about 3 minutes. (Or bake in 400°F/ 200°C oven for 15 minutes.)

Makes 8 servings.

PER SERVING: about 276 cal, 13 g pro, 13 g total fat (7 g sat. fat), 27 g carb, 3 g fibre, 37 mg chol, 657 mg sodium, 723 mg potassium. % RDI: 26% calcium, 11% iron, 17% vit A, 38% vit C, 23% folate.

• **Filet mignon** (a.k.a. tournedo or entrecôte) is cut from the tenderloin and is the most tender, expensive steak. It's not as flavourful, so it may need extra seasoning. That's why it's often wrapped in bacon.

• **A rib-eye steak** is a classic butcher's favourite. It's cut from the rib section, between the short loin and the chuck. It has an extremely rich, deep beef flavour and is very tender. If you like prime rib, you'll like rib-eye, because it's the same cut in steak form.

Beef and Green Bean Stew

Choose an outside or inside round oven roast or shoulder pot roast. Starting with one piece of meat rather than precut stewing beef means that all the chunks will be similar in size and texture, and will require the same cooking time.

2½ lb (1.25 kg) **beef outside round oven roast**

¼ tsp (1 mL) each **salt** and **pepper**

¼ cup (60 mL) **olive oil**

1 **onion,** chopped

2 cloves **garlic,** minced

2 tsp (10 mL) **ground allspice**

2½ cups (625 mL) **beef broth**

½ cup (125 mL) **tomato paste**

1 **bay leaf**

1 lb (500 g) **green beans,** trimmed

Trim roast and cut into 1-inch (2.5 cm) cubes. Toss together beef, salt and pepper. In large Dutch oven, heat oil over medium-high heat; brown beef in batches. Transfer to plate.

Drain any fat from pan and reduce heat to medium; cook onion and garlic, stirring occasionally, until onion is softened, about 5 minutes. Add allspice; cook, stirring, for 1 minute. Whisk in beef broth, tomato paste and bay leaf; bring to boil. Return beef and any accumulated juices to pan.

Reduce heat, cover and simmer until beef is tender, 2 to 2½ hours.

Meanwhile, in pot of boiling salted water, cook beans until tender-crisp, 5 to 7 minutes. Drain and rinse in cold water. Drain; cut in half on diagonal. Add beans to pan; simmer, uncovered and stirring occasionally, for 5 minutes. Discard bay leaf.

Makes 6 to 8 servings.

PER EACH OF 8 SERVINGS: about 262 cal, 28 g pro, 13 g total fat (3 g sat. fat), 9 g carb, 2 g fibre, 54 mg chol, 510 mg sodium. % RDI: 4% calcium, 24% iron, 7% vit A, 22% vit C, 13% folate.

VARIATION

Slow-Cooker Beef and Green Bean Stew: Follow first 2 paragraphs; transfer to slow-cooker. Cover and cook on low until beef is tender, 6 to 8 hours. Cook beans as directed and add to slow-cooker; cover and cook for 15 minutes. Discard bay leaf.

easy beef mains

Have-It-Your-Way Steak and Pepper Fajitas

Wrap the tortillas in foil and warm on the barbecue rack (not over direct flame) or in a warm oven while the steak is cooking.

1 lb (500 g) **beef strip loin grilling steak,** 1 inch (2.5 cm) thick

2 tbsp (30 mL) **vegetable oil**

1 **onion,** sliced

1 each **sweet red, green** and **yellow pepper,** sliced

¼ tsp (1 mL) **salt**

4 cups (1 L) sliced **mushrooms**

1 clove **garlic,** minced

¼ tsp (1 mL) **dried thyme**

6 small **whole wheat tortillas** (6 inches/15 cm)

CHILI RUB:

2 tsp (10 mL) **chili powder**

½ tsp (2 mL) **salt**

¼ tsp (1 mL) each **ground cumin** and **pepper**

GARNISHES:

Salsa, sour cream and shredded **Cheddar cheese**

Chili Rub: Stir together chili powder, salt, cumin and pepper; rub all over steak. Wrap in plastic wrap and refrigerate for up to 24 hours.

Place steak on greased grill over medium-high heat or in skillet; close lid and grill, turning once, until medium-rare, about 8 minutes. Transfer to cutting board and tent with foil; let stand for 5 minutes before slicing thinly across the grain.

Meanwhile, in skillet, heat 1 tbsp (15 mL) of the oil over medium-high heat; sauté onion for 2 minutes.

Add red, green and yellow peppers and pinch of the salt; sauté, adding 2 tbsp (30 mL) water halfway through, until peppers are tender-crisp, about 5 minutes. Transfer to bowl; keep warm.

In same skillet, heat remaining oil over medium-high heat; cook mushrooms, garlic, thyme and remaining salt until golden and no liquid remains, about 6 minutes. Transfer to separate bowl; keep warm.

Garnishes: Serve steak, peppers, mushrooms, salsa, sour cream and cheese in separate bowls for guests to roll up in tortillas as desired.

Makes 6 servings.

PER SERVING: about 250 cal, 17 g pro, 13 g total fat (4 g sat. fat), 20 g carb, 3 g fibre, 40 mg chol, 434 mg sodium. % RDI: 2% calcium, 20% iron, 10% vit A, 132% vit C, 13% folate.

Quick Ground Beef Curry
Serve this speedy weeknight dish over rice or with naan bread. Garnish with fresh mint or coriander, if desired.

3 tbsp (45 mL) **vegetable oil**

2 **onions,** diced

1 tbsp (15 mL) each minced **garlic** and **gingerroot**

2 tbsp (30 mL) **Madras curry powder**

2 tbsp (30 mL) **tomato paste**

¾ tsp (4 mL) **salt**

Pinch **hot pepper flakes**

1 lb (500 g) **lean ground beef**

1 lb (500 g) **Yukon Gold potatoes,** peeled and diced

1 can (14 oz/398 mL) **diced tomatoes**

1 tbsp (15 mL) **sodium-reduced soy sauce**

1 cup (250 mL) **frozen green peas**

In large shallow Dutch oven, heat oil over medium heat; cook onions, stirring occasionally, until golden, about 12 minutes.

Add garlic and ginger; cook for 3 minutes. Add curry powder, tomato paste, salt and hot pepper flakes; cook, stirring, for 2 minutes. Add beef, breaking up with spoon; cook until browned. Add potatoes; cook for 2 minutes.

Add tomatoes, soy sauce and 1 cup (250 mL) water; bring to boil. Reduce heat, cover and simmer until potatoes are tender, about 15 minutes. Stir in peas; cook for 5 minutes.

Makes 4 to 6 servings.

PER EACH OF 6 SERVINGS: about 328 cal, 19 g pro, 18 g total fat (5 g sat. fat), 25 g carb, 4 g fibre, 45 mg chol, 548 mg sodium, 712 mg potassium. % RDI: 6% calcium, 24% iron, 6% vit A, 30% vit C, 16% folate.

Sirloin Tip Oven Roast With Porcini Mushroom Jus

This economical oven roast is perfect for Sunday family dinner, then as leftovers the following day. Though juicy and flavourful, it is best cooked to no more than medium.

6 cloves **garlic**

½ tsp (2 mL) **salt**

1 tbsp (15 mL) **vegetable oil** or olive oil

½ tsp (2 mL) each **dried thyme** and **pepper**

3 lb (1.5 kg) **beef sirloin tip oven roast**

PORCINI MUSHROOM JUS:

1 pkg (14 g) **dried porcini mushrooms**

1 tbsp (15 mL) **vegetable oil** or olive oil

1 clove **garlic,** minced

Pinch **dried thyme**

Pinch **salt**

1 tbsp (15 mL) **brandy** or sodium-reduced beef broth

1½ cups (375 mL) **sodium-reduced beef broth**

On cutting board, finely mince garlic; sprinkle with salt. Using side of chef's knife, smash and scrape garlic to form paste. Scrape into small bowl.

Mix oil, thyme and pepper into garlic paste; rub all over top and sides of roast.

Place roast on rack in small roasting pan; add 1½ cups (375 mL) water. Roast in 500°F (260°C) oven for 30 minutes. Reduce heat to 275°F (140°C); roast for about 1½ hours more or until meat thermometer registers 140°F (60°C) for medium-rare, or 155°F (68°C) for medium.

Transfer to cutting board and tent with foil; let stand for 15 minutes before slicing thinly.

Porcini Mushroom Jus: Meanwhile, soak mushrooms in 1 cup (250 mL) boiling water for 20 minutes. Remove mushrooms and chop. Strain liquid and set aside.

Skim fat from roasting pan juices. Place pan over medium-high heat; add mushroom liquid and bring to boil, scraping up browned bits on bottom of pan. Strain and set pan juices aside.

In saucepan, heat oil over medium heat; fry garlic, thyme, salt and mushrooms until softened, about 2 minutes. Add brandy; cook, stirring, until no liquid remains.

Add broth and reserved pan juices; bring to boil. Reduce heat and simmer, uncovered, until reduced to about 2 cups (500 mL), about 8 minutes. Serve with roast.

Makes 8 servings.

PER SERVING: about 276 cal, 37 g pro, 11 g total fat (4 g sat. fat), 3 g carb, trace fibre, 85 mg chol, 322 mg sodium, 375 mg potassium. % RDI: 1% calcium, 29% iron, 2% vit C, 4% folate.

sunday roast
beef dinner

Roasted Fall Vegetables

Roasting a colourful array of fall vegetables brings out their natural sweetness. If you can't find golden beets, use all red.

Half **acorn squash**

2 **carrots**

2 **parsnips**

12 oz (375 g) each **red** and **golden beets** (about 3 each), trimmed

8 **shallots** or small onions

3 sprigs **fresh rosemary** (or 1 tsp/5 mL dried)

2 tbsp (30 mL) **extra-virgin olive oil**

½ tsp (2 mL) each **salt** and **pepper**

Cut squash into 4 wedges; cut each lengthwise into thirds. Place in large bowl.

Peel carrots, parsnips and beets. Cut carrots and parsnips into 1-inch (2.5 cm) pieces; cut beets into wedges. Add vegetables to bowl. Halve shallots; add to bowl. Add rosemary, oil, salt and pepper; toss to coat.

Roast on large foil- or parchment paper–lined rimmed baking sheet in 400°F (200°C) oven until tender and browned, about 1 hour.

Makes 8 servings.

PER SERVING: about 109 cal, 2 g pro, 4 g total fat (1 g sat. fat), 19 g carb, 3 g fibre, 0 mg chol, 203 mg sodium. % RDI: 4% calcium, 8% iron, 48% vit A, 15% vit C, 33% folate.

best tips:

In a convection oven, a fan blows heated air around the food throughout the cooking process. This means the food cooks more quickly and evenly than in a conventional oven. Cooking this way is more economical, thanks to these shorter cooking times and because you can set the oven to a slightly lower temperature to achieve the same result – both of which save energy.

While you should always consult the manufacturer's instructions, here are some general rules for converting conventional oven recipes for a convection oven.

Smashed Leek Potatoes

6 **Yukon Gold potatoes** (3 lb/1.5 kg)

3 tbsp (45 mL) **butter**

2 **leeks** (white and light green parts only)

¾ tsp (4 mL) each **salt** and **pepper**

Pinch **dried thyme**

1⅓ cups (325 mL) **buttermilk**

Scrub potatoes; cut into 2-inch (5 cm) cubes. In large saucepan of boiling salted water, cover and cook potatoes until tender, about 15 minutes. Drain and return to pot.

Meanwhile, in small skillet, melt 1 tbsp (15 mL) of the butter over medium heat; cook leeks, pinch each of the salt and pepper, and thyme until tender, about 5 minutes.

Add buttermilk and remaining butter, salt and pepper to potatoes; smash with potato masher until smooth with a few large pieces remaining. Stir in leek mixture.

Makes 8 servings.

PER SERVING: about 186 cal, 4 g pro, 5 g total fat (3 g sat. fat), 32 g carb, 3 g fibre, 13 mg chol, 632 mg sodium. % RDI: 6% calcium, 11% iron, 4% vit A, 32% vit C, 10% folate.

•When roasting, cook at the same temperature indicated in the original recipe, but reduce cooking time by 25 per cent.

•When baking, reduce baking temperature by 25°F (13°C), especially for items that cook in less than 15 minutes. Cook for the same amount of time indicated in the original recipe.

•Remember to write down the new convection cooking time and/or oven temperature on the conventional recipe for future reference.

Philly Cheese Steak Pizza

1 tbsp (15 mL) **extra-virgin olive oil**

1 **sweet green pepper,** sliced

2 cloves **garlic,** minced

Half **sweet onion,** sliced

2 cups (500 mL) sliced **mushrooms**

1 tsp (5 mL) **dried oregano**

¼ tsp (1 mL) each **salt** and **pepper**

1 lb (500 g) **pizza dough**

½ cup (125 mL) **pizza sauce** or tomato pasta sauce

8 slices **provolone cheese**

1 cup (250 mL) thinly sliced cooked **Sirloin Tip Oven Roast**
   (page 69) or cooked roast beef

In large skillet, heat oil over medium-high heat; sauté green pepper, garlic, onion, mushrooms, oregano, salt and pepper until onion is golden and no liquid remains, about 5 minutes.

Meanwhile, on floured surface, roll out dough into circle large enough to fit 12-inch (30 cm) pizza pan. Spread with pizza sauce. Arrange half of the cheese over sauce; spoon vegetable mixture over top. Top with roast beef and remaining cheese.

Bake in bottom third of 475°F (240°C) oven until crust is golden and cheese is bubbly, 15 to 18 minutes.

Makes 8 slices.

PER SLICE: about 390 cal, 25 g pro, 17 g total fat (8 g sat. fat), 33 g carb, 2 g fibre, 51 mg chol, 786 mg sodium. % RDI: 29% calcium, 21% iron, 13% vit A, 20% vit C, 15% folate.

best roast beef leftovers

Pub-Style Beef Dip

Caramelized onions elevate leftover roast beef in this satisfying supper sandwich. Use a favourite mustard, such as Dijon or grainy.

2 tbsp (30 mL) **vegetable oil**

2 large **onions,** thinly sliced

1 tbsp (15 mL) **white wine vinegar**

Pinch each **salt** and **pepper**

Pinch **granulated sugar**

1 **sourdough baguette**

¼ cup (60 mL) **mustard**

Half **Sirloin Tip Oven Roast** (page 69),
   heated and thinly sliced

1 cup (250 mL) **Porcini Mushroom Jus**
   (page 69), heated

In skillet, heat oil over medium-low heat; fry onions, vinegar, salt, pepper and sugar, stirring often, until very soft and caramelized, 15 to 20 minutes.

Meanwhile, cut baguette into quarters; cut each horizontally in half and spread with 1 tbsp (15 mL) mustard. Top with beef and onions. Serve with hot jus for dipping.

Makes 4 servings.

PER SERVING: about 571 cal, 39 g pro, 23 g total fat (5 g sat. fat), 50 g carb, 4 g fibre, 67 mg chol, 1,164 mg sodium. % RDI: 9% calcium, 37% iron, 8% vit C, 42% folate.

Beef Pot Pie

This pie offers a delicious way to use leftovers. You can also try 2 cups (500 mL) frozen vegetables instead of cooked diced vegetables. Use a sharper, more aged Cheddar for maximum flavour.

3 cups (750 mL) cubed cooked **roast beef**

2 cups (500 mL) cooked diced **vegetables**

2 cups (500 mL) **gravy** or Porcini Mushroom Jus (page 69)

¼ tsp (1 mL) each **salt** and **pepper**

BISCUIT TOPPING:

⅔ cup (150 mL) **butter,** softened

½ cup (125 mL) **boiling water**

1 **egg yolk**

1 cup (250 mL) **whole wheat flour**

1 cup (250 mL) **all-purpose flour**

1 cup (250 mL) shredded **Cheddar cheese**

2 tsp (10 mL) **baking powder**

½ tsp (2 mL) **salt**

Biscuit Topping: In large bowl, stir butter with boiling water until melted. Let cool.

Meanwhile, in 9-inch (2.5 L) square cake pan, combine roast beef, vegetables, gravy, salt and pepper. Set aside.

Stir egg yolk into butter mixture. In separate bowl, whisk together whole wheat and all-purpose flours, cheese, baking powder and salt. Add to butter mixture. Mix with fork until dough clumps together.

On floured surface with floured hands, knead dough about 3 times until smooth with ragged edges. Pat dough into 8-inch (20 cm) square; cut into 9 squares. Lay squares over filling.

Bake in 400°F (200°C) oven until filling is bubbly and biscuits are no longer doughy underneath, about 40 minutes.

Makes 6 to 8 servings.

PER EACH OF 8 SERVINGS: about 544 cal, 26 g pro, 36 g total fat (18 g sat. fat), 31 g carb, 4 g fibre, 145 mg chol, 815 mg sodium. % RDI: 15% calcium, 29% iron, 50% vit A, 8% vit C, 24% folate.

Stuffed Beef and Cheddar Burgers

These juicy burgers hold a melted cheese surprise in each satisfying mouthful. Serve with lettuce and bacon, or your favourite toppings. You can make and refrigerate the patties up to 24 hours ahead.

1 **egg**

2 tbsp (30 mL) **water**

¼ cup (60 mL) **dry bread crumbs**

1 small **onion,** grated

2 tsp (10 mL) **Dijon mustard**

½ tsp (2 mL) each **dried thyme** and **salt**

¼ tsp (1 mL) **pepper**

1 lb (500 g) **lean ground beef**

½ cup (125 mL) shredded **old Cheddar cheese**

4 **hamburger buns**

In large bowl, beat egg with water; stir in bread crumbs, onion, mustard, thyme, salt and pepper. Mix in beef just until combined.

Divide into quarters; shape into balls. With finger, make well in each; place one-quarter of the cheese in each well. Press meat over to enclose cheese. Press into four ½-inch (1 cm) thick patties.

Place patties on greased grill over medium heat; close lid and grill, turning once, until instant-read thermometer inserted sideways into centre registers 160°F (71°C), 12 to 14 minutes. Serve on buns.

Makes 4 servings.

PER SERVING: about 464 cal, 32 g pro, 20 g total fat (8 g sat. fat), 37 g carb, 2 g fibre, 121 mg chol, 867 mg sodium. % RDI: 20% calcium, 34% iron, 6% vit A, 2% vit C, 38% folate.

best burger night

Crispy French Fries With Mustard Mayonnaise

Blanching the fries before frying or baking makes them extra golden and crisp.

3 lb (1.5 kg) **baking potatoes**

Vegetable oil for deep-frying

½ tsp (2 mL) **salt**

MUSTARD MAYONNAISE:

1 cup (250 mL) **mayonnaise**

2 tbsp (30 mL) **grainy mustard**

¾ tsp (4 mL) **lemon juice**

Scrub potatoes. With paring knife, cut out any eyes or dark spots. Cut unpeeled potatoes lengthwise into ¼-inch (5 mm) thick slices. Stacking 2 or 3 slices at a time, cut lengthwise into ¼-inch (5 mm) wide sticks.

Stir potatoes into large pot of boiling salted water; return to boil. Blanch until no longer raw in centre, 1 to 2 minutes. Drain and pat dry on towel.

Mustard Mayonnaise: Whisk together mayonnaise, mustard and lemon juice; set aside.

In deep-fryer or deep pot, pour in enough oil to come at least two-thirds of the way up side; heat to 375°F (190°C) on deep-fryer thermometer. In batches, fry potatoes until golden brown, 4 to 5 minutes per batch. Using slotted spoon, transfer to paper towel–lined baking sheet to drain; sprinkle with salt. Serve with Mustard Mayonnaise.

Makes 8 servings.

PER SERVING: about 409 cal, 3 g pro, 32 g total fat (4 g sat. fat), 29 g carb, 2 g fibre, 10 mg chol, 691 mg sodium. % RDI: 2% calcium, 10% iron, 2% vit A, 28% vit C, 7% folate.

VARIATION

Crispy Oven Fries with Mustard Mayonnaise: Toss blanched potato sticks with 2 tbsp (30 mL) vegetable oil and ½ tsp (2 mL) salt. Bake on large baking sheet in 450°F (230°C) oven, turning once, until crisp and golden, 35 to 40 minutes.

Caramelized Onions

Burgers are always better when topped with these golden onions.

1 tbsp (15 mL) **vegetable oil** or olive oil

1 **Spanish onion,** thinly sliced

1 tbsp (15 mL) **wine vinegar**

1 tsp (5 mL) **granulated sugar**

2 cloves **garlic,** thinly sliced

1 tsp (5 mL) **dried thyme**

¼ tsp (1 mL) each **salt** and **pepper**

In skillet, heat oil over medium-low heat; cook onion, vinegar, sugar, garlic, thyme, salt and pepper, stirring occasionally, until very soft, golden and caramelized, about 25 minutes.

Makes 1 cup (250 mL).

PER 2 TBSP (30 ML): about 35 cal, trace pro, 2 g total fat (trace sat. fat), 5 g carb, 1 g fibre, 0 mg chol, 73 mg sodium, 60 mg potassium. % RDI: 1% calcium, 2% iron, 3% folate.

Horseradish Aïoli **Add some zip to your burger by topping it with this zesty condiment.**

½ cup (125 mL) **light mayonnaise**

1 small clove **garlic,** minced

2 tsp (10 mL) **prepared horseradish**

1 tsp (5 mL) **lemon juice**

Pinch **salt**

Mix together mayonnaise, garlic, horseradish, lemon juice and salt.

Makes about ½ cup (125 mL).

PER 1 TBSP (15 ML): about 50 cal, trace pro, 5 g total fat (1 g sat. fat), 2 g carb, 0 g fibre, 5 mg chol, 105 mg sodium, 11 mg potassium. % RDI: 1% iron, 1% vit A, 2% vit C.

best tips:

• Try a large sweet onion, such as a Vidalia, and omit the sugar. Using balsamic vinegar in place of wine vinegar also adds nice depth of flavour.

• If you like extra zing, increase the amount of horseradish in the aïoli.

Old-Fashioned Barbecued Drumsticks

Drumsticks are very inexpensive and a favourite with kids and adults alike, especially when the chicken is smothered in homemade Cajun barbecue sauce. You can refrigerate the sauce for up to a week.

1 cup (250 mL) **tomato sauce**

⅓ cup (75 mL) **tomato paste**

¼ cup (60 mL) packed **brown sugar**

¼ cup (60 mL) **cider vinegar**

¼ cup (60 mL) **Dijon mustard**

1 **onion,** chopped

3 cloves **garlic,** minced

2 tbsp (30 mL) **fancy molasses**

1 tbsp (15 mL) **Cajun seasoning** or chili powder

1 tsp (5 mL) **Worcestershire sauce**

8 **chicken drumsticks** (1¾ lb/875 g), skinned

In saucepan, bring tomato sauce, tomato paste, sugar, vinegar, mustard, onion, garlic, molasses, Cajun seasoning and Worcestershire sauce to boil, stirring often. Reduce heat to medium-low; simmer for 10 minutes. Let cool for 10 minutes. Pour into blender; purée until smooth.

Set aside ⅔ cup (150 mL) sauce to serve with drumsticks. Transfer remaining sauce to large bowl.

Place chicken on greased grill over medium heat; close lid and grill, turning once, until juices run clear when chicken is pierced, about 30 minutes. Add to bowl of barbecue sauce; toss to coat. Return chicken to grill; grill until slightly crusty but still saucy, about 5 minutes. Serve with reserved sauce.

Makes 4 servings.

PER SERVING: about 294 cal, 25 g pro, 7 g total fat (2 g sat. fat), 35 g carb, 2 g fibre, 87 mg chol, 785 mg sodium. % RDI: 9% calcium, 27% iron, 18% vit A, 32% vit C, 8% folate.

easy chicken mains

Paprika Chicken

Use sweet or mild paprika or, for a hint of smokiness, try smoked paprika (see Best Tips, page 156, for tips on buying this spice). Serve with buttered egg noodles or rice.

1 tbsp (15 mL) **vegetable oil**

8 **boneless skinless chicken thighs**

1 **onion,** chopped

2 cloves **garlic,** minced

1 tbsp (15 mL) **paprika**

¼ tsp (1 mL) each **salt** and **pepper**

1 can (19 oz/540 mL) **whole tomatoes,** chopped

2 tbsp (30 mL) **tomato paste**

1 **sweet green pepper,** diced

½ cup (125 mL) **light sour cream** or regular sour cream

2 tbsp (30 mL) minced **fresh parsley**

In large skillet, heat oil over medium-high heat; brown chicken, in batches. Transfer to plate.

Drain fat from pan. Fry onion, garlic, paprika, salt and pepper over medium heat, stirring often, until onion is softened, about 5 minutes. Add tomatoes and tomato paste; bring to boil, stirring and scraping up browned bits from bottom of pan. Reduce heat and simmer for 10 minutes.

Return chicken and any accumulated juices to pan. Add green pepper; cover and simmer until slightly thickened, about 10 minutes.

Garnish with sour cream and parsley.

Makes 4 servings.

PER SERVING: about 268 cal, 26 g pro, 11 g total fat (3 g sat. fat), 17 g carb, 3 g fibre, 99 mg chol, 478 mg sodium. % RDI: 12% calcium, 21% iron, 26% vit A, 87% vit C, 14% folate.

VARIATION

Slow Cooker Paprika Chicken: Use bone-in skin-on chicken thighs. After browning chicken, transfer to slow cooker. Continue with recipe, reserving tomato paste until later and scraping tomato mixture into slow cooker. Cover and cook on low for 4 hours. Stir green pepper and tomato paste into slow cooker; cover and cook on high until thickened, about 15 minutes. Remove chicken skin if desired. Garnish with sour cream and parsley.

20-Minute Chicken Linguine

2 **boneless skinless chicken breasts**

¾ tsp (4 mL) each **salt** and **pepper**

3 tbsp (45 mL) **extra-virgin olive oil**

2 cups (500 mL) **cherry tomatoes** or grape tomatoes

1 small **onion,** sliced

8 cloves **garlic,** sliced

1 tsp (5 mL) **dried oregano**

2 cups (500 mL) firmly packed coarsely
shredded **radicchio**

4 **green onions,** sliced

12 oz (375 g) **linguine**

¼ cup (60 mL) grated **Parmesan cheese**

Cut chicken crosswise into strips; season with half each of the salt and pepper. In large skillet, heat 1 tbsp (15 mL) of the oil over medium-high heat; sauté chicken until golden, about 3 minutes. Transfer to plate.

Add tomatoes, onion, garlic, oregano and remaining oil, salt and pepper to skillet; sauté for 2 minutes. Add radicchio; sauté until tomatoes begin to split and soften, about 2 minutes. Return chicken to skillet; add green onions and cook until heated through.

Meanwhile, in large pot of boiling salted water, cook pasta until al dente, 10 minutes. Drain and return to pot; add sauce and toss to coat. Serve sprinkled with Parmesan cheese.

Makes 4 servings.

PER SERVING: about 546 cal, 30 g pro, 15 g total fat (3 g sat. fat), 72 g carb, 5 g fibre, 44 mg chol, 821 mg sodium. % RDI: 13% calcium, 22% iron, 6% vit A, 28% vit C, 65% folate.

best tips:

Radicchio adds lovely colour and a nice, slightly bitter flavour. You can replace it with 2 cups (500 mL) thinly sliced Swiss chard or 3 cups (750 mL) packed spinach or arugula leaves, if you like.

Spinach Ricotta-Stuffed Chicken Breasts

Be sure the chicken has an ample covering of skin to hold in the stuffing.

6 **bone-in, skin-on chicken breasts** (about 2½ lb/1.25 kg)

1 tbsp (15 mL) **butter,** melted

STUFFING:

1 tbsp (15 mL) **butter**

1 small **onion,** finely chopped

1 small clove **garlic,** minced

1½ cups (375 mL) packed chopped **fresh spinach**

2 tbsp (30 mL) chopped **fresh parsley**

1 tbsp (15 mL) chopped **fresh basil** (or ½ tsp/2 mL dried)

½ cup (125 mL) **ricotta cheese**

½ cup (125 mL) shredded **mozzarella cheese**

2 tbsp (30 mL) grated **Parmesan cheese**

1 **egg yolk**

¼ tsp (1 mL) **salt**

Pinch each **nutmeg** and **pepper**

Stuffing: In large skillet, heat butter over medium heat; cook onion and garlic, stirring often, until softened, 3 to 5 minutes. Add spinach, parsley and basil; cook, stirring, until spinach is wilted and no liquid remains, 2 minutes. Let cool completely.

Mix together spinach mixture, ricotta, mozzarella and Parmesan cheeses, egg yolk, salt, nutmeg and pepper.

Using sharp knife, bone chicken, leaving skin attached. Gently loosen skin from 1 long side of each breast, leaving skin attached at curved side. Stuff about ¼ cup (60 mL) stuffing under skin, pressing to spread evenly. Tuck ends of skin and meat underneath.

Place on greased rack in foil-lined pan. Brush with butter. Bake in 375°F (190°C) oven, basting occasionally, until golden and chicken is no longer pink inside, 40 minutes.

Makes 6 servings.

PER SERVING: about 350 cal, 37 g pro, 21 g total fat (9 g sat. fat), 3 g carb, trace fibre, 164 mg chol, 288 mg sodium, 476 mg potassium. % RDI: 13% calcium, 9% iron, 21% vit A, 3% vit C, 12% folate.

chicken three ways

Chinese Sesame Noodles With Chicken

You can put together this scrumptious main course quickly using leftover chicken. Soba noodles or spaghetti can replace the Chinese wheat noodles.

7 cups (1.75 L) finely shredded **napa cabbage**
  or green cabbage

¾ tsp (4 mL) **salt**

4 ribs **celery**

10 oz (300 g) **Chinese wheat noodles**

2 tsp (10 mL) **sesame oil**

2 cups (500 mL) shredded **cooked chicken**

8 **radishes,** thinly sliced

2 **green onions,** sliced

SESAME SAUCE:

½ cup (125 mL) **sesame paste** or tahini

3 tbsp (45 mL) **unseasoned rice vinegar** or cider vinegar

2 tbsp (30 mL) **sesame oil**

4 tsp (20 mL) **soy sauce**

2 tsp (10 mL) **granulated sugar**

2 tsp (10 mL) **Dijon mustard** or hot mustard

¼ tsp (1 mL) each **salt** and **pepper**

2 cloves **garlic,** minced

Sesame Sauce: In food processor, purée together sesame paste, vinegar, sesame oil, soy sauce, sugar, mustard, salt, pepper and ⅓ cup (75 mL) water. Stir in garlic.

In bowl, mix cabbage with salt; let stand for 20 minutes. By handfuls, squeeze out moisture; set cabbage aside in colander.

Meanwhile, in large pot of boiling salted water, blanch celery for 30 seconds; remove with tongs and chill under cold water. Drain and slice thinly; set aside.

In same pot, boil noodles until tender but firm, about 5 minutes. Drain and chill under cold water; drain well and place in large shallow bowl. Toss with sesame oil to coat.

Top noodles with cabbage, celery, chicken, radishes and green onions. Top with sauce; toss just before serving.

Makes 4 servings.

PER SERVING: about 765 cal, 34 g pro, 43 g total fat (11 g sat. fat), 64 g carb, 9 g fibre, 59 mg chol, 1,274 mg sodium. % RDI: 26% calcium, 35% iron, 18% vit A, 75% vit C, 76% folate.

best tips:

Look for sesame paste in Chinese and Japanese grocery stores. It's richer in flavour than tahini, which will do in a pinch.

Island Chicken and Rice

Eating this tender chicken steeped in Caribbean flavour makes you feel like you're on an island vacation, no matter the time of the year. Use breasts, thighs or legs, or a combination of chicken pieces.

4 **bone-in chicken breasts** (about 2 lb/1 kg)

¾ tsp (4 mL) each **salt** and **pepper**

½ tsp (2 mL) **ground allspice**

¼ tsp (1 mL) **ground ginger**

1 tbsp (15 mL) **vegetable oil**

5 cloves **garlic,** minced

1 tbsp (15 mL) minced **jalapeño pepper**

1½ cups (375 mL) **long-grain rice**

1 **sweet red pepper,** chopped

1 can (400 mL) **coconut milk**

1 cup (250 mL) **chicken broth**

½ cup (125 mL) chopped **fresh coriander**

1 **green onion,** chopped

Remove skin from chicken; trim off any fat. Sprinkle with ¼ tsp (1 mL) each of the salt and pepper, the allspice and ginger.

In large shallow Dutch oven, heat oil over medium-high heat; brown chicken. Transfer to plate.

Add garlic, jalapeño and remaining salt and pepper to pan; cook over medium heat, stirring, until garlic is golden, about 1 minute. Add rice and red pepper; stir in coconut milk and broth, scraping up browned bits from bottom of pan. Bring to boil.

Return chicken (bone side up) and any accumulated juices to pan. Reduce heat, cover and simmer, turning chicken once, until no longer pink inside and no liquid remains, about 25 minutes.

Stir in all but 2 tbsp (30 mL) of the coriander. Sprinkle with remaining coriander and green onion.

Makes 4 servings.

PER SERVING: about 661 cal, 43 g pro, 27 g total fat (19 g sat. fat), 61 g carb, 2 g fibre, 86 mg chol, 726 mg sodium. % RDI: 6% calcium, 34% iron, 14% vit A, 97% vit C, 14% folate.

Pan-Roasted Cherry Tomatoes

1 tbsp (15 mL) **extra-virgin olive oil**

4 cups (1 L) **cherry tomatoes** or grape tomatoes

1 clove **garlic,** minced

1 tsp (5 mL) **dried Italian herb seasoning**

¼ tsp (1 mL) **salt**

Pinch **granulated sugar**

Pinch **hot pepper flakes**

2 **green onions,** sliced

2 tsp (10 mL) **balsamic vinegar**

In large skillet, heat oil over medium-high heat; fry tomatoes, garlic, Italian herb seasoning, salt, sugar, hot pepper flakes and green onions, stirring occasionally, until tomatoes are shrivelled, about 5 minutes. Stir in vinegar.

Makes 4 servings.

PER SERVING: about 63 cal, 2 g pro, 4 g total fat (1 g sat. fat), 7 g carb, 2 g fibre, 0 mg chol, 152 mg sodium. % RDI: 2% calcium, 5% iron, 13% vit A, 32% vit C, 9% folate.

VARIATION
Pan-Roasted Cherry Tomatoes with Corn and Zucchini: Replace Italian seasoning with ½ tsp (2 mL) each paprika and dried oregano. Add 1 small zucchini, cut into 1-inch (2.5 cm) pieces, and ½ cup (125 mL) frozen corn kernels, thawed. Replace balsamic with cider vinegar, if desired.

roast chicken dinner

Lemon Herb Roast Chickens

It's just as easy to cook two birds as one. Serve one and refrigerate any remaining chicken and gravy for another use.

2 **chickens** (each 3½ to 5 lb/1.75 to 2.2 kg)

2 **lemons**

1 **onion,** halved

1 head **garlic,** cut in half

1 bunch **fresh parsley**

6 sprigs **fresh rosemary**

2 tbsp (30 mL) **extra-virgin olive oil**

2 tsp (10 mL) **salt**

1 tsp (5 mL) **pepper**

GRAVY:

2 tbsp (30 mL) **all-purpose flour**

1 cup (250 mL) **sodium-reduced chicken broth**

Remove giblets and necks from chickens.

Halve lemons; squeeze out juice and set aside. Divide lemon halves, onion, garlic and parsley between chicken cavities. Tie legs together with kitchen string; tuck wings under backs. Place, breast side up, on rack in large roasting pan. Tuck rosemary under chickens.

Stir together reserved lemon juice, oil, salt and pepper; pour over chickens. Pour ¾ cup (175 mL) water into pan. Roast in 375°F (190°C) oven, basting occasionally and adding ¾ cup (175 mL) water halfway through, until meat thermometer inserted in thigh registers 185°F (85°C), 1½ to 2 hours.

Discard contents of cavities; tip juices from cavities into pan drippings. Transfer chickens to platter and tent with foil; let stand for 20 minutes before carving.

Gravy: Skim fat from pan juices. Sprinkle with flour; cook over medium-high heat, stirring, for 1 minute. Pour in broth and any juices from platter; boil, stirring, until thickened, about 3 minutes. Strain into warmed gravy boat. Serve with chickens.

Makes 12 servings.

PER SERVING (WITHOUT SKIN): about 225 cal, 23 g pro, 13 g total fat (3 g sat. fat), 3 g carb, trace fibre, 82 mg chol, 552 mg sodium. % RDI: 1% calcium, 7% iron, 3% vit A, 7% vit C, 5% folate.

Two-Tone Mashed Potato Crisp

8 **Yukon Gold potatoes** (about 2½ lb/1.25 kg)

4 **sweet potatoes** (about 2½ lb/1.25 kg)

1 cup (250 mL) each **milk** and **sour cream**

¼ cup (60 mL) **butter,** softened

1 tsp (5 mL) **salt**

½ tsp (2 mL) each **ground nutmeg** and **white pepper**

TOPPING:

2 cups (500 mL) cubed **crusty bread**

2 tbsp (30 mL) chopped **fresh parsley**

2 tbsp (30 mL) **butter,** melted

Keeping separate, peel and cut Yukon Gold and sweet potatoes into chunks. In 2 large pots of boiling salted water, cover and cook potatoes separately until tender, about 20 minutes. Drain and return potatoes to each pot. Divide milk, sour cream, butter, salt, nutmeg and pepper between pots; mash until smooth.

Spread mashed sweet potatoes evenly in greased 13- x 9-inch (3 L) baking dish; spread mashed Yukon Gold potatoes evenly over top.

Topping: Meanwhile, in food processor, pulse bread until in pea-size pieces; pulse in parsley and butter. Sprinkle over potatoes. Bake in 400°F (200°C) oven until golden and knife inserted in centre comes out hot, about 20 minutes.

Makes 12 servings.

PER SERVING: about 251 cal, 4 g pro, 9 g total fat (6 g sat. fat), 38 g carb, 3 g fibre, 27 mg chol, 673 mg sodium. % RDI: 7% calcium, 6% iron, 151% vit A, 33% vit C, 10% folate.

best tips:

To make this lovely potato side dish ahead of time, spoon potatoes into dish as directed. Let cool for 30 minutes; refrigerate until cold. Cover with plastic wrap; refrigerate for up to 24 hours. Uncover and microwave on high for 10 to 12 minutes, or cover with foil and bake in 400°F (200°C) oven until hot, about 30 minutes. Uncover and sprinkle with topping.

Asian Chicken Noodle Soup

6 cups (1.5 L) **sodium-reduced chicken broth**

1 tbsp (15 mL) **fish sauce** or soy sauce

4 slices **gingerroot**

2 cloves **garlic,** smashed

4 oz (125 g) **large rice stick noodles**

2 cups (500 mL) shredded **cooked chicken**

6 **grape tomatoes** or cherry tomatoes, cut in quarters

3 **green onions,** chopped

¾ cup (175 mL) **fresh coriander leaves,** or
   fresh basil or mint leaves

1 **hot green pepper,** thinly sliced

Lime wedges

In large pot or Dutch oven, bring chicken broth, fish sauce, ginger and garlic to boil; reduce heat, cover and simmer for 10 minutes. Discard ginger.

Meanwhile, in large saucepan of boiling water, cook noodles until tender but firm, about 5 minutes. Drain and rinse under cold water; toss to drain well. Divide among soup bowls.

Ladle hot broth over noodles. Sprinkle with shredded chicken, tomatoes, green onions, coriander and hot pepper. Serve with lime wedges.

Makes 6 servings.

PER SERVING: about 180 cal, 18 g pro, 4 g total fat (1 g sat. fat), 18 g carb, 1 g fibre, 42 mg chol, 879 mg sodium, 176 mg potassium. % RDI: 3% calcium, 6% iron, 3% vit A, 5% vit C, 5% folate.

best roast chicken leftovers

Make-Your-Own Chicken Quesadillas

Set out bowls of sour cream and salsa as accompaniments to this family favourite.

1 tbsp (15 mL) **vegetable oil**

1 **onion,** sliced

3 cups (750 mL) sliced **mushrooms**

1 **sweet green pepper,** sliced

2 tsp (10 mL) **chili powder**

¼ tsp (1 mL) each **salt** and **pepper**

1½ lb (750 g) **roasted chicken** (see Best Tips, below)

½ cup (125 mL) **barbecue sauce**

2 cups (500 mL) shredded **Monterey Jack cheese**

1 cup (250 mL) frozen **corn kernels,** thawed

4 **green onions,** sliced

8 large **tortillas** (10 inches/25 cm)

In large skillet, heat oil over medium-high heat; fry onion, mushrooms, green pepper, chili powder, salt and pepper until liquid is evaporated, about 8 minutes. Scrape into bowl.

Meanwhile, remove and discard any skin from chicken. Remove meat from bones and shred into separate bowl. Add barbecue sauce and stir to coat. Set out cheese, corn and green onions in separate bowls.

To serve, add desired ingredients to half of each tortilla. Fold tortilla over; press onto filling. Bake on rimmed baking sheets in 400°F (200°C) oven, turning once, until golden and cheese is melted, about 20 minutes. Cut into halves or quarters.

Makes 4 servings.

PER SERVING: about 692 cal, 49 g pro, 33 g total fat (14 g sat. fat), 52 g carb, 5 g fibre, 132 mg chol, 1,069 mg sodium. % RDI: 45% calcium, 36% iron, 26% vit A, 50% vit C, 55% folate.

best tips:

When time is tight, picking up a supermarket deli-roasted chicken on your way home is a smart solution. Or cook up our Lemon Herb Roast Chickens (page 90) and use the extra one for this recipe. In total, you'll need about 3 cups (750 mL) shredded cooked chicken.

Artichoke Chicken Flatbread
You can replace the flatbread with a thin pizza crust or two naan flatbreads.

1 jar (370 mL) **roasted red peppers,** drained

2 cloves **garlic,** smashed

2 tbsp (30 mL) **extra-virgin olive oil**

½ tsp (2 mL) **salt**

1 thin-crust 12-inch (30 cm) **flatbread**

1 cup (250 mL) shredded **mozzarella cheese** or crumbled goat cheese

1¾ cups (425 mL) sliced **cooked chicken**

Half small **red onion,** thinly sliced

1 jar (6 oz/175 mL) **marinated artichoke hearts,** drained

¼ cup (60 mL) sliced **black olives** (optional)

½ tsp (2 mL) **dried oregano**

In food processor, purée together roasted red peppers, garlic, oil and salt; spread evenly over flatbread. Transfer to baking sheet or pizza stone.

Sprinkle with half of the cheese. Scatter chicken, onion, artichokes, olives (if using) and oregano over top; sprinkle with remaining cheese.

Bake in bottom third of 500°F (260°C) oven until golden and cheese is bubbly, about 15 minutes. (Or bake according to flatbread package instructions.)

Makes 4 servings.

PER SERVING: about 486 cal, 31 g pro, 23 g total fat (7 g sat. fat), 39 g carb, 4 g fibre, 80 mg chol, 947 mg sodium. % RDI: 19% calcium, 22% iron, 27% vit A, 162% vit C, 16% folate.

Roast Turkey Breast With Peppers and Rosemary Garlic Butter

3 lb (1.5 kg) **boneless single turkey breast**

1 tbsp (15 mL) **lemon juice**

3 **sweet red, orange** and/or **yellow peppers**

16 cloves **garlic**

4 sprigs **fresh rosemary,** halved

1 tbsp (15 mL) **extra-virgin olive oil**

ROSEMARY GARLIC BUTTER:

2 cloves **garlic**

¼ tsp (1 mL) **salt**

2 tbsp (30 mL) **butter,** softened

1½ tsp (7 mL) chopped **fresh rosemary**

½ tsp (2 mL) grated **lemon rind**

¼ tsp (1 mL) **pepper**

Rosemary Garlic Butter: On cutting board, coarsely chop garlic; sprinkle with salt. With side of chef's knife or fork, mash into paste; scrape into small bowl. Mix in butter, rosemary, lemon rind and pepper.

With fingers, loosen skin at thickest part of turkey. Slide fingers under skin to make pocket, leaving skin intact on 3 sides. Press butter mixture into pocket, pressing skin to spread mixture evenly.

Place turkey, skin side up, in small shallow roasting pan. Drizzle with lemon juice. Roast in 325°F (160°C) oven for 45 minutes.

Meanwhile, quarter and seed sweet peppers; cut each quarter crosswise into thirds. Toss together peppers, garlic, rosemary and oil to coat. Arrange around turkey.

Roast until meat thermometer inserted in thickest part of breast registers 185°F (85°C), about 45 minutes. Transfer turkey to cutting board; tent with foil and let stand for 15 minutes before slicing.

Return pepper mixture to oven; continue roasting until peppers are tender, about 15 minutes. Serve with turkey.

Makes 8 servings.

PER SERVING: about 310 cal, 38 g pro, 14 g total fat (5 g sat. fat), 6 g carb, 1 g fibre, 105 mg chol, 185 mg sodium. % RDI: 4% calcium, 16% iron, 14% vit A, 122% vit C, 7% folate.

Turkey con Queso Bake

Chili con queso is typically served as an appetizer with tortilla chips or vegetables. This dish borrows that idea and combines it with a turkey wrap. The amount of sauce may initially seem too generous, but it eventually thickens enough to spoon over the rolls.

3 tbsp (45 mL) **butter**

1 **onion,** chopped

2 cloves **garlic,** minced

¼ cup (60 mL) **all-purpose flour**

1½ cups (375 mL) **chicken broth**

1 cup (250 mL) **milk**

3 cups (750 mL) shredded **old Cheddar cheese**

½ tsp (2 mL) each **salt** and **pepper**

FILLING:

2 cups (500 mL) diced **cooked turkey**

2 **tomatoes,** seeded and diced

¼ cup (60 mL) chopped **green olives**

3 **green onions,** chopped

2 tbsp (30 mL) chopped **fresh coriander**

1 **jalapeño pepper,** seeded and chopped

8 small **tortillas** (6 inches/15 cm)

In saucepan, melt butter over medium heat; fry onion and garlic, stirring occasionally, until softened, about 2 minutes.

Add flour; cook, stirring, for 2 minutes. Whisk in broth and milk; bring to boil, stirring. Reduce heat and simmer until thickened, about 5 minutes. Remove from heat. Stir in 2½ cups (625 mL) of the cheese, salt and pepper; set aside.

Filling: In large bowl, combine turkey, tomatoes, olives, onions, coriander and jalapeño pepper; stir in ½ cup (125 mL) of the cheese sauce. Spoon ¾ cup (175 mL) into greased 13- x 9-inch (3 L) baking dish.

Divide remaining filling evenly down centre of each tortilla; roll up loosely. Place, seam side down, on sauce in dish. Spoon remaining sauce over top. Sprinkle with remaining cheese.

Bake in 350°F (180°C) oven until golden and bubbly, 35 to 40 minutes. Let stand for 10 minutes before serving.

Makes 8 servings.

PER SERVING: about 463 cal, 28 g pro, 25 g total fat (13 g sat. fat), 32 g carb, 2 g fibre, 87 mg chol, 813 mg sodium. % RDI: 35% calcium, 21% iron, 22% vit A, 13% vit C, 35% folate.

best tips:

You can replace the turkey with diced cooked chicken, steak or pork; shrimp; or black beans.

Cranberry Turkey Cutlets

½ cup (125 mL) **dry bread crumbs**

1 tsp (5 mL) crumbled **dried sage** (or 1 tbsp/15 mL chopped fresh sage)

¼ tsp (1 mL) each **salt** and **pepper**

2 tbsp (30 mL) **vegetable oil** or olive oil

4 **turkey cutlets** (1 lb/500 g total)

SAUCE:

½ cup (125 mL) **cranberry sauce**

1 tsp (5 mL) grated **orange rind**

Pinch each **salt** and **pepper**

In shallow dish, mix together bread crumbs, sage, salt and pepper. Brush 1 tbsp (15 mL) of the oil all over cutlets; press into crumb mixture, turning to coat.

In nonstick skillet, heat remaining oil over medium heat; fry cutlets, turning once, until golden and no longer pink inside, 4 to 5 minutes. Transfer to plate; keep warm.

Sauce: Add cranberry sauce, 2 tbsp (30 mL) water, orange rind, salt and pepper to pan; simmer until hot, about 2 minutes. Serve with cutlets.

Makes 4 servings.

PER SERVING: about 238 cal, 13 g pro, 10 g total fat (2 g sat. fat), 24 g carb, 1 g fibre, 39 mg chol, 314 mg sodium. % RDI: 4% calcium, 14% iron, 2% vit C, 3% folate.

best tips: Buy turkey cutlets or make your own by cutting a single turkey breast crosswise into 1-inch (2.5 cm) thick slices. Pound slices to ½-inch (1 cm) thickness. You can also use chicken, pork or veal cutlets.

Pineapple-Mustard Glazed Ham With Caramelized Pineapple

7 lb (3.15 kg) **fully cooked bone-in ham**

Whole cloves

¼ cup (60 mL) **liquid honey**

¼ cup (60 mL) **pineapple juice**

1 tbsp (15 mL) **butter**

1 tbsp (15 mL) **Dijon mustard**

Caramelized Pineapple (recipe follows)

Place ham, fat side up, on rack in roasting pan; pour in 2 cups (500 mL) water. Cover pan tightly with foil; roast in 325°F (160°C) oven for 2 hours, adding more water if necessary to maintain level. Pour off drippings, reserving ¼ cup (60 mL).

If ham has skin, peel off. Trim fat layer to ¼-inch (5 mm) thickness. Diagonally score fat to form diamond pattern. Stud centre of each diamond with clove.

In small saucepan, heat honey, pineapple juice and butter over medium heat, stirring occasionally, until syrupy and reduced to ½ cup (125 mL). Stir in mustard and reserved ham drippings; let cool slightly. Brush about half over ham.

Roast ham, uncovered and brushing several times with remaining glaze, until meat thermometer inserted in centre registers 140°F (60°C), about 40 minutes. Transfer to cutting board and tent with foil; let stand for 15 minutes before carving. Serve with Caramelized Pineapple.

Makes 8 to 10 servings.

PER EACH OF 10 SERVINGS: about 328 cal, 40 g pro, 12 g total fat (5 g sat. fat), 16 g carb, 1 g fibre, 94 mg chol, 2,119 mg sodium, 568 mg potassium. % RDI: 2% calcium, 12% iron, 2% vit A, 22% vit C, 5% folate.

Caramelized Pineapple: Peel, core and cut 1 pineapple into quarters; cut crosswise into slices. In skillet, melt 1 tbsp (15 mL) butter over medium heat; in batches, brown pineapple, turning occasionally, until caramelized, about 6 minutes.

Makes 8 to 10 servings.

Crunchy Scalloped Potatoes

The best part of these crunchy-topped potatoes in a creamy sauce is that you can make them up to a day ahead and reheat them to serve. There's less to fuss about when you have at least one vegetable that just needs to warm and crisp while you carve the ham.

2½ lb (1.25 kg) **Yukon Gold potatoes** (about 7), peeled and halved crosswise

2 tbsp (30 mL) **butter**

1½ cups (375 mL) sliced **leeks** (white and light green parts only)

3 tbsp (45 mL) **all-purpose flour**

½ tsp (2 mL) **salt**

¼ tsp (1 mL) **pepper**

Pinch **dried thyme**

1¾ cups (425 mL) **milk**

TOPPING:

½ cup (125 mL) **fine fresh bread crumbs**

2 tbsp (30 mL) grated **Parmesan cheese**

1 tbsp (15 mL) **butter,** melted

In large pot of boiling salted water, cover and cook potatoes until almost tender, about 10 minutes. Drain and let cool. Cut crosswise into ¼-inch (5 mm) thick slices.

Meanwhile, in large saucepan, melt butter over medium heat; cover and cook leeks, stirring occasionally, until tender, about 7 minutes.

Stir in flour, salt, pepper and thyme; cook, stirring, for 1 minute. Gradually whisk in milk; cook, whisking, until thick enough to coat back of spoon, about 5 minutes. Remove from heat. Gently stir in potatoes to coat. Spread in 8-cup (2 L) casserole or square baking dish.

Topping: Stir together bread crumbs, cheese and butter until crumbly; sprinkle over potatoes. Bake, uncovered, in 425°F (220°C) oven until heated through and topping is browned, about 20 minutes.

Makes 8 servings.

PER SERVING: about 194 cal, 5 g pro, 6 g total fat (4 g sat. fat), 31 g carb, 2 g fibre, 17 mg chol, 243 mg sodium, 487 mg potassium. % RDI: 9% calcium, 6% iron, 7% vit A, 17% vit C, 12% folate.

best tips:

To carve ham, cut down to bone into ¼-inch (5 mm) thick slices. With knife parallel to bone, cut off slices along bone. Turn remaining meaty portion up; repeat carving.

Boston Lettuce and Mâche Salad With Buttermilk Dill Dressing

Mâche, also known as lamb's lettuce, is a small, sweet leafy green.

2 small heads **Boston lettuce**

4 cups (1 L) **mâche,** baby spinach or arugula leaves

4 **radishes,** thinly sliced

1 **green onion,** sliced

BUTTERMILK DILL DRESSING:

⅔ cup (150 mL) **buttermilk**

¼ cup (60 mL) **light mayonnaise**

2 tbsp (30 mL) minced **fresh parsley**

1 tsp (5 mL) **cider vinegar**

½ tsp (2 mL) **Dijon mustard**

¼ tsp (1 mL) **dried dillweed**

Pinch each **salt** and **pepper**

Buttermilk Dill Dressing: Whisk together buttermilk, mayonnaise, parsley, vinegar, mustard, dillweed, salt and pepper.

Cut each head of Boston lettuce into quarters. Keeping lettuce wedges intact, arrange mâche between leaves. Place each on salad plate; sprinkle with radishes and green onion. Drizzle with dressing.

Makes 8 servings.

PER SERVING: about 45 cal, 2 g pro, 3 g total fat (trace sat. fat), 4 g carb, 1 g fibre, 3 mg chol, 85 mg sodium. % RDI: 5% calcium, 6% iron, 25% vit A, 28% vit C, 18% folate.

Glazed Carrots With Thyme

You can assemble this versatile side dish hours in advance and cook it just before serving. It requires only a few minutes of attention at the end, when the carrots are browning.

8 **carrots** (about 1 lb/500 g)

1 tbsp (15 mL) **olive oil**

2 tsp (10 mL) chopped **fresh thyme**

2 tsp (10 mL) **granulated sugar**

½ tsp (2 mL) **salt**

Cut carrots into 2-inch (5 cm) pieces. In nonstick skillet, combine carrots, ¾ cup (175 mL) water, oil, thyme, sugar and salt. Bring to boil; cover and cook over medium heat until carrots are tender and water is evaporated, 10 to 12 minutes.

Uncover and cook, shaking pan often, until carrots are glazed and lightly browned, 6 to 10 minutes.

Makes 6 servings.

PER SERVING: about 57 cal, 1 g pro, 2 g total fat (0 g sat. fat), 9 g carb, 2 g fibre, 0 mg chol, 237 mg sodium. % RDI: 2% calcium, 4% iron, 171% vit A, 3% vit C, 5% folate.

Curried Pork Burgers

While the grilled red onion is delicious, these juicy, zesty burgers are also nice without them.

1 lb (500 g) **lean ground pork**

½ cup (125 mL) chopped **fresh coriander**

⅓ cup (75 mL) crumbled **feta cheese**

2 tbsp (30 mL) **mild curry paste**

2 cloves **garlic,** minced

2 tsp (10 mL) minced **gingerroot**

1 **jalapeño pepper,** seeded and minced

¾ tsp (4 mL) **ground cumin**

¼ tsp (1 mL) each **salt** and **pepper**

4 leaves **Boston lettuce**

4 **soft buns**

GRILLED RED ONION:

Half large **red onion**

1 tsp (5 mL) **vegetable oil**

Pinch each **salt** and **pepper**

Mix together pork, coriander, feta, curry paste, garlic, ginger, jalapeño, cumin, salt and pepper. Divide into quarters; shape into patties. Cover and refrigerate for 10 minutes or up to 4 hours.

Place patties on greased grill over medium-high heat; close lid and grill, turning once, until instant-read thermometer inserted sideways into centre of each registers 160°F (71°C), about 10 minutes.

Grilled Red Onion: Meanwhile, cut onion crosswise into ½-inch (1 cm) thick slices. Insert small skewer horizontally through each slice to keep rings intact. Brush both sides with oil; sprinkle with salt and pepper.

Place onion on greased grill over medium-high heat; close lid and cook, turning once, until softened and lightly charred, about 5 minutes. Sandwich onion, lettuce and burgers in buns.

Makes 4 servings.

PER SERVING: about 472 cal, 29 g pro, 22 g total fat (7 g sat. fat), 38 g carb, 3 g fibre, 84 mg chol, 889 mg sodium, 516 mg potassium. % RDI: 17% calcium, 25% iron, 4% vit A, 10% vit C, 36% folate.

Pork Saltimbocca

Pork Saltimbocca In Italian, *saltimbocca* means "to jump in the mouth," which accurately describes the exciting flavours of this dish. It most often features veal, but is delicious using pork.

1½ lb (750 g) **boneless pork loin**
½ tsp (2 mL) **pepper**
8 slices **prosciutto**
8 large **fresh sage leaves**
2 tbsp (30 mL) **all-purpose flour**
2 tbsp (30 mL) **extra-virgin olive oil**
⅔ cup (150 mL) **sodium-reduced chicken broth**
⅓ cup (75 mL) **Marsala wine**
1 tbsp (15 mL) finely chopped **fresh chives** or parsley

Cut pork into 8 pieces. Between plastic wrap and using flat side of mallet, pound each piece to ¼-inch (5 mm) thickness. Sprinkle each with pepper; top each with 1 slice prosciutto. Place 1 sage leaf on prosciutto at short end; roll up crosswise and secure with toothpick. Place in bowl.

Sprinkle rolls with flour, tossing to coat. In large skillet, heat oil over medium-high heat. Shaking off excess flour, sear rolls on all sides until golden, about 3 minutes. Transfer to plate.

Drain fat from pan. Add broth and Marsala; bring to boil, scraping up browned bits on bottom of pan. Return rolls to pan; cover and simmer until juices run clear when pork is pierced and just a hint of pink remains inside, about 3 minutes. Transfer to platter; remove toothpicks.

Boil liquid until reduced to ⅓ cup (75 mL), about 3 minutes. Strain over rolls. Sprinkle with chives.

Makes 4 servings.

PER SERVING: about 337 cal, 45 g pro, 12 g total fat (3 g sat. fat), 7 g carb, trace fibre, 119 mg chol, 575 mg sodium. % RDI: 5% calcium, 14% iron, 1% vit A, 3% vit C, 7% folate.

best tips:

Marsala is a fortified sweet wine. It is delicious for sipping on its own or as an ingredient in a number of Italian dishes.

Pork and Pepper Stir-Fry

This quick stir-fry is great sprinkled with chopped toasted cashews or peanuts. It's delicious served over rice.

1 lb (500 g) **pork tenderloin**

1 tbsp (15 mL) **cornstarch**

1 tbsp (15 mL) **soy sauce**

2 cloves **garlic,** minced

2 tsp (10 mL) **sesame oil**

1 tsp (5 mL) finely grated **gingerroot**

Pinch **pepper**

2 tbsp (30 mL) **vegetable oil**

1 large **white onion,** sliced

1 each **sweet red** and **green pepper,** sliced

¼ cup (60 mL) **sodium-reduced beef broth**

2 tbsp (30 mL) **oyster sauce**

¼ cup (60 mL) chopped **fresh coriander**

Thinly slice pork across the grain into strips. Toss together pork, cornstarch, soy sauce, garlic, 1 tsp (5 mL) of the sesame oil, ginger and pepper; let stand for 20 minutes.

In wok or large skillet, heat vegetable oil over high heat; stir-fry pork mixture, in batches, until lightly browned, about 1 minute. Transfer to plate.

Add onion and red and green peppers to pan; stir-fry until onion is softened, about 3 minutes.

Return pork and accumulated juices to pan. Stir in broth and oyster sauce; cook until thickened, about 1 minute. Stir in remaining sesame oil. Garnish with coriander.

Makes 4 servings.

PER SERVING: about 317 cal, 27 g pro, 16 g total fat (3 g sat. fat), 16 g carb, 2 g fibre, 66 mg chol, 600 mg sodium. % RDI: 5% calcium, 11% iron, 13% vit A, 125% vit C, 13% folate.

around the world

Grilled Calamari With Lemon and Oregano

Mild-tasting calamari is most often sold in 2-lb (1 kg) boxes, frozen or thawed. Moist and tender, it can toughen with overcooking, so watch your grilling time.

¼ cup (60 mL) **olive oil**

4 cloves **garlic,** minced

½ tsp (2 mL) grated **lemon rind**

3 tbsp (45 mL) **lemon juice**

2 tbsp (30 mL) chopped **fresh oregano**

½ tsp (2 mL) each **salt** and **pepper**

1 lb (500 g) **calamari,** cleaned (see Best Tips, page 112)

Lemon wedges

In large bowl, whisk together oil, garlic, lemon rind and juice, oregano, salt and pepper. Cut calamari tentacles from tubes; score top layer of each tube crosswise, 2 inches (5 cm) apart. Add tentacles and tubes to bowl; toss to coat. Cover and refrigerate for 30 minutes.

Place on greased grill or grill pan over high heat; close lid or cover and cook, turning once, until firm, about 2 minutes. Serve with lemon wedges to squeeze over top.

Makes 4 servings.

PER SERVING: about 172 cal, 17 g pro, 10 g total fat (1 g sat. fat), 4 g carb, trace fibre, 54 mg chol, 440 mg sodium. % RDI: 6% calcium, 39% iron, 5% vit A, 13% vit C, 7% folate.

VARIATION

Grilled Shrimp with Lemon and Oregano: Substitute large shrimp, peeled and deveined, for the calamari. Thread onto 8 skewers. Place on greased grill over medium-high heat; close lid and cook, turning once, until pink, about 5 minutes.

greek take-out at home

Chicken Souvlaki
Make your own tzatziki with our recipe (below) or look for it in the dairy aisle in your supermarket.

12 oz (375 g) **boneless skinless chicken breasts**

1 tsp (5 mL) grated **lemon rind**

2 tbsp (30 mL) **lemon juice**

1 tbsp (15 mL) **extra-virgin olive oil**

1 tsp (5 mL) **dried oregano**

¼ tsp (1 mL) each **salt** and **pepper**

Half **red onion,** cut into 1-inch (2.5 cm) wedges

Half **cucumber**

¼ cup (60 mL) **Greek Tzatziki** (right)

4 whole wheat or white **pocketless pitas**

1 **tomato,** cut in chunks

1 cup (250 mL) shredded **romaine lettuce**

Cut chicken into 1-inch (2.5 cm) cubes. In large bowl, toss together chicken, lemon rind and juice, oil, oregano, salt and pepper; let stand for 10 minutes.

Alternately thread chicken and onion onto 4 metal skewers. Broil on foil-lined rimmed baking sheet, turning once, until chicken is no longer pink inside, about 10 minutes.

Meanwhile, cut cucumber in half lengthwise; thinly slice crosswise to make 1 cup (250 mL). Spread tzatziki over half of each pita. Push chicken and onion off skewers onto pitas. Top with tomato, cucumber and lettuce; fold over.

Makes 4 servings.

PER SERVING: about 392 cal, 29 g pro, 8 g total fat (2 g sat. fat), 55 g carb, 8 g fibre, 51 mg chol, 668 mg sodium. % RDI: 5% calcium, 25% iron, 11% vit A, 20% vit C, 29% folate.

Greek Tzatziki: In refrigerator, drain 2 cups (500 mL) Balkan-style plain yogurt in cheesecloth-lined sieve set over bowl for at least 2 hours or up to 6 hours. Mix in 1 small clove garlic, minced; 1 tbsp (15 mL) chopped fresh mint; 1 tbsp (15 mL) extra-virgin olive oil; and ¼ tsp (1 mL) salt. Stir in ½ cup (125 mL) finely diced and patted dry seeded peeled cucumber.

Makes about 2 cups (500 mL).

best tips:

To clean squid, cut off tentacles above where they attach and just under eye. Push out hard beak from centre; discard. Rinse off any grit. Pull eye and innards out of body tube (also known as hood); discard. Reach in and pull out cellophane-like quill (backbone); discard. If desired, loosen corner and pull off purple skin (if it's slippery, grasp with paper towel); discard.

Great Big Hothouse Greek Salad

Half **English cucumber**

1 **sweet green pepper**

1 large **ripe tomato**

Half **red onion,** chopped

½ cup (125 mL) **Kalamata olives**

2 tbsp (30 mL) **extra-virgin olive oil**

4 tsp (20 mL) **red wine vinegar**

1 tbsp (15 mL) chopped **fresh oregano**
   (or 1 tsp/5 mL dried)

Pinch each **salt** and **pepper**

3 oz (90 g) **feta cheese,** cubed or sliced

Quarter cucumber lengthwise; cut into ¾-inch (2 cm) chunks. Core, seed and cut green pepper into same-size pieces. Core and cut tomato into same-size chunks.

In bowl, toss together cucumber, pepper, tomato, onion and olives. Sprinkle with oil, vinegar, oregano, salt and pepper; toss to combine. Top each serving with cheese.

Makes 4 servings.

PER SERVING: about 214 cal, 5 g pro, 18 g total fat (5 g sat. fat), 11 g carb, 3 g fibre, 20 mg chol, 808 mg sodium. % RDI: 13% calcium, 8% iron, 9% vit A, 67% vit C, 15% folate.

best tips:

• Feta cheese is usually made from sheep's milk, goat's milk or a blend, though it's occasionally made with cow's milk. You can buy feta that ranges from mild to sharp, and soft to hard.

• Feta is sold in blocks and usually kept in brine so that it won't dry out. You can buy feta already crumbled, but whole pieces can be a bit moister.

• Before you use feta, rinse the brine off and pat the cheese dry with a paper towel to reduce the saltiness.

Help-Yourself Turkey Tacos

Serve these tasty, weeknight-friendly tacos with the chopped plum tomatoes or substitute some of the Fresh Tomato Salsa (below).

1 lb (500 g) **lean ground turkey**

2 cloves **garlic,** minced

1 tbsp (15 mL) **chili powder**

2 tsp (10 mL) **dried oregano**

½ tsp (2 mL) each **salt** and **pepper**

4 **green onions,** thinly sliced

¼ cup (60 mL) **chili sauce,** salsa or Fresh Tomato Salsa (below)

1 cup (250 mL) shredded **lettuce**

2 small **plum tomatoes,** chopped

1 cup (250 mL) shredded **Cheddar cheese**

½ cup (125 mL) **light sour cream**

1 small **avocado,** peeled, pitted and chopped

8 **taco shells**

In large nonstick skillet, sauté turkey over medium-high heat, breaking up with spoon, until no longer pink, about 5 minutes. Drain off any fat.

Add garlic, chili powder, oregano, salt and pepper; fry over medium heat until liquid is evaporated, about 6 minutes. Stir in green onions and chili sauce. Scrape into serving bowl.

At the table, spoon meat mixture, lettuce, tomatoes, cheese, sour cream and avocado into taco shells as desired.

Makes 4 servings.

PER SERVING: about 544 cal, 33 g pro, 33 g total fat (11 g sat. fat), 32 g carb, 6 g fibre, 108 mg chol, 921 mg sodium. % RDI: 33% calcium, 26% iron, 22% vit A, 25% vit C, 40% folate.

Fresh Tomato Salsa: In bowl, stir together 2 plum tomatoes, diced; ¼ cup (60 mL) chopped fresh coriander; 1 tbsp (15 mL) minced jalapeño pepper; 1 green onion, finely chopped; 1 tbsp (15 mL) lime juice or wine vinegar; 1 tbsp (15 mL) vegetable oil; and ¼ tsp (1 mL) each salt and pepper.

Makes about 1½ cups (375 mL).

best taco night

Layered Guacamole

Serve this chunky dip with store-bought tortilla chips or treat yourself to some homemade Baked Tortilla Chips (below). For ease, you can make and store the chips in an airtight container up to 24 hours ahead.

4 ripe **avocados,** peeled, pitted and cubed

½ cup (125 mL) minced **red onion**

2 tbsp (30 mL) minced seeded **jalapeño pepper**

2 tbsp (30 mL) **lime juice**

2 tbsp (30 mL) **extra-virgin olive oil**

3 cloves **garlic,** minced

¾ tsp (4 mL) each **salt** and **pepper**

1 **plum tomato,** diced

2 tbsp (30 mL) minced **fresh coriander**

Gently toss together avocados, onion, jalapeño pepper, lime juice, 1 tbsp (15 mL) of the oil, garlic and ½ tsp (2 mL) each of the salt and pepper.

Toss together tomato, coriander and remaining oil, salt and pepper; sprinkle over avocado mixture.

Makes about 3½ cups (875 mL).

PER 1 TBSP (15 mL): about 29 cal, trace pro, 3 g total fat (trace sat. fat), 1 g carb, 1 g fibre, 0 mg chol, 32 mg sodium. % RDI: 1% iron, 1% vit A, 3% vit C, 4% folate.

Baked Tortilla Chips: Brush 5 small flour tortillas with 1 tbsp (15 mL) vegetable oil; cut each into 12 wedges. Spread out on rimmed baking sheet; bake in 375°F (190°C) oven until crisp and golden, about 10 minutes.

Makes 60 pieces.

best tips: If your avocados need ripening, place them in a paper bag and let stand at room temperature for 2 to 3 days. If you want to speed things up even more, put an apple in the bag. It will give off natural ethylene gas, which speeds ripening.

Herbed Rice

Cooking rice in broth adds flavour. Another great option is half water and half tomato juice.

1½ cups (375 mL) **sodium-reduced chicken broth** or water

1 cup (250 mL) **long-grain rice**

¼ tsp (1 mL) **salt**

⅓ cup (75 mL) minced **fresh coriander** or parsley

1 **green onion,** finely chopped

1 small clove **garlic,** minced

1 tbsp (15 mL) **extra-virgin olive oil**

In saucepan, bring broth, rice and salt to boil. Reduce heat to low; cover and simmer until rice is tender, about 20 minutes.

Stir in coriander, green onion, garlic and olive oil. Let stand, covered, for 5 minutes.

Makes 4 servings.

PER SERVING: about 206 cal, 5 g pro, 4 g total fat (1 g sat. fat), 37 g carb, 1 g fibre, 0 mg chol, 368 mg sodium, 65 mg potassium. % RDI: 2% calcium, 3% iron, 1% vit A, 2% vit C, 3% folate.

best tips:

For extra crunch and colour, stir in ½ cup (125 mL) diced sweet red pepper along with green onion and herbs. Sprinkle with 2 tbsp (30 mL) pepitas.

Thai Mango Salad

½ cup (125 mL) coarsely chopped **peanuts**

2 firm **mangoes** (about 2 lb/1 kg total)

1 **sweet red pepper**

2 **carrots,** coarsely grated

4 cups (1 L) torn **mixed greens**

¼ cup (60 mL) thinly sliced **green onions**

2 tbsp (30 mL) coarsely chopped **fresh mint**

DRESSING:

¼ cup (60 mL) **vegetable oil**

1 tsp (5 mL) grated **lime rind**

2 tbsp (30 mL) **lime juice**

1 tbsp (15 mL) **fish sauce** or soy sauce

2 tsp (10 mL) **granulated sugar**

1 tsp (5 mL) minced seeded **hot pepper**
   (or Asian chili paste)

¼ tsp (1 mL) each **salt** and **pepper**

In dry small skillet, toast peanuts over medium heat, shaking pan often, until fragrant and golden, 5 minutes. Set aside.

Peel, pit and thinly slice mangoes lengthwise. Seed, core and thinly slice red pepper. Set aside.

Dressing: In large bowl, whisk together oil, lime rind and juice, fish sauce, sugar, hot pepper, salt and pepper.

Add mangoes, red pepper, carrots, mixed greens, green onions and mint to dressing; toss to coat. Serve sprinkled with peanuts.

Makes 6 servings.

PER SERVING: about 251 cal, 5 g pro, 15 g total fat (2 g sat. fat), 28 g carb, 5 g fibre, 0 mg chol, 403 mg sodium. % RDI: 6% calcium, 8% iron, 136% vit A, 128% vit C, 34% folate.

best thai take-out

Fresh Avocado Spring Rolls With Sweet Thai Dipping Sauce

These rolls are a healthier choice than their deep-fried counterparts, and can be made and refrigerated up to 6 hours ahead of time. Squeeze some lemon juice over the avocado to keep it bright green.

5 oz (150 g) **rice vermicelli noodles**

2 **carrots,** shredded

1½ cups (375 mL) julienned **cucumber**

½ cup (125 mL) lightly packed **fresh mint leaves,** chopped

½ cup (125 mL) lightly packed **fresh coriander leaves,** chopped

¼ cup (60 mL) **seasoned rice vinegar**

4 tsp (20 mL) **fish sauce**

2 large **avocados**

24 **rice paper wrappers** (8¼ inches/21 cm round)

SWEET THAI DIPPING SAUCE:

1 cup (250 mL) **granulated sugar**

½ cup (125 mL) **cider vinegar** or unseasoned rice vinegar

4 cloves **garlic,** minced

2 **Thai bird's-eye chilies,** thinly sliced

½ tsp (2 mL) **salt**

Sweet Thai Dipping Sauce: In saucepan, bring sugar, vinegar, ½ cup (125 mL) water, garlic, chilies and salt to boil. Reduce heat and simmer until reduced to 1 cup (250 mL), 15 to 20 minutes. Let cool completely.

In large bowl, cover noodles with boiling water; let stand until softened, about 10 minutes. Drain and chill under cold water; drain and return to bowl. Using scissors, cut into thirds. Add carrots, cucumber, mint, coriander, vinegar and fish sauce; toss to combine. Peel and pit avocados; cut into ½-inch (1 cm) thick slices.

Fill 9-inch (23 cm) pie plate with warm water. Dip each rice paper wrapper into water until pliable, about 10 seconds; pat dry on towel. Onto centre of each wrapper, spoon scant ¼ cup (60 mL) noodle mixture; form into log shape. Top each with 1 slice avocado. Fold bottom then sides of wrapper over filling; roll into cylinder. Place on damp towel–lined baking sheet; cover with damp towel to prevent drying out. Serve with dipping sauce.

Makes 24 pieces.

PER PIECE: about 107 cal, 1 g pro, 3 g total fat (trace sat. fat), 21 g carb, 1 g fibre, 0 mg chol, 222 mg sodium. % RDI: 1% calcium, 3% iron, 21% vit A, 8% vit C, 7% folate.

best tips:

"To julienne" means to cut into matchstick-size strips.

Chicken Pad Thai
For added flavour, toss 8 oz (250 g) peeled deveined shrimp in with the chicken.

Half pkg (14 oz/400 g pkg) **wide rice stick noodles**

⅔ cup (150 mL) **chicken broth**

½ cup (125 mL) **ketchup**

¼ cup (60 mL) **fish sauce**

2 tbsp (30 mL) **granulated sugar**

2 tbsp (30 mL) **cornstarch**

1 tsp (5 mL) grated **lime rind**

2 tbsp (30 mL) **lime juice**

1 tsp (5 mL) **hot pepper sauce** or Asian chili paste

4 tsp (20 mL) **vegetable oil**

2 **eggs,** lightly beaten

1 lb (500 g) **boneless skinless chicken breasts,** thinly sliced

4 small **carrots,** thinly sliced

1 **sweet red pepper,** thinly sliced

2 cloves **garlic,** minced

1 tbsp (15 mL) minced **gingerroot**

2 cups (500 mL) **bean sprouts**

2 **green onions,** sliced

¼ cup (60 mL) chopped **unsalted peanuts**

In large bowl, soak noodles in warm water for 20 minutes; drain and set aside.

Meanwhile, whisk together broth, ketchup, fish sauce, sugar, cornstarch, lime rind and juice, and hot pepper sauce; set aside.

In wok or large skillet, heat 2 tsp (10 mL) of the oil over medium heat; cook eggs, stirring often, until scrambled and set, about 2 minutes. Transfer to plate.

Wipe out wok; add remaining oil. Brown chicken, in batches, over medium-high heat. Transfer to separate plate.

Add carrots, red pepper, garlic and ginger to pan; cook, stirring, until slightly softened, about 3 minutes. Add noodles; stir gently for 1 minute.

Return chicken and any accumulated juices to pan. Stir sauce mixture and pour into pan; cook, stirring, until sauce is thickened, noodles are tender and chicken is no longer pink inside, about 3 minutes.

Return egg mixture to wok along with bean sprouts; toss gently until heated through, about 1 minute. Serve sprinkled with green onions and peanuts.

Makes 4 servings.

PER SERVING: about 590 cal, 40 g pro, 14 g total fat (2 g sat. fat), 76 g carb, 5 g fibre, 174 mg chol, 2,079 mg sodium. % RDI: 9% calcium, 21% iron, 202% vit A, 108% vit C, 39% folate.

best tips: Thai cuisine usually consists of lightly cooked dishes with strong aromatic components. The balance of flavours and textures is very important. When you think about flavour balance, think of these 4 S's: salty, sweet, sour and spicy. Taste your dishes as you cook and make adjustments to your seasonings to keep all the elements in harmony.

Jerk Pork Chops

Serve these fragrant, juicy Jamaican-inspired chops with Peas, Pepper and Rice (below). You can also make this dish with 8 boneless skinless chicken thighs instead of the pork. The prepared meat can be refrigerated for up to 24 hours before roasting.

1 tbsp (15 mL) **soy sauce**

1 tbsp (15 mL) **orange juice**

1 tbsp (15 mL) **extra-virgin olive oil**

2 cloves **garlic,** minced

3 **green onions,** minced

1 tsp (5 mL) each **ground allspice** and **dried thyme**

¼ tsp (1 mL) each **salt** and **pepper**

¼ tsp (1 mL) **ground ginger**

Pinch **cayenne pepper**

4 **pork loin centre chops**

Stir together soy sauce, orange juice, oil, garlic, green onions, allspice, thyme, salt, pepper, ginger and cayenne; rub all over pork chops.

In small roasting pan, roast pork in 375°F (190°C) oven, turning halfway through, until juices run clear when pork is pierced and just a hint of pink remains inside, about 18 minutes.

Makes 4 servings.

PER SERVING: about 190 cal, 21 g pro, 10 g total fat (3 g sat. fat), 3 g carb, 1 g fibre, 58 mg chol, 453 mg sodium. % RDI: 3% calcium, 10% iron, 1% vit A, 7% vit C, 5% folate.

Peas, Pepper and Rice: In saucepan, heat 1 tbsp (15 mL) vegetable oil over medium-high heat; fry 1 small onion, chopped, stirring occasionally, until softened, about 3 minutes. Add 1 sweet red pepper, diced, and ¾ cup (175 mL) parboiled rice; stir for 1 minute. Add 1½ cups (375 mL) chicken broth, and ¼ tsp (1 mL) each cinnamon, salt and pepper; bring to boil. Reduce heat, cover and simmer until rice is tender and liquid is absorbed, about 20 minutes. With fork, stir in ¾ cup (175 mL) frozen peas; heat through.

Makes 4 servings.

quick and easy
caribbean

Grilled Pineapple

Don't worry about coring the pineapple for this recipe – just eat around it.

1 **golden pineapple** (about 3½ lb/1.75 kg)
2 tbsp (30 mL) **vegetable oil**
¼ tsp (1 mL) each **salt** and **pepper**
¼ tsp (1 mL) **hot pepper sauce**
2 tbsp (30 mL) chopped **fresh coriander**

Cut top and bottom off pineapple. Stand on flat end; with sharp knife, cut off skin. Remove eyes. Cut pineapple crosswise into ½-inch (1 cm) thick slices.

Stir together oil, salt, pepper and hot pepper sauce; brush half over 1 side of pineapple slices. Place, oiled side down, on greased grill over medium heat; brush with remaining oil mixture. Close lid and grill, turning once, until browned, about 4 minutes. Transfer to platter; sprinkle with coriander.

Makes 8 servings.

PER SERVING: about 79 cal, trace pro, 3 g total fat (trace sat. fat), 13 g carb, 1 g fibre, 0 mg chol, 66 mg sodium. % RDI: 1% calcium, 3% iron, 20% vit C, 3% folate.

best tips:

Golden pineapple is juicy and sweet. If unavailable, add 1 tbsp (15 mL) liquid honey to oil mixture.

Ginger Beer Shandy

Created by the British in the 19th century, a shandy is a popular drink in the Caribbean and a refreshing beverage in your backyard.

Ice cubes (optional)
Quarter **lime**
4 oz (120 mL) chilled **lager beer**
4 oz (120 mL) chilled **ginger beer**

Fill glass halfway with ice (if using). Squeeze lime over top, twisting rind to release oils. Add lager and ginger beer; stir to combine.

Makes 1 serving.

PER SERVING: about 177 cal, 1 g pro, trace total fat (0 g sat. fat), 37 g carb, 0 g fibre, 0 mg chol, 10 mg sodium. % RDI: 1% calcium, 1% iron, 5% vit C, 6% folate.

best tips:

Multiply this recipe to make as many servings as needed. In a pinch, ginger ale can stand in for ginger beer.

Spring Salad Cups With Tarragon Dressing

2 heads **Bibb lettuce** or Boston lettuce

8 cups (2 L) **baby spinach** or mixed baby greens

8 **radishes,** thinly sliced

3 **green onions,** thinly sliced

TARRAGON DRESSING:

⅓ cup (75 mL) **extra-virgin olive oil** or vegetable oil

2 tbsp (30 mL) **light mayonnaise**

1 tbsp (15 mL) chopped **fresh tarragon**

1 tbsp (15 mL) **white wine vinegar**

2 tsp (10 mL) **Dijon mustard**

¼ tsp (1 mL) **salt**

Pinch **pepper**

Tarragon Dressing: Whisk together oil, mayonnaise, tarragon, vinegar, mustard, salt and pepper.

Separate lettuce leaves; set aside 12 of the best large cups. Tear remaining lettuce into bite-size pieces; place in large bowl. Add spinach and half each of the radishes and green onions. Add dressing; toss to coat.

Mound salad in each lettuce cup. Sprinkle with remaining radishes and green onions.

Makes 12 servings.

PER SERVING: about 76 cal, 2 g pro, 7 g total fat (1 g sat. fat), 3 g carb, 1 g fibre, 1 mg chol, 110 mg sodium. % RDI: 5% calcium, 9% iron, 28% vit A, 25% vit C, 44% folate.

easy french dinner

Golden Onion Tart As easy to make as pizza, this Alsatian-inspired pie can be enjoyed warm or at room temperature.

2 tbsp (30 mL) **vegetable oil**

6 cups (1.5 L) sliced **sweet onions** (about 2½ lb/1.25 kg)

¼ tsp (1 mL) **caraway seeds**

2 tbsp (30 mL) **wine vinegar**

¾ tsp (4 mL) each **salt** and **pepper**

2 cloves **garlic,** minced

1 lb (500 g) **pizza dough**

1 **egg,** beaten

⅓ cup (75 mL) **sour cream**

1 **green onion,** chopped

In large shallow Dutch oven, heat oil over medium heat; fry sliced onions, stirring occasionally, until softened and golden, 12 to 15 minutes.

Meanwhile, using mortar and pestle or back of heavy skillet, crush caraway seeds; add to pan along with vinegar, salt, pepper and garlic. Cook, stirring and scraping up any browned bits from bottom of pan, for 1 minute. Scrape into large bowl; let cool slightly.

On lightly floured surface, roll out dough into 14-inch (35 cm) circle. Place on greased 12-inch (30 cm) pizza pan. Roll up overhang to form lip, pinching to seal.

Add egg, sour cream and green onion to cooked onion mixture; mix thoroughly. Spread evenly over dough, leaving lip uncovered. Bake in 350°F (180°C) oven until crust is golden and filling is set in centre, about 30 minutes. Let stand for 5 minutes before cutting into wedges.

Makes 4 to 6 servings.

PER EACH OF 6 SERVINGS: about 341 cal, 9 g pro, 11 g total fat (3 g sat. fat), 53 g carb, 4 g fibre, 39 mg chol, 671 mg sodium. % RDI: 7% calcium, 17% iron, 3% vit A, 13% vit C, 23% folate.

best tips:

You can add onions and garlic to almost any dish. To save time, peel a whole head of garlic at once and keep the peeled cloves in a small airtight container in the refrigerator for up to 1 week. Avoid prechopping the cloves because there is a danger of food poisoning. Plus, freshly chopped garlic is always superior in flavour.

En Papillote Salmon Packages

1 small **fennel bulb**

4 **roasted red peppers,** peeled, drained and sliced

4 **salmon fillets** (1½ lb/750 g)

2 tbsp (30 mL) chopped **fresh Italian parsley**

2 tbsp (30 mL) **olive oil**

2 tbsp (30 mL) **Pernod** or other licorice-flavoured
   liqueur, or vegetable broth

4 cloves **garlic,** minced

1 tsp (5 mL) grated **lemon rind**

½ tsp (2 mL) each **salt** and **pepper**

Lemon wedges

Cut stalks off fennel. Halve fennel from top to root end; core. Cut into thin slices. Place one-quarter of the slices on 1 side of each of four 18-inch (45 cm) long pieces of parchment paper or foil. Sprinkle with red peppers. Top with salmon.

Stir together parsley, oil, Pernod, garlic, lemon rind, salt and pepper; spoon over salmon. Fold paper over top. Fold open edges over in small pleats to seal and form semicircular package.

Bake on rimmed baking sheet in 425°F (220°C) oven until fennel is tender and fish flakes easily when tested, 15 to 20 minutes. Serve with lemon wedges.

Makes 4 servings.

PER SERVING: about 422 cal, 36 g pro, 26 g total fat (5 g sat. fat), 12 g carb, 3 g fibre, 100 mg chol, 414 mg sodium. % RDI: 4% calcium, 10% iron, 44% vit A, 345% vit C, 31% folate.

Crème Brûlée If your brown sugar is lumpy, press through a fine-mesh sieve before sprinkling over tops of custards.

3 cups (750 mL) **whipping cream**

8 **egg yolks**

⅓ cup (75 mL) **granulated sugar**

1½ tsp (7 mL) **vanilla**

½ cup (125 mL) packed **brown sugar**

In saucepan, heat cream over medium-high heat until steaming. In bowl, whisk egg yolks with granulated sugar; gradually whisk in cream. Whisk in vanilla. Skim off foam.

Divide among eight ¾-cup (175 mL) ramekins or custard cups. Place in 2 large shallow pans; pour in enough boiling water to come halfway up sides of ramekins.

Bake in 350°F (180°C) oven until edge is set but centre still jiggles and knife inserted in centre comes out creamy, about 20 minutes. Remove from water; let cool on racks. Cover and refrigerate until chilled and set, about 2 hours.

Place cups on rimmed baking sheet; sprinkle brown sugar evenly over custards. Using blowtorch or broiler, broil until sugar bubbles and darkens, about 6 minutes (watch carefully if using broiler and remove each dish as it's ready). Chill, uncovered, for at least 30 minutes before serving or for up to 3 hours.

Makes 8 servings.

PER SERVING: about 438 cal, 5 g pro, 37 g total fat (21 g sat. fat), 24 g carb, 0 g fibre, 318 mg chol, 45 mg sodium, 139 mg potassium. % RDI: 9% calcium, 6% iron, 36% vit A, 13% folate.

Pasta With White Beans and Rapini

1 bunch **rapini** or broccoli

4 cups (1 L) **whole wheat penne**

3 tbsp (45 mL) **extra-virgin olive oil**

1½ cups (375 mL) **fresh bread crumbs**

4 cloves **garlic,** minced

¼ tsp (1 mL) **salt**

Pinch **hot pepper flakes**

1 can (19 oz/540 mL) **romano beans** or
white kidney beans, drained and rinsed

Trim base of rapini stalks. In large pot of boiling water, cover and cook rapini until tender, about 2 minutes. With slotted spoon, transfer to colander; let drain. Cut into 1-inch (2.5 cm) pieces; set aside.

In same pot of boiling water, cook pasta until al dente, 8 to 10 minutes. Reserving ½ cup (125 mL) of the cooking liquid, drain and return to pot.

Meanwhile, in large skillet, heat 1 tsp (5 mL) of the oil over medium heat; fry bread crumbs and one-quarter of the garlic, stirring, until golden, about 3 minutes. Transfer to bowl.

In same skillet, heat remaining oil over medium heat; fry remaining garlic, salt and hot pepper flakes, stirring, until golden, about 1 minute.

Stir in rapini and beans; cook until heated through, about 3 minutes. Add to pasta; toss to coat, adding some of the reserved cooking liquid, if desired. Serve sprinkled with bread crumb mixture.

Makes 4 servings.

PER SERVING: about 552 cal, 24 g pro, 13 g total fat (2 g sat. fat), 92 g carb, 17 g fibre, 0 mg chol, 611 mg sodium. % RDI: 20% calcium, 51% iron, 28% vit A, 30% vit C, 82% folate.

italian family-style feast

Roasted Loin of Pork With Porchetta Flavours

Porchetta, a spit-roasted whole baby pig, is usually the centrepiece of joyous Roman outdoor celebrations. This loin of pork won't feed the whole neighbourhood, but it provides plenty of succulent slices for a Saturday night meal with friends.

3 lb (1.5 kg) **boneless pork loin centre roast (single loin)**

3 tbsp (45 mL) **extra-virgin olive oil**

4 cloves **garlic,** minced

2 tbsp (30 mL) minced **fresh rosemary**

1 tbsp (15 mL) **dry white vermouth** or white balsamic vinegar

4 tsp (20 mL) minced **fresh sage**

¾ tsp (4 mL) **fennel seeds,** crushed

½ tsp (2 mL) **salt**

¼ tsp (1 mL) **pepper**

Place pork, fat side up, on cutting board. Starting at right side with knife parallel to board, cut loin in half almost but not all the way through; open like book. Starting in centre of opened loin and with knife parallel to board, cut in half on left side almost but not all the way through. Repeat on right side. Open flat. Cover with waxed paper; pound with mallet to even thickness.

In small skillet, heat half of the oil over medium-low heat; fry garlic, stirring often, until softened, about 5 minutes. Scrape into large bowl. Stir in remaining oil, rosemary, vermouth, sage, fennel, salt and pepper. Spread about three-quarters over inside of loin, leaving 1-inch (2.5 cm) border along 1 short end. Starting at other end, roll up firmly toward border. Tie with kitchen string at 1-inch (2.5 cm) intervals.

Place tied roast in remaining garlic mixture in bowl, turning to coat. Cover and marinate in refrigerator, turning occasionally, for 2 hours or up to 24 hours.

Place roast on rack in roasting pan. Roast in 375°F (190°C) oven until meat thermometer inserted in centre registers 160°F (71°C), about 1¼ to 1½ hours.

Transfer to cutting board and tent with foil; let rest for 15 minutes. Remove string and slice thinly across the grain.

Makes 8 servings.

PER SERVING: about 261 cal, 33 g pro, 13 g total fat (4 g sat. fat), 1 g carb, trace fibre, 90 mg chol, 219 mg sodium. % RDI: 3% calcium, 9% iron, 3% vit C, 2% folate.

Balsamic Grilled Vegetables

If you have a grill pan, this is the ideal place to use it, as it will keep the vegetables from slipping through wider grates. These vegetables are delicious at room temperature, so grill them before starting the loin of pork (opposite).

4 mixed **sweet peppers** (red, yellow, orange and/or green)

2 large **zucchini**

1 **red onion**

BALSAMIC DRESSING:

⅓ cup (75 mL) **extra-virgin olive oil**

3 tbsp (45 mL) **white balsamic vinegar** or balsamic vinegar

1 tsp (5 mL) minced **fresh oregano** or rosemary

½ tsp (2 mL) each **salt** and **pepper**

Core and seed sweet peppers; cut into 1-inch (2.5 cm) wide slices; place in large bowl. Cut zucchini lengthwise into ¼-inch (5 mm) thick strips; add to bowl. Cut onion into ½-inch (1 cm) thick rings; skewer to keep rings intact. Set aside on plate.

Balsamic Dressing: Whisk together oil, vinegar, oregano, salt and pepper; toss half with vegetables, brushing some over onions. Let stand for 10 minutes.

Place vegetables on greased grill over medium-high heat; close lid and grill, turning once, until tender and lightly charred, 10 to 15 minutes. Remove to platter, peeling skins from peppers if desired. Drizzle with remaining dressing.

Makes 6 servings.

PER SERVING: about 154 cal, 1 g pro, 12 g total fat (2 g sat. fat), 11 g carb, 2 g fibre, 0 mg chol, 197 mg sodium. % RDI: 2% calcium, 6% iron, 21% vit A, 210% vit C, 12% folate.

Spinach Miso Soup White or cremini mushrooms, shiitake caps, trimmed enoki mushrooms or a combination would be great in this soup.

¾ cup (175 mL) **white miso** (see Best Tips, page 137)

1 small **zucchini**

3 cups (750 mL) thinly sliced **mushrooms**

1 pkg (454 g) **medium-firm tofu**

1 pkg (6 oz/170 g) **fresh baby spinach**

1 cup (250 mL) **bean sprouts**

1 **green onion,** thinly sliced

In large saucepan, bring 5 cups (1.25 L) water to boil; reduce heat to simmer. Whisk miso with 1 cup (250 mL) water; add to water.

Meanwhile, cut zucchini lengthwise in half; cut crosswise into ½-inch (1 cm) thick slices. Add to pan along with mushrooms; cover and simmer until vegetables are softened, about 5 minutes.

Meanwhile, drain tofu; cut into ½-inch (1 cm) cubes. Add to pan along with spinach; simmer until spinach wilts, about 1 minute. Serve soup garnished with bean sprouts and green onion.

Makes 4 servings.

PER SERVING: about 228 cal, 18 g pro, 9 g total fat (1 g sat. fat), 25 g carb, 8 g fibre, 0 mg chol, 1,933 mg sodium. % RDI: 27% calcium, 40% iron, 35% vit A, 20% vit C, 66% folate.

Smoked Salmon Maki Rolls
Slice the rolls just before serving and accompany with sushi soy sauce, which is milder and sweeter than regular soy sauce.

1 ripe **avocado**

Half **lemon**

6 **roasted nori sheets**

1 pkg (150 g) sliced **smoked salmon**

Half bunch **watercress,** tough stems trimmed

SUSHI RICE:

1 cup (250 mL) **medium-grain sushi rice**

3 tbsp (45 mL) **unseasoned rice vinegar**

4 tsp (20 mL) **granulated sugar**

¾ tsp (4 mL) **salt**

WASABI CREAM:

4 tsp (20 mL) **light mayonnaise**

1½ tsp (7 mL) each **wasabi powder** and **water**

½ tsp (2 mL) **unseasoned rice vinegar**

Sushi Rice: In fine sieve, rinse rice in 4 changes of cold water, stirring vigorously until water runs clear. Drain well. In saucepan, bring rice and 1¼ cups (300 mL) cold water to boil over high heat; reduce heat to low, cover and simmer for 13 minutes. Remove from heat. Uncover and drape tea towel over top; replace lid, letting edges of towel hang over side. Let stand for 10 minutes. Transfer rice to large bowl.

Meanwhile, in microwaveable bowl, combine vinegar, sugar and salt; microwave at high for 20 to 30 seconds or just until hot. Stir until sugar dissolves; let cool completely. Drizzle over rice; gently toss with wooden spoon to coat grains. Spread over surface of bowl; loosely cover with tea towel and let cool completely at room temperature, about 30 minutes. Do not refrigerate.

Wasabi Cream: Stir together mayonnaise, wasabi powder, water and vinegar; set aside.

Pit and peel avocado; cut into thin slices and squeeze lemon juice over top. Set aside.

Place 1 nori sheet, shiny side down and with long side closest, on bamboo sushi rolling mat. With moistened fingers, lightly spread about ½ cup (125 mL) of the rice in even layer on nori sheet, leaving ½-inch (1 cm) border along each long side.

Drizzle about ½ tsp (2 mL) wasabi cream in horizontal line about 2 inches (5 cm) from closest long edge. Lay one-sixth of the salmon on wasabi cream. Top with one-sixth of the avocado, then one-sixth of the watercress.

Working with closest edge of bamboo mat, lift and roll up nori, firmly encasing filling. Set aside, seam side down. Repeat with remaining ingredients to make 6 rolls.

With sharp knife, cut each roll into 8 slices, wiping knife with wet cloth between cuts.

Makes 48 pieces.

PER PIECE: about 28 cal, 1 g pro, 1 g total fat (trace sat. fat), 4 g carb, trace fibre, 1 mg chol, 66 mg sodium. % RDI: 1% iron, 2% vit A, 3% vit C, 2% folate.

best tips:

These rolls can be made and refrigerated up to 4 hours ahead. Wrap each unsliced roll in paper towel, then plastic wrap. Slice just before serving.

Edamame

These green soybeans are a healthy snack. To eat them, press the pods to pop out the beans, the same way you would fresh peas.

1 pkg (1 lb/500 g) frozen **edamame in pods**
1 tsp (5 mL) **sea salt** or table salt (approx)

Bring pot of water to boil over medium-high heat. Add edamame and salt; return to boil and cook until hot and tender, 2 to 3 minutes.

Drain well and transfer to serving bowl. Sprinkle with additional salt, if desired. Serve warm or cold.

Makes 6 servings.

PER SERVING: about 57 cal, 5 g pro, 2 g total fat (trace sat. fat), 5 g carb, 2 g fibre, 0 mg chol, 114 mg sodium, 205 g potassium. % RDI: 3% calcium, 8% iron, 5% vit C, 66% folate.

best tips: Miso is fermented soybean paste and is used in many traditional Japanese dishes. Look for it in Japanese or other Asian markets, natural food stores and some supermarkets. The white variety has a delicate flavour that's perfect for soup, but there many different varieties, such as red miso (stronger flavour; perfect for rubs on fish) and ones made from barley or brown rice.

Tabbouleh Salad

Chickpeas provide protein and are a nice addition to this otherwise traditional fresh and zesty salad. Or use 1 lb (500 g) cooked shrimp or chicken strips instead of the chickpeas.

1 cup (250 mL) **bulgur** (medium or coarse), rinsed and drained

1 can (19 oz/540 mL) **chickpeas,** drained and rinsed

2 **tomatoes,** seeded and chopped

1 cup (250 mL) diced **English cucumber**

1 cup (250 mL) minced **fresh parsley**

½ cup (125 mL) thinly sliced **green onions**

¼ cup (60 mL) chopped **fresh mint**

DRESSING:

¼ cup (60 mL) **lemon juice**

2 tbsp (30 mL) **extra-virgin olive oil**

2 cloves **garlic,** minced

1 tsp (5 mL) **salt**

½ tsp (2 mL) **pepper**

In saucepan, bring 1¾ cups (425 mL) water to boil; stir in bulgur. Reduce heat to low, cover and simmer until no liquid remains, about 10 minutes. Transfer to large bowl; fluff with fork. Let cool to room temperature.

Add chickpeas, tomatoes, cucumber, parsley, onions and mint.

Dressing: Whisk together lemon juice, oil, garlic, salt and pepper; pour over bulgur mixture and toss to combine.

Makes 4 servings.

PER SERVING: about 336 cal, 13 g pro, 9 g total fat (1 g sat. fat), 56 g carb, 9 g fibre, 0 mg chol, 803 mg sodium. % RDI: 8% calcium, 29% iron, 14% vit A, 60% vit C, 56% folate.

best middle eastern take-out

Mini Falafel

Not just for vegetarians, this bite-size version of the Middle Eastern specialty will become a favourite for entertaining.

½ cup (125 mL) **dried chickpeas**

½ cup (125 mL) finely chopped **onion**

2 tbsp (30 mL) chopped **fresh parsley**

1 clove **garlic,** minced

2 tbsp (30 mL) **all-purpose flour**

2 tsp (10 mL) **ground cumin**

1 tsp (5 mL) **baking powder**

1 tsp (5 mL) **salt**

1 tsp (5 mL) **lemon juice**

Vegetable oil for frying

12 **mini pitas**

1 large **radish,** thinly sliced

TAHINI YOGURT SAUCE:

⅓ cup (75 mL) **Balkan-style plain yogurt**

¼ cup (60 mL) **tahini**

2 tbsp (30 mL) **lemon juice**

1 tbsp (15 mL) minced **fresh parsley**

1 tbsp (15 mL) **extra-virgin olive oil**

¼ tsp (1 mL) each **salt** and **cayenne pepper**

In bowl, pour enough cold water over chickpeas to cover by 1 inch (2.5 cm); cover and soak for at least 4 hours or up to 24 hours. Drain well.

In food processor, chop together chickpeas, onion, half of the parsley and the garlic to form coarse paste.

Add flour, cumin, baking powder, salt and lemon juice; pulse just until blended, about 10 seconds. Shape by heaping tablespoonfuls (15 mL) into balls; flatten to ½-inch (1 cm) thickness. Arrange in single layer on rimmed baking sheet; cover and refrigerate for 2 hours or up to 12 hours.

Pour enough oil into heavy skillet to come ¼ inch (5 mm) up side of pan; heat over medium-high heat. Fry falafel, turning once, until golden, about 4 minutes. With slotted spoon, transfer to paper towel–lined plate; let drain.

Tahini Yogurt Sauce: Meanwhile, whisk together yogurt, tahini, lemon juice, parsley, oil, salt and cayenne pepper.

Cut one-third off top of each pita; open to form pocket. Stuff each with falafel and radish slice. Drizzle with yogurt sauce; sprinkle with remaining parsley.

Makes 12 pieces.

PER SERVING: about 163 cal, 4 g pro, 11 g total fat (1 g sat. fat), 13 g carb, 2 g fibre, 1 mg chol, 318 mg sodium. % RDI: 5% calcium, 10% iron, 1% vit A, 5% vit C, 22% folate.

best tips:

• You can turn these hors d'oeuvres into regular-size sandwiches. Cut the top third off 4 regular-size pitas with pockets. Stuff 3 falafels into each and drizzle with sauce.

• To make these appetizers ahead, let fried falafels cool; cover and refrigerate for up to 24 hours. To reheat, bake on greased rimmed baking sheet in 350°F (180°C) oven until hot, about 10 minutes.

Roasted Garlic and Eggplant Dip Serve with flatbread
crackers or wedges of warm soft pita bread for dipping.

2 **eggplants** (about 2 lb/1 kg total)

6 cloves **garlic** (unpeeled)

½ cup (125 mL) **light sour cream**

1 tbsp (15 mL) **Dijon mustard**

2 tsp (10 mL) **balsamic vinegar** or red wine vinegar

¼ tsp (1 mL) each **salt** and **pepper**

1 tbsp (15 mL) chopped **fresh coriander**

1 tbsp (15 mL) chopped **fresh basil**

With fork, prick eggplants all over; place on lightly greased baking sheet. Bake in 400°F (200°C) oven for 35 minutes. Add garlic to pan. Bake until eggplants are very tender and garlic is golden and soft, about 25 minutes. Slit eggplant lengthwise and let cool enough to handle.

Peel garlic. With spoon, scoop eggplant flesh into food processor along with garlic. Add sour cream, mustard, vinegar, salt and pepper; purée until smooth.

Stir in coriander and basil; scrape into serving bowl. Cover and refrigerate for at least 1 hour or up to 3 days.

Makes about 3 cups (750 mL).

PER 2 TBSP (30 ML): about 20 cal, 1 g pro, trace total fat (trace sat. fat), 4 g carb, 1 g fibre, 1 mg chol, 37 mg sodium, 62 mg potassium. % RDI: 1% calcium, 1% iron, 2% vit C, 2% folate.

best tips:
For a more authentic, dairy-free variation, omit sour cream and add ¼ cup (60 mL) extra-virgin olive oil.

Best-Ever Spaghetti and Meatballs Serve in warmed pasta bowls with grated Romano or Parmesan cheese to sprinkle over top.

2 tbsp (30 mL) **extra-virgin olive oil**

2 **onions,** chopped

3 cloves **garlic,** minced

1 **egg**

½ cup (125 mL) **ricotta cheese**

2 tsp (10 mL) **fennel seeds,** lightly crushed

1¼ tsp (6 mL) **salt**

¾ tsp (4 mL) **pepper**

¼ tsp (1 mL) each **ground cinnamon, cloves**
   and **nutmeg**

1 cup (250 mL) coarse **fresh bread crumbs**

¼ cup (60 mL) minced **fresh parsley**

¼ cup (60 mL) grated **Romano cheese** or
   Parmesan cheese

8 oz (250 g) **lean ground beef**

8 oz (250 g) **lean ground pork**

½ cup (125 mL) **dry red wine** or sodium-reduced
   beef broth

1 can (28 oz/796 mL) **diced tomatoes**

1½ cups (375 mL) **canned crushed tomatoes**

½ cup (125 mL) coarsely chopped **fresh basil**
   (or 2 tsp/10 mL dried)

¼ tsp (1 mL) **granulated sugar**

1½ lb (750 g) **spaghetti**

In large skillet, heat half of the oil over medium heat; fry onions and garlic, stirring occasionally, until onions are softened, about 6 minutes. Transfer to bowl.

In large bowl, whisk together egg, ricotta cheese, fennel seeds, ¾ tsp (4 mL) of the salt, pepper, cinnamon, cloves and nutmeg. Stir in bread crumbs, parsley, Romano cheese and half of the onion mixture; mix in beef and pork. Refrigerate for 30 minutes.

With wet hands, form meat mixture by rounded tablespoonfuls (15 mL) into balls. Add remaining oil to pan. Brown meatballs, in batches, over medium-high heat; with slotted spoon, transfer to plate. Drain off fat.

Add wine to pan; bring to boil, stirring and scraping up browned bits. Transfer to Dutch oven; stir in remaining onion mixture, diced and crushed tomatoes, half of the basil (or all dried, if using), the remaining salt and sugar. Add meatballs. Cover and simmer over low heat, stirring occasionally, for 25 minutes.

Meanwhile, in large pot of boiling salted water, cook pasta until al dente, 8 to 10 minutes. Drain; return to pot. Add about 1 cup (250 mL) of the sauce; toss to coat.

Serve with remaining sauce and meatballs spooned over top. Garnish with remaining basil.

Makes 6 servings.

PER SERVING: about 781 cal, 37 g pro, 23 g total fat (8 g sat. fat), 105 g carb, 8 g fibre, 91 mg chol, 1,227 mg sodium. % RDI: 21% calcium, 46% iron, 21% vit A, 58% vit C, 92% folate.

best spaghetti night

Bitter Greens Salad

A simply dressed salad makes an excellent showcase for locally grown greens. Peruse the market stalls for your favourites and keep an eye out for locally made vinegars as well.

4 cups (1 L) torn **Boston lettuce**

4 cups (1 L) torn **radicchio**

2 cups (500 mL) sliced **Belgian endive**

2 cups (500 mL) torn **escarole** or frisée

1 **green onion,** sliced

⅓ cup (75 mL) **extra-virgin olive oil**

¼ cup (60 mL) **wine vinegar,** cider vinegar or fruit vinegar

¼ tsp (1 mL) **sea salt** or salt

¼ tsp (1 mL) **pepper**

In large bowl, toss together Boston lettuce, radicchio, endive, escarole and green onion. Sprinkle with oil, vinegar, salt and pepper; toss to combine.

Makes 6 to 8 servings.

PER EACH OF 8 SERVINGS: about 93 cal, 1 g pro, 9 g total fat (1 g sat. fat), 3 g carb, 1 g fibre, 0 mg chol, 58 mg sodium. % RDI: 2% calcium, 3% iron, 6% vit A, 10% vit C, 21% folate.

Cheddar Garlic Bread

1 **baguette**

¼ cup (60 mL) **butter,** softened

2 cloves **garlic,** minced

2 tbsp (30 mL) chopped **fresh parsley**

Pinch each **salt** and **pepper**

1 cup (250 mL) shredded **Cheddar cheese,** or Asiago or
    Fontina cheese

Cut baguette in half crosswise; cut each in half horizontally.

Stir together butter, garlic, parsley, salt and pepper; spread over cut sides of baguette.

Place baguette on rimmed baking sheet; sprinkle with cheese. Bake in 425°F (220°C) oven until cheese is bubbly and bread is golden, about 12 minutes.

Makes 8 servings.

PER SERVING: about 201 cal, 6 g pro, 11 g total fat (7 g sat. fat), 19 g carb, 1 g fibre, 27 mg chol, 389 mg sodium. % RDI: 13% calcium, 7% iron, 9% vit A, 1% vit C, 13% folate.

Butter Chicken

Serve this restaurant favourite with pappadams and lime or lemon wedges. If using unsalted butter, add about ¼ tsp (1 mL) salt to sauce. Use bone-in or boneless chicken breasts and halve them, if desired.

2 cups (500 mL) **Balkan-style plain yogurt**

6 cloves **garlic,** minced

1 piece (1 inch/2.5 cm) **gingerroot,** minced

1 tbsp (15 mL) **Garam Masala** (page 149)

1 tbsp (15 mL) **lime juice**

1 tbsp (15 mL) **medium curry paste**

2 tsp (10 mL) each **paprika, ground cumin**
   and **ground coriander**

½ tsp (2 mL) **salt**

8 **chicken breasts,** with wings if desired

BUTTER SAUCE:

1 tbsp (15 mL) **vegetable oil**

1 **onion,** chopped

1 tbsp (15 mL) **Garam Masala** (page 149)

2 tsp (10 mL) **paprika**

2 tsp (10 mL) **medium curry paste**

1 can (28 oz/796 mL) **tomatoes**

¾ cup (175 mL) **whipping cream**

⅓ cup (75 mL) cold **butter,** cubed

¼ cup (60 mL) chopped **fresh coriander**

Line sieve with cheesecloth; set over bowl. Add yogurt; drain in refrigerator for 1 hour. Discard liquid. In large bowl, whisk together yogurt, garlic, ginger, Garam Masala, lime juice, curry paste, paprika, cumin, coriander and salt. Add chicken to bowl and turn to coat; cover and refrigerate for 24 hours, turning occasionally.

Place chicken, skin side up, on rack in large shallow roasting pan; spoon yogurt mixture over top. Roast in 400°F (200°C) oven until no longer pink inside, about 45 minutes. Transfer to platter and tent with foil; let stand for 10 minutes. Skim fat from pan juices, reserving juices in pan.

Butter Sauce: Meanwhile, in large skillet, heat oil over medium heat; fry onion until deep golden, about 10 minutes. Add Garam Masala, paprika and curry paste; cook, stirring often, until fragrant and beginning to stick to pan, about 5 minutes. Mash in tomatoes, stirring and scraping up browned bits from bottom of pan. Simmer until thickened, about 15 minutes. Let cool slightly. In food processor or blender, purée until smooth.

Pour sauce into roasting pan; bring to boil over medium heat, scraping up any brown bits from bottom of pan. Add cream and butter, a few pieces at a time, cooking just until each is melted. Pour over chicken. Garnish with coriander.

Makes 8 servings.

PER SERVING (WITHOUT SKIN): about 439 cal, 37 g pro, 26 g total fat (13 g sat. fat), 12 g carb, 2 g fibre, 176 mg chol, 508 mg sodium. % RDI: 15% calcium, 24% iron, 34% vit A, 33% vit C, 9% folate.

Vegetable Biryani

This quick vegetarian version of a classic intricately spiced and slow-simmered dish is ready in about half an hour – perfect for weeknights.

¾ cup (175 mL) **dried green lentils**

2 tbsp (30 mL) **extra-virgin olive oil**

1 **onion,** chopped

3 **carrots,** diced

2 cloves **garlic,** minced

1 tbsp (15 mL) mild, medium or biryani **curry paste**

¼ tsp (1 mL) each **salt** and **pepper**

2 cups (500 mL) small **cauliflower florets**

1 cup (250 mL) **basmati rice**

¼ cup (60 mL) **raisins**

2¼ cups (550 mL) **vegetable broth**

1 cup (250 mL) **frozen peas,** thawed

¼ cup (60 mL) toasted **sliced almonds** (optional)

In saucepan of boiling water, cook lentils for 10 minutes; drain. Meanwhile, in Dutch oven, heat oil over medium-high heat; sauté onion until deep golden, 6 minutes. Add carrots, garlic, curry paste, salt and pepper; sauté until fragrant, 3 minutes. Stir in cauliflower, rice, raisins and lentils to coat. Add broth; bring to boil. Reduce heat, cover and simmer until rice and vegetables are tender, 20 minutes. Stir in peas; cook until heated through, 4 minutes. Sprinkle with almonds (if using).

Makes 4 servings.

PER SERVING: about 476 cal, 17 g pro, 10 g total fat (1 g sat. fat), 82 g carb, 10 g fibre, 0 mg chol, 871 mg sodium. % RDI: 7% calcium, 35% iron, 106% vit A, 48% vit C, 111% folate.

VARIATION

Chicken Biryani: Omit cauliflower. Cube 2 boneless skinless chicken breasts (12 oz/375 g). Brown in 1 tbsp (15 mL) vegetable oil; set aside. Return to pan along with rice.

Cucumber Yogurt

Known as *raita*, this cooling side dish is great alongside fiery curries.

1 cup (250 mL) **Balkan-style plain yogurt**
½ cup (125 mL) grated peeled **cucumber**
1 **green onion,** thinly sliced
1 tsp (5 mL) **lemon juice**
½ tsp (2 mL) each **salt** and **granulated sugar**

Stir together yogurt, cucumber, green onion, lemon juice, salt and granulated sugar. Let stand for 10 minutes before serving.

Makes 1⅓ cups (325 mL).

PER 2 TBSP (30 mL): about 21 cal, 1 g pro, 1 g total fat (1 g sat. fat), 2 g carb, trace fibre, 5 mg chol, 119 mg sodium, 48 mg potassium. % RDI: 3% calcium, 2% vit C, 1% folate.

Garam Masala

Store any unused portion of this spice mixture in an airtight jar for up to 1 month.

1 tbsp (15 mL) broken **cinnamon sticks**
1 tbsp (15 mL) **cardamom pods**
1 tbsp (15 mL) **black peppercorns**
1 tbsp (15 mL) **whole cloves**
1 tbsp (15 mL) **fennel seeds**

In small skillet, toast cinnamon sticks, cardamom, peppercorns and cloves over medium-low heat, shaking pan often, until fragrant, about 5 minutes.

Add fennel seeds; toast for 1 minute. Let cool. In spice grinder, or in mortar with pestle, grind to fine powder.

Makes about ¼ cup (60 mL).

Sweet-and-Sour Pineapple Chicken

You can replace the canned pineapple with 1 fresh pineapple, peeled, cored and cut in ½-inch (1 cm) pieces. Serve over hot rice.

1 lb (500 g) **boneless skinless chicken breasts,** cut into
   1-inch (2.5 cm) cubes

1 **egg white**

2 tbsp (30 mL) **cornstarch**

2 tbsp (30 mL) **all-purpose flour**

¼ tsp (1 mL) **salt**

¼ tsp (1 mL) **white pepper** or black pepper

⅓ cup (75 mL) **vegetable oil**

⅓ cup (75 mL) **sodium-reduced chicken broth**

3 tbsp (45 mL) **ketchup**

1 tbsp (15 mL) **dry sherry** (optional)

1 tbsp (15 mL) **sodium-reduced soy sauce**

1 tbsp (15 mL) **unseasoned rice vinegar**

2 tsp (10 mL) minced **gingerroot**

1 tsp (5 mL) **granulated sugar**

1 **onion,** cut into ¾-inch (2 cm) cubes

1 each **sweet red** and **green pepper,** cut into
   ¾-inch (2 cm) cubes

1 cup (250 mL) drained canned **pineapple chunks**

Stir together chicken, egg white, cornstarch, flour, salt and pepper; let stand for 10 minutes.

In wok or large skillet, heat oil over medium-high heat. Reserving cornstarch mixture in bowl, stir-fry chicken, in batches, until golden, about 3 minutes. Transfer chicken to plate.

Add broth, ⅓ cup (75 mL) water, ketchup, sherry (if using), soy sauce, vinegar, ginger and sugar to reserved cornstarch mixture; whisk to combine.

Drain off all but 1 tbsp (15 mL) fat from wok. Stir-fry onion and red and green peppers over medium-high heat until tender-crisp, about 3 minutes.

Add chicken and any juices, pineapple and cornstarch mixture to wok; stir-fry until sauce is glossy and thickened and chicken is coated, 2 to 3 minutes.

Makes 4 servings.

PER SERVING: about 273 cal, 29 g pro, 7 g total fat (1 g sat. fat), 25 g carb, 2 g fibre, 66 mg chol, 548 mg sodium. % RDI: 3% calcium, 9% iron, 13% vit A, 125% vit C, 12% folate.

chinese take-out
at home

Baked Egg Rolls
You can assemble and refrigerate these up to 12 hours before baking. Serve with plum sauce or homemade Chinese Plum Sauce (opposite).

1 lb (500 g) **lean ground pork**

3 **green onions,** chopped

2 cloves **garlic,** minced

1 **carrot,** grated

½ cup (125 mL) chopped **water chestnuts**

2 tbsp (30 mL) **soy sauce**

1 tbsp (15 mL) **cornstarch**

1 tsp (5 mL) **sesame oil**

½ tsp (2 mL) **pepper**

12 large (5½-inch/13 cm) **egg roll wrappers**

1 tsp (5 mL) **vegetable oil**

In nonstick skillet, cook pork over medium-high heat, breaking up with wooden spoon, until no longer pink, about 5 minutes; drain off fat. Add onions, garlic, carrot and water chestnuts; cook over medium heat, stirring occasionally, until onions are softened, about 3 minutes.

In small bowl, whisk together soy sauce, cornstarch, 1 tbsp (15 mL) water, sesame oil and pepper; pour into pan and toss well. Let cool slightly.

Forming 1 roll at a time, place wrapper on work surface; brush with water. Spoon scant 3 tbsp (45 mL) pork mixture on bottom third, leaving ½-inch (1 cm) borders on bottom and sides. Pull bottom edge up over filling and roll up; pinch ends to seal. Place, seam side down, on greased rimmed baking sheet; brush with oil. Bake in 375°F (190°C) oven until golden and crisp, about 20 minutes.

Makes 12 pieces.

PER PIECE: about 110 cal, 8 g pro, 5 g total fat (2 g sat. fat), 8 g carb, 1 g fibre, 25 mg chol, 243 mg sodium. % RDI: 2% calcium, 6% iron, 15% vit A, 2% vit C, 5% folate.

Chinese Plum Sauce

When plums are in season, make a batch or two of this delicious sauce. It's also great on roast pork or chicken.

8 cups (2 L) halved **pitted plums** (3 lb/1.5 kg)
1 cup (250 mL) chopped **onions**
1 cup (250 mL) **water**
1 tsp (5 mL) minced **gingerroot**
1 clove **garlic,** minced
¾ cup (175 mL) **granulated sugar**
½ cup (125 mL) **unseasoned rice vinegar** or cider vinegar
1 tsp (5 mL) **ground coriander**
½ tsp (2 mL) **salt**
½ tsp (2 mL) **cinnamon**
¼ tsp (1 mL) **cayenne pepper**
¼ tsp (1 mL) **ground cloves**

In large heavy saucepan, bring plums, onions, water, ginger and garlic to boil over medium heat; reduce heat to low, cover and simmer, stirring occasionally, until plums and onions are very tender, about 30 minutes.

Press through food mill or sieve; transfer to clean pan. Stir in sugar, vinegar, coriander, salt, cinnamon, cayenne and cloves. Bring to boil, stirring; reduce heat to low and simmer until mixture is consistency of applesauce, about 45 minutes.

Pour into 2-cup (500 mL) canning jars, leaving ½-inch (1 cm) headspace. Cover with prepared lids; screw on bands until resistance is met; increase to fingertip tight. Boil in boiling water canner for 30 minutes.

Makes 4 cups (1 L).

PER 1 TBSP (15 mL): about 22 cal, trace pro, trace total fat (0 g sat. fat), 5 g carb, trace fibre, 0 mg chol, 18 mg sodium, 37 mg potassium. % RDI: 1% vit A, 2% vit C.

Ginger Green Beans

Cooking the beans right in the skillet with their sauce not only saves a pan but also infuses the beans with the wonderful zing of ginger.

1 tsp (5 mL) **sesame seeds**
1 tbsp (15 mL) **vegetable oil** or olive oil
1 clove **garlic,** minced
1 tbsp (15 mL) minced **gingerroot**
¼ tsp (1 mL) each **salt** and **pepper**
1 lb (500 g) **green beans,** trimmed
⅓ cup (75 mL) **vegetable broth** or chicken broth

In dry large skillet over medium heat, toast sesame seeds, shaking pan occasionally, until golden, about 3 minutes. Transfer to bowl.

In same pan, heat oil over medium heat; fry garlic, ginger, salt and pepper until fragrant, about 30 seconds. Add beans; cook, stirring, for 2 minutes. Add broth; cover and steam for 6 minutes.

Uncover and cook until liquid is evaporated and beans are tender-crisp, about 2 minutes. Sprinkle with sesame seeds.

Makes 4 servings.

PER SERVING: about 74 cal, 2 g pro, 4 g total fat (trace sat. fat), 9 g carb, 2 g fibre, 0 mg chol, 199 mg sodium. % RDI: 4% calcium, 10% iron, 7% vit A, 17% vit C, 15% folate.

VARIATION

If you prefer less ginger and a stronger hit of sesame, reduce ginger to 1 tsp (5 mL) and substitute sesame oil for the vegetable oil. For extra crunch, substitute ¼ cup (60 mL) toasted slivered almonds for the sesame seeds.

best tips:

Toasting sesame seeds brings out their nutty flavour. Toast a large amount, then refrigerate cooled seeds in an airtight container for up to 1 month. Sprinkle on salads, granola and more.

Scallops and Shrimp With Sherry Paprika

This simple yet elegant dish makes a hearty, Spanish-inspired main course. Serve over rice for a main course or with crusty bread as an appetizer. Sweet paprika can replace the smoked paprika.

⅔ cup (150 mL) drained chopped **roasted red peppers**

⅓ cup (75 mL) **dry sherry**

2 tbsp (30 mL) **10% cream**

2 tsp (10 mL) **smoked paprika** (see Best Tips, page 156)

1 tsp (5 mL) chopped **fresh rosemary**

½ tsp (2 mL) each **salt** and **pepper**

16 **sea scallops** (8 oz/250 g)

10 oz (300 g) **raw large shrimp,** peeled and deveined

2 tbsp (30 mL) **butter**

3 cloves **garlic,** minced

1 tbsp (15 mL) chopped **fresh parsley**

In blender, purée together peppers, sherry, cream, paprika, rosemary, salt and pepper; set aside.

Remove tough muscle from side of each scallop if necessary; pat scallops and shrimp dry.

In large skillet, melt butter over medium heat; cook garlic until softened but not browned, about 1 minute. Add scallops and shrimp; cook over high heat, stirring, until shrimp begin to turn pink, about 1 minute.

Stir in pepper mixture; cover and cook until shrimp are pink and scallops are opaque, about 3 minutes. Sprinkle with parsley.

Makes 4 servings.

PER SERVING: about 202 cal, 21 g pro, 8 g total fat (4 g sat. fat), 7 g carb, 1 g fibre, 117 mg chol, 749 mg sodium. % RDI: 7% calcium, 17% iron, 27% vit A, 95% vit C, 7% folate.

Marinated Olives with Garlic

1 jar (12 oz/375 mL) **green olives**

¼ cup (60 mL) **sherry vinegar** or red wine vinegar

3 cloves **garlic,** smashed

1 thin slice **lemon**

Half **dried hot pepper** (optional)

1 sprig **fresh rosemary** or thyme
  (or ½ tsp/2 mL dried)

½ tsp (2 mL) **dried marjoram** or oregano

½ tsp (2 mL) **ground cumin**

Drain olives. With side of chef's knife or bottom of heavy pan, lightly crush olives; return to jar. Add vinegar, garlic, lemon, hot pepper (if using), rosemary, marjoram and cumin; seal and shake well.

Uncover and pour in enough water to reach top; shake to mix. Seal and refrigerate for at least 3 days before serving, or for up to 2 weeks.

Makes about 1½ cups (375 mL), or 8 servings.

PER SERVING: about 23 cal, trace pro, 2 g total fat (trace sat. fat), 1 g carb, trace fibre, 0 mg chol, 401 mg sodium. % RDI: 1% calcium, 4% iron, 1% vit A, 3% vit C.

Summer Sangria

1 **nectarine** (unpeeled), pitted and sliced

1 **orange** (unpeeled), sliced

1 **lemon** (unpeeled), sliced

2 tbsp (30 mL) **granulated sugar**

2 **whole cloves**

1 **cinnamon stick,** broken

2 oz (30 mL) **brandy**

1 bottle (1 L) **dry red wine**

Ice cubes

1½ cups (375 mL) **soda water,** chilled (approx)

In large pitcher, combine nectarine, orange, lemon, sugar, cloves, cinnamon, brandy and 1 cup (250 mL) of the wine. Cover and chill pitcher and remaining wine separately for 2 to 8 hours.

To serve, add ice cubes to fruit mixture in pitcher; stir in chilled wine. Stir in soda water, adding more, if desired. Serve immediately.

Makes 6 to 8 servings.

PER EACH OF 8 SERVINGS: about 130 cal, 1 g pro, trace total fat (0 g sat. fat), 10 g carb, 1 g fibre, 0 mg chol, 16 mg sodium, 215 mg potassium. % RDI: 2% calcium, 5% iron, 1% vit A, 22% vit C, 4% folate.

best tips:

• Spanish paprika (called *pimentón*) is made from a variety of different dried peppers and comes in three grades. *Dulce,* or sweet, is mild. *Agridulce* is medium-hot. *Picante* is hot.

• Smoked Spanish paprika is made from smoked dried peppers and is labelled the same way. *Dulce* is mild, dark red and silky. *Agridulce* has a distinct bitterness. *Picante* has a spicy kick.

Cheese and Chorizo Puffs
Light and flaky, these quick, five-ingredient tapas-size pastries will disappear faster than you can say "Olé!"
If your puff pastry is not prerolled, on floured surface, roll out dough into 10-inch (25 cm) square about ¼ inch (5 mm) thick.

Half pkg (450 g pkg) frozen **all-butter puff pastry,** thawed

¾ cup (175 mL) finely chopped **chorizo sausage**
   (3 oz/90 g)

½ cup (125 mL) shredded **Manchego cheese,** or Asiago or
   Monterey Jack cheese

1 **egg**

1 tsp (5 mL) **paprika**

On floured surface, unroll pastry. Using 3-inch (8 cm) round cutter, cut out 16 rounds, gathering and rerolling scraps as necessary.

In bowl, mix chorizo with cheese; place scant 1 tbsp (15 mL) in centre of each round. Lightly brush edges with water; fold pastry over to create half-moon shapes. Pinch edges to seal. Place on parchment paper–lined rimmed baking sheet. Or freeze on baking sheet until firm; layer between waxed paper in airtight container and freeze for up to 1 month.

In small bowl, whisk together egg, 2 tsp (10 mL) water and paprika; brush over tops of puffs. Bake in centre of 450°F (230°C) oven until puffed and golden, 10 to 12 minutes.

Makes 16 pieces.

PER PIECE: about 98 cal, 3 g pro, 7 g total fat (3 g sat. fat), 6 g carb, trace fibre, 25 mg chol, 133 mg sodium. % RDI: 3% calcium, 4% iron, 4% vit A, 1% folate.

lighten up!

Crispy Fish Fillets With Tartar Sauce

Panko is coarse Japanese bread crumbs used for coating; it becomes a super-crunchy crust when cooked. You'll find panko in Asian markets and most supermarkets.

1 tbsp (15 mL) **vegetable oil**

1 **egg**

2 tsp (10 mL) **Dijon mustard**

1 cup (250 mL) **panko**

¼ tsp (1 mL) each **salt** and **pepper**

4 **catfish fillets** or tilapia fillets (1½ lb/750 g total)

TARTAR SAUCE:

¼ cup (60 mL) **light mayonnaise**

2 tbsp (30 mL) **dill pickle relish**

1 tsp (5 mL) drained **capers**

Pinch **pepper**

Brush oil on rimmed baking sheet; heat in 450°F (230°C) oven for 5 minutes.

Meanwhile, in shallow dish, whisk together egg, 1 tbsp (15 mL) water and mustard. In second shallow dish, combine panko, salt and pepper. Dip fish into egg mixture then into panko mixture, turning to coat. Place on hot baking sheet; bake, turning once halfway through, until golden and fish flakes easily when tested, about 15 minutes.

Tartar Sauce: Meanwhile, stir together mayonnaise, relish, capers and pepper. Serve with fish.

Makes 4 servings.

PER SERVING: about 437 cal, 32 g pro, 24 g total fat (5 g sat. fat), 21 g carb, 1 g fibre, 132 mg chol, 660 mg sodium. % RDI: 7% calcium, 18% iron, 5% vit A, 2% vit C, 23% folate.

family favourites made healthy

Sweet Potato Fries With Curry Mayonnaise

4 **sweet potatoes** (2½ lb/1.25 kg)

2 **egg whites**

1 tbsp (15 mL) **vegetable oil**

1 tsp (5 mL) each **ground cumin** and **paprika**

½ tsp (2 mL) each **salt** and **pepper**

CURRY MAYONNAISE:

½ cup (125 mL) **light mayonnaise**

1 tsp (5 mL) **lime juice**

¼ tsp (1 mL) **mild curry paste**

Peel potatoes; trim ends and sides to create rectangles. Cut lengthwise into ½-inch (1 cm) thick slices; cut each lengthwise into ½-inch (1 cm) wide strips.

In large bowl, whisk egg whites until frothy; whisk in oil, cumin, paprika, salt and pepper. Add potatoes, tossing to coat. Spread on 2 parchment paper–lined rimmed baking sheets.

Bake in top and bottom thirds of 425°F (220°C) oven, rotating and switching pans halfway through, until tender and edges are browned and crisp, 30 to 35 minutes.

Curry Mayonnaise: Meanwhile, whisk together mayonnaise, lime juice and curry paste until smooth; serve with potatoes.

Makes 4 to 6 servings.

PER EACH OF 6 SERVINGS: about 209 cal, 4 g pro, 9 g total fat (1 g sat. fat), 29 g carb, 4 g fibre, 7 mg chol, 385 mg sodium. % RDI: 4% calcium, 11% iron, 240% vit A, 33% vit C, 5% folate.

best tips:

For maximum nutrition, choose sweet potatoes that are deep orange. One medium sweet potato provides more than 100 per cent of the recommended daily allowance (RDA) for vitamin A, about 33 per cent of the RDA for vitamin C, 20 per cent of the RDA for vitamin B₆, and 400 mg of potassium. Sweet potatoes are also a source of fibre.

Phyllo Cluster Apple Tarts

4 **apples**

3 tbsp (45 mL) **liquid honey**

½ tsp (2 mL) **cinnamon**

½ tsp (2 mL) grated **lemon rind**

3 sheets **phyllo pastry**

2 tbsp (30 mL) **canola oil,** vegetable oil or butter, melted

3 tbsp (45 mL) sliced **almonds,** toasted

Peel, core and slice apples. In large nonstick skillet, bring apples, ½ cup (125 mL) water, honey, cinnamon and lemon rind to simmer over medium heat; cover and cook, stirring occasionally, until tender, about 15 minutes. Let cool.

Place 1 sheet of phyllo on work surface; brush lightly with oil. Repeat twice, using all but about 1 tsp (5 mL) of the oil. Using sharp knife, cut into quarters. Gently press each into large greased muffin cup, separating layers to ruffle edges.

Divide apple mixture among cups; sprinkle with almonds. Brush remaining oil over ruffled edges of phyllo. Bake in 350°F (180°C) oven until pastry is light golden, about 15 minutes. Let cool slightly in pan on rack. Serve warm.

Makes 4 servings.

PER SERVING: about 265 cal, 3 g pro, 11 g total fat (1 g sat. fat), 43 g carb, 4 g fibre, 0 mg chol, 91 mg sodium. % RDI: 2% calcium, 7% iron, 7% vit C, 7% folate.

best tips:

• An average slice of apple pie contains 450 calories and 22 grams of fat. These spiced apples nestled in crisp phyllo pastry have only 265 calories and 11 grams of fat, of which only 1 gram is saturated.

• Use firm pie apples, such as Northern Spy, Idared or Golden Delicious, for the best texture.

Halibut and Spinach Curry

1½ lb (750 g) **halibut** (or other firm-fleshed white fish)

2 tbsp (30 mL) **vegetable oil**

1 small **onion,** diced

2 cloves **garlic,** minced

2 tbsp (30 mL) **mild curry paste**

1 tbsp (15 mL) minced **gingerroot**

Half **jalapeño pepper** (optional), minced

1 tsp (5 mL) **ground coriander**

½ tsp (2 mL) **salt**

¼ tsp (1 mL) **ground turmeric**

4 cups (1 L) **baby spinach** (about one 170 g bag)

¾ cup (175 mL) **canned crushed tomatoes**

1 tbsp (15 mL) **lemon juice**

Remove skin (if any) from halibut; cut fish into 1½-inch (4 cm) cubes. Set aside.

In large skillet, heat oil over medium heat; cook onion, garlic, curry paste, ginger, jalapeño (if using), coriander, salt and turmeric, stirring occasionally, until onion is softened, about 6 minutes.

Add spinach; cook, stirring, until wilted, about 2 minutes.

Stir in tomatoes and 1 cup (250 mL) water; bring to boil. Add fish; reduce heat and simmer, stirring occasionally, until fish flakes easily when tested, about 8 minutes. Stir in lemon juice.

Makes 4 servings.

PER SERVING: about 310 cal, 35 g pro, 15 g total fat (1 g sat. fat), 9 g carb, 3 g fibre, 50 mg chol, 625 mg sodium. % RDI: 14% calcium, 26% iron, 52% vit A, 15% vit C, 38% folate.

Quinoa Barley Salad With Ginger Vinaigrette

Gluten-free quinoa contains calcium, phosphorus, magnesium, iron, potassium, copper, manganese and zinc. It has a natural coating called saponin, which can taste bitter, so rinse it well under cold water before cooking.

½ tsp (2 mL) **salt**

⅔ cup (150 mL) **pot barley**

⅔ cup (150 mL) **quinoa,** rinsed

1 tbsp (15 mL) **olive oil**

½ cup (125 mL) each diced **carrot** and **celery**

½ cup (125 mL) diced **sweet red pepper**

1 cup (250 mL) diced **cucumber**

2 **green onions,** thinly sliced

1 tbsp (15 mL) each chopped **fresh parsley** and **mint**

GINGER VINAIGRETTE:

⅓ cup (75 mL) **extra-virgin olive oil**

2 tbsp (30 mL) **cider vinegar**

1 tbsp (15 mL) grated **gingerroot**

2 tsp (10 mL) **Dijon mustard**

¼ tsp (1 mL) each **salt** and **pepper**

In saucepan, bring 1½ cups (375 mL) water and half of the salt to boil; add barley. Reduce heat, cover and simmer until tender and liquid is absorbed, about 40 minutes. Let cool.

Meanwhile, in separate saucepan, bring 1⅓ cups (325 mL) water and remaining salt to boil; add quinoa. Reduce heat, cover and simmer until tender and liquid is absorbed, about 15 minutes. Let cool.

Meanwhile, in skillet, heat oil over medium heat; fry carrot, celery and red pepper, stirring occasionally, until tender-crisp, about 4 minutes. Let cool.

Ginger Vinaigrette: Whisk together oil, vinegar, ginger, mustard, salt and pepper.

In large bowl, combine barley, quinoa, vegetable mixture, cucumber, green onions, parsley and mint; toss with dressing to coat. Serve immediately or cover and refrigerate for up to 24 hours.

Makes 6 servings.

PER SERVING: about 286 cal, 6 g pro, 16 g total fat (2 g sat. fat), 32 g carb, 6 g fibre, 0 mg chol, 333 mg sodium, 363 mg potassium. % RDI: 4% calcium, 22% iron, 24% vit A, 40% vit C, 11% folate.

best tips:

•Spinach is high in vitamin A and lutein, two antioxidants that help protect your eyesight. Spinach also contains iron, which helps make red blood cells.

•Tomatoes are rich in lycopene, an antioxidant that may help protect against prostate and breast cancers.

Blueberry Oatmeal Squares

2½ cups (625 mL) **rolled oats** (not instant)

1¼ cups (300 mL) **all-purpose flour**

1 cup (250 mL) packed **brown sugar**

1 tbsp (15 mL) grated **orange rind**

¼ tsp (1 mL) **salt**

1 cup (250 mL) cold **butter,** cubed

FILLING:

3 cups (750 mL) **fresh blueberries**

½ cup (125 mL) **granulated sugar**

⅓ cup (75 mL) **orange juice**

4 tsp (20 mL) **cornstarch**

Filling: In saucepan, bring blueberries, sugar and juice to boil; reduce heat and simmer until tender, 10 minutes. Whisk cornstarch with 2 tbsp (30 mL) water; whisk into blueberries. Boil, stirring, until thickened, 1 minute. Place plastic wrap directly on surface; refrigerate until cooled, 1 hour.

In large bowl, whisk together oats, flour, sugar, orange rind and salt; with pastry blender, cut in butter until in coarse crumbs. Press half into parchment paper–lined 8-inch (2 L) square cake pan; spread with blueberry filling. Sprinkle with remaining oat mixture, pressing lightly.

Bake in 350°F (180°C) oven until light golden, 45 minutes. Let cool in pan on rack before cutting into squares. Or cover and refrigerate for up to 2 days, or overwrap with heavy-duty foil and freeze for up to 2 weeks.

Makes 24 squares.

PER SQUARE: about 193 cal, 2 g pro, 8 g total fat (5 g sat. fat), 28 g carb, 2 g fibre, 20 mg chol, 84 mg sodium. % RDI: 2% calcium, 7% iron, 7% vit A, 5% vit C, 8% folate.

best tips:

• Blueberries rank No. 1 in antioxidant activity when compared to 60 other fresh fruits and vegetables. They may help lower your risk for age-related diseases such as Parkinson's and Alzheimer's.

• Blueberries freeze very well. Here's how: Rinse, then let berries dry in a single layer on towels. Freeze in a single layer on rimmed baking sheets. Seal in freezer-safe containers for up to 1 year.

Use them straight from the freezer in your morning cereal, blend them into a smoothie, or mix them into pancake or muffin batter.

Grilled Pickerel With Charmoulah

Charmoulah – a traditional Moroccan dipping sauce – is fantastic on any grilled meat or vegetable.

1½ lb (750 g) **skin-on pickerel fillets,** or skin-on perch or other freshwater fish fillets

¼ tsp (1 mL) each **salt** and **pepper**

CHARMOULAH:

½ cup (125 mL) each chopped **fresh parsley** and **coriander**

2 **green onions,** finely chopped

¼ cup (60 mL) **extra-virgin olive oil**

3 tbsp (45 mL) **lemon juice**

2 cloves **garlic,** minced

1 tsp (5 mL) each **ground cumin** and **paprika**

¼ tsp (1 mL) **cayenne pepper**

¼ tsp (1 mL) each **salt** and **pepper**

Charmoulah: Mix together parsley, coriander, green onions, oil, lemon juice, garlic, cumin, paprika, cayenne pepper, salt and pepper. Set aside.

Divide fish into 4 servings. Skewer each crosswise on pair of skewers; sprinkle with salt and pepper.

Place fish, skin side down, on greased grill over medium-high heat. Close lid and grill, turning once, until fish flakes easily when tested, about 5 minutes per ½ inch (1 cm) thickness. Serve topped with charmoulah.

Makes 4 servings.

PER SERVING: about 274 cal, 30 g pro, 16 g total fat (2 g sat. fat), 3 g carb, 1 g fibre, 129 mg chol, 374 mg sodium. % RDI: 18% calcium, 24% iron, 15% vit A, 27% vit C, 18% folate.

Citrus Quinoa

The amount of liquid used for cooking quinoa varies, so check the package instructions for best results. If you have any vegetable stock or broth on hand, use it in place of water to give the quinoa even more flavour.

2 tbsp (30 mL) **butter**

1 tsp (5 mL) **canola oil** or vegetable oil

4 **shallots,** minced

Grated rind of 1 each **lemon, lime** and **orange**

2 cups (500 mL) **quinoa,** rinsed

¼ cup (60 mL) **buckwheat honey** or other liquid honey

¼ tsp (1 mL) each **salt** and **pepper**

In large saucepan, heat 1 tsp (5 mL) of the butter and oil over low heat; cook shallots, stirring occasionally, until caramelized, about 20 minutes.

Add lemon, lime and orange rinds; cook for 1 minute. Transfer to bowl.

Add quinoa to pan; cook, stirring, until toasted, about 4 minutes. Add 4 cups (1 L) water and bring to boil; reduce heat, cover and simmer until liquid is almost absorbed, about 12 minutes.

Uncover and cook, stirring, for 2 minutes. Stir in shallot mixture, honey, salt, pepper and remaining butter.

Makes 6 servings.

PER SERVING: about 305 cal, 8 g pro, 8 g total fat (3 g sat. fat), 53 g carb, 5 g fibre, 10 mg chol, 139 mg sodium. % RDI: 5% calcium, 39% iron, 4% vit A, 12% vit C, 14% folate.

best tips:

• Raspberries are rich in ellagic acid, an antioxidant that may help prevent cervical cancer.

• Raspberries are so perishable that only three per cent of Canada's crop is sold fresh. The other 97 per cent are used to make jam, baked goods and other delicacies.

Cucumber Herb Salad

Inexpensive field cucumbers are perfect for this light and fresh salad.

4 **cucumbers** (about 3 lb/1.5 kg)

½ cup (125 mL) **fresh coriander leaves**

4 **green onions,** sliced

2 tbsp (30 mL) chopped **fresh mint**

DRESSING:

3 tbsp (45 mL) **extra-virgin olive oil**

2 tbsp (30 mL) **lemon juice**

1 tbsp (15 mL) **white wine vinegar**

1 **shallot,** minced

1 clove **garlic,** minced

¼ tsp (1 mL) each **salt** and **pepper**

Peel, quarter and seed cucumbers; chop and place in large bowl. Coarsely chop coriander; add to bowl along with green onions and mint.

Dressing: Whisk together oil, lemon juice, vinegar, shallot, garlic, salt and pepper; toss with salad. Refrigerate for 2 hours before serving.

Makes 8 servings.

PER SERVING: about 60 cal, 1 g pro, 5 g total fat (1 g sat. fat), 3 g carb, 1 g fibre, 0 mg chol, 76 mg sodium. % RDI: 2% calcium, 4% iron, 2% vit A, 8% vit C, 8% folate.

Raspberry Iced Tea

Serve this tart, fruity tea with lime slices or raspberry ice cubes (see Best Tips, below).

4 bags **black tea** (such as Darjeeling or orange pekoe)

2 cups (500 mL) **raspberries** (fresh or frozen)

½ cup (125 mL) **granulated sugar**

Ice cubes

Steep tea in 8 cups (2 L) boiling water for 4 minutes. Discard bags.

Meanwhile, in large saucepan, bring raspberries, sugar and 1 cup (250 mL) water to boil. Reduce heat to medium-low; simmer, stirring, until raspberries break up. Add to tea; let cool to room temperature, about 30 minutes. Refrigerate until cold, about 2 hours.

Strain through cheesecloth-lined sieve into pitcher, pressing solids gently so liquid remains clear. Serve over ice cubes.

Makes 8 cups (2 L), or 6 to 8 servings.

PER EACH OF 8 SERVINGS: about 62 cal, trace pro, trace total fat (0 g sat. fat), 15 g carb, 0 g fibre, 0 mg chol, 8 mg sodium. % RDI: 1% calcium, 1% iron, 10% vit C, 7% folate.

VARIATION

Raspberry Iced Green Tea: Replace black tea bags with 5 green tea bags; steep for 5 minutes.

best tips:

Need a pretty garnish for your favourite drinks? Fill ice-cube tray halfway with water and freeze until solid. Top each cube with fruit (such as blueberries, raspberries or citrus slices), then top with more water and freeze again. Turn out of tray and store in resealable freezer bags. Or, do the same with herbs, such as mint leaves, rosemary or thyme flowers.

Cranberry Flax Muffins

These muffins are filled to the brim with dried fruit and flaxseeds. If cranberry isn't your fruit, switch it up by using dried cherries or chopped dried apricots instead.

1 cup (250 mL) **flaxseeds**

1 cup (250 mL) **all-purpose flour**

1 cup (250 mL) **whole wheat flour**

1 cup (250 mL) **natural bran**

1 tbsp (15 mL) **baking powder**

1 tsp (5 mL) each **baking soda** and **cinnamon**

½ tsp (2 mL) **salt**

2 **eggs**

1½ cups (375 mL) **buttermilk**

1 cup (250 mL) packed **brown sugar**

⅓ cup (75 mL) **vegetable oil**

1½ cups (375 mL) **dried cranberries**

Set aside 2 tbsp (30 mL) of the flaxseeds. In food processor, finely grind remaining flaxseeds; transfer to large bowl. Add all-purpose and whole wheat flours, bran, baking powder, baking soda, cinnamon and salt; whisk to combine.

Whisk together eggs, buttermilk, sugar and oil; pour over dry ingredients. Sprinkle with cranberries; stir just until combined.

Spoon into 12 greased or paper-lined muffin cups; sprinkle with reserved flaxseeds. Bake in 375°F (190°C) oven until tops are firm to the touch, about 20 minutes. Let cool in pan on rack for 5 minutes. Transfer to rack; let cool completely.

Makes 12 muffins.

PER MUFFIN: about 338 cal, 8 g pro, 12 g total fat (1 g sat. fat), 54 g carb, 7 g fibre, 32 mg chol, 315 mg sodium. % RDI: 12% calcium, 25% iron, 2% vit A, 5% vit C, 29% folate.

energy snacks

Power Bars

These nutrient-packed snack bars can be made and stored in the refrigerator in an airtight container for up to 5 days. Or freeze for up to 1 month.

2 cups (500 mL) **whole wheat flour**

½ cup (125 mL) packed **brown sugar**

¼ cup (60 mL) **skim milk powder**

¼ cup (60 mL) **wheat germ**

1 tsp (5 mL) **baking powder**

1½ cups (375 mL) chopped **dried apricots** or raisins

½ cup (125 mL) unsalted **sunflower seeds**

2 **eggs**

½ cup (125 mL) **vegetable oil**

½ cup (125 mL) **fancy molasses**

⅓ cup (75 mL) **peanut butter**

In large bowl, whisk together flour, sugar, skim milk powder, wheat germ and baking powder; stir in apricots and sunflower seeds. Stir together eggs, oil, molasses and peanut butter; stir into dry ingredients until well combined.

Spread in greased 9-inch (2.5 L) square cake pan. Bake in 350°F (180°C) oven until golden and firm to the touch, about 35 minutes. Let cool completely. Cut into bars.

Makes 24 bars.

PER BAR: about 184 cal, 4 g pro, 9 g total fat (1 g sat. fat), 25 g carb, 3 g fibre, 16 mg chol, 45 mg sodium, 334 mg potassium. % RDI: 4% calcium, 10% iron, 4% vit A, 9% folate.

Make-Your-Own Hummus

You'll never buy ready-made again once you see how quick and easy hummus is to make.

1 can (19 oz/540 mL) **chickpeas,** drained and rinsed
⅓ cup (75 mL) **tahini**
3 tbsp (45 mL) each **lemon juice** and **water**
1 tbsp (15 mL) **olive oil**
¾ tsp (4 mL) **ground cumin**
¼ tsp (1 mL) **salt**
1 or 2 cloves **garlic,** minced

In food processor, purée together chickpeas, tahini, lemon juice, water, olive oil, cumin and salt. Stir in garlic.

Makes 2 cups (500 mL).

PER 2 TBSP (30 mL): about 72 cal, 2 g pro, 4 g total fat (1 g sat. fat), 8 g carb, 2 g fibre, 0 mg chol, 115 mg sodium, 68 mg potassium. % RDI: 3% calcium, 6% iron, 3% vit C, 10% folate.

Pita Chips

These are the perfect accompaniment to hummus. Store them in an airtight container for up to 3 days.

4 **pitas** with pockets (8 inches/20 cm)
2 tbsp (30 mL) **vegetable oil**
¼ tsp (1 mL) **salt**

Using scissors, cut pitas around edge to make 8 rounds; cut each into 8 triangles.

Toss together pita triangles, oil and salt to coat. Spread on baking sheets; bake in 350°F (180°C) oven until crisp and golden, about 8 minutes.

Makes 64 pieces.

PER PIECE: about 14 cal, trace pro, trace total fat (0 g sat. fat), 2 g carb, 0 g fibre, 0 mg chol, 29 mg sodium. % RDI: 1% iron, 1% folate.

Green and Yellow Bean Salad

To keep the beans colourful and crisp, toss this salad with the dressing as close to serving time as possible.

12 oz (375 g) **green beans,** trimmed

12 oz (375 g) **yellow beans,** trimmed

2 tbsp (30 mL) chopped **fresh oregano**

2 tbsp (30 mL) **extra-virgin olive oil**

2 tbsp (30 mL) **wine vinegar**

2 tsp (10 mL) **grainy mustard**

1 clove **garlic,** minced

½ tsp (2 mL) each **salt** and **pepper**

Half **red onion,** thinly sliced

Fill large bowl with ice water; set aside. In large pot of boiling salted water, blanch green beans until tender-crisp, 3 to 4 minutes. Using slotted spoon, transfer beans to ice water, stirring until cold. Remove beans to towel-lined plate; let drain. Repeat with yellow beans.

In large bowl, whisk together oregano, oil, vinegar, mustard, garlic, salt and pepper; add onion and green and yellow beans. Toss to combine.

Makes 6 servings.

PER SERVING: about 96 cal, 3 g pro, 5 g total fat (1 g sat. fat), 12 g carb, 3 g fibre, 0 mg chol, 482 mg sodium. % RDI: 6% calcium, 12% iron, 8% vit A, 22% vit C, 20% folate.

lighten up!
dinner

Apple Trout Fillets

The flavours of tart mustard and sweet apple combine into the perfect brushing sauce for the fish.

4 **rainbow trout fillets** (about 2 lb/1 kg)

2 tbsp (30 mL) thawed **apple juice concentrate**

1 tbsp (15 mL) **Dijon mustard**

1 tsp (5 mL) **cider vinegar**

½ tsp (2 mL) **paprika**

¼ tsp (1 mL) **pepper**

Pinch **salt**

Pat fillets dry; arrange, skin side down, on plate. Stir together apple juice concentrate, mustard, vinegar, paprika, pepper and salt; brush some of the sauce onto fillets.

Place fillets, skin side down, on greased grill over medium heat; close lid and cook, brushing once with remaining sauce, until fish flakes easily when tested, 12 to 14 minutes.

Makes 4 servings.

PER SERVING: about 287 cal, 47 g pro, 8 g total fat (2 g sat. fat), 4 g carb, trace fibre, 129 mg chol, 113 mg sodium. % RDI: 15% calcium, 33% iron, 6% vit A, 25% vit C, 8% folate.

Cucumber Mustard Salad

This simple salad comes together in just a few minutes.

2 **English cucumbers** (about 2 lb/1 kg)

½ tsp (2 mL) **salt**

½ cup (125 mL) thinly sliced **red onion**

4 tsp (20 mL) **white wine vinegar**

1 tbsp (15 mL) **Dijon mustard**

Pinch each **pepper** and **granulated sugar**

½ cup (125 mL) **fresh parsley leaves**

Halve cucumbers lengthwise and scoop out seeds; cut crosswise into ¼-inch (5 mm) thick slices. In bowl, sprinkle cucumbers with salt; let stand for 20 minutes.

Stir in onion, vinegar, mustard, pepper and sugar; toss to combine. Sprinkle with parsley; toss before serving.

Makes 8 servings.

PER SERVING: about 23 cal, 1 g pro, trace total fat (0 g sat. fat), 5 g carb, 1 g fibre, 0 mg chol, 173 mg sodium. % RDI: 3% calcium, 5% iron, 4% vit A, 15% vit C, 6% folate.

best tips: **No grill? Broil the trout fillets on a greased baking sheet, watching closely, for about 8 minutes.**

Raspberry Snow Cones

Just one bite of these refreshing, fruity ice desserts will whisk you back to your childhood. You'll need a blender that can withstand crushing ice to get the right texture.

2 cups (500 mL) fresh or frozen **raspberries**
    or blueberries
¼ cup (60 mL) **granulated sugar**
½ cup (125 mL) **orange juice**
5 cups (1.25 L) **ice cubes**

In food processor or blender, purée raspberries with sugar; strain through fine sieve into bowl to remove seeds. Stir in orange juice.

In blender, crush ice to make about 4 cups (1 L). Mound ice into cone shape in each of 4 chilled dessert dishes; drizzle with raspberry mixture.

Makes 4 servings.

PER SERVING: about 78 cal, 1 g pro, trace total fat (0 g sat. fat), 19 g carb, trace fibre, 0 mg chol, 6 mg sodium. % RDI: 2% calcium, 2% iron, 1% vit A, 40% vit C, 12% folate.

Chicken and Swiss Chard Fusilli This pasta dish is also delicious with broccoli instead of chard. Use 1 bunch, adding stems in place of ribs and florets in place of leaves.

1 lb (500 g) **Swiss chard**

2 tbsp (30 mL) **olive oil**

2 **boneless skinless chicken breasts,** thinly sliced

1 **onion,** chopped

5 cloves **garlic,** minced

2 **sweet red peppers,** sliced

2 tbsp (30 mL) **balsamic vinegar** or red wine vinegar

1 tsp (5 mL) chopped **fresh rosemary**

4 cups (1 L) **fusilli pasta** (12 oz/375 g)

4 tsp (20 mL) **cornstarch**

1½ cups (375 mL) **chicken broth**

¼ cup (60 mL) grated **Parmesan cheese**

Cut chard into ribs and leaves; chop each and set aside separately.

In large skillet, heat half of the oil over high heat; cook chicken, stirring often, until no longer pink inside, about 4 minutes. Transfer to plate; keep warm.

Reduce heat to medium-high; add remaining oil to pan. Cook onion, garlic, red peppers and chard ribs until softened, about 5 minutes. Return chicken to pan. Add vinegar, rosemary and chard leaves; cover and cook, stirring occasionally, until chard is wilted, about 4 minutes.

Meanwhile, in large pot of boiling salted water, cook pasta until al dente, about 8 minutes. Drain well and return to pot; add chard mixture and toss to combine.

Whisk cornstarch into broth; add to skillet and cook over high heat, whisking, until thickened. Stir into pasta. Serve sprinkled with Parmesan cheese.

Makes 4 servings.

PER SERVING: 553 cal, 32 g pro, 12 g total fat (3 g sat. fat), 80 g carb, 7 g fibre, 39 mg chol, 843 mg sodium. % RDI: 17% calcium, 31% iron, 53% vit A, 195% vit C, 19% folate.

Pasta With Lemon and Spinach Any small pasta shape would be great for this dish, including fusilli and bow ties.

4 cups (1 L) **penne pasta** (about 12 oz/375 g)

1 tbsp (15 mL) **butter** or extra-virgin olive oil

1 clove **garlic,** minced

1 cup (250 mL) **extra-smooth light ricotta cheese**

¼ cup (60 mL) grated **Parmesan cheese**

1 tsp (5 mL) grated **lemon rind**

2 tbsp (30 mL) **lemon juice**

½ tsp (2 mL) each **salt** and **pepper**

Half bag (10-oz/284 g bag) **fresh spinach**
   (about 5 cups/1.25 L)

½ cup (125 mL) finely diced **sweet red pepper**

In large saucepan of boiling salted water, cook pasta until al dente, about 10 minutes. Reserving ½ cup (125 mL) of the cooking liquid, drain pasta; set aside.

In same saucepan, melt butter over medium heat; fry garlic until fragrant, about 1 minute. Add reserved cooking liquid, ricotta cheese, half of the Parmesan cheese, the lemon rind and juice, salt and pepper; bring to simmer.

Add spinach and red pepper; stir until spinach is wilted, about 2 minutes. Return pasta to pot; toss to coat. Sprinkle with remaining Parmesan cheese.

Makes 4 servings.

PER SERVING: about 447 cal, 21 g pro, 9 g total fat (5 g sat. fat), 69 g carb, 5 g fibre, 33 mg chol, 798 mg sodium. % RDI: 29% calcium, 25% iron, 44% vit A, 63% vit C, 80% folate.

best tips:

• Choose garlic heads that are firm with no dark, powdery mould patches on the cloves.
• As garlic ages, it shrivels and shrinks, making it easier to peel.

• Store unpeeled garlic in an open container in a cool, dry place away from other foods. Refrigerate peeled garlic cloves in a sealed container for up to 1 week. If you have garlic in an oil-based salad dressing, store it in the fridge for no more than 1 week – never at room temperature. Deadly bacteria can grow quickly in the oxygen-starved environment that oil provides.

Linguine With Garlic Shrimp and Sun-Dried Tomato Pesto This decadent and elegant dish is fabulous for quick entertaining or any dinner occasion.

1 lb (500 g) **linguine**

Sun-Dried Tomato Pesto (right)

4 tsp (20 mL) **extra-virgin olive oil**

3 cloves **garlic,** thinly sliced

1 lb (500 g) **large shrimp,** peeled and deveined

1 cup (250 mL) chopped **fresh basil**

¼ tsp (1 mL) **hot pepper flakes**

Pinch **salt**

In large pot of boiling salted water, cook pasta until al dente, about 7 minutes. Drain and transfer to large bowl; toss with pesto.

Meanwhile, in skillet, heat oil over medium-low heat; cook garlic until softened, about 3 minutes. Add shrimp, basil, hot pepper flakes and salt; cook until shrimp are pink, about 5 minutes. Toss with pasta.

Makes 4 servings.

PER SERVING: about 791 cal, 42 g pro, 28 g total fat (4 g sat. fat), 93 g carb, 7 g fibre, 176 mg chol, 659 mg sodium, 677 mg potassium. % RDI: 15% calcium, 61% iron, 13% vit A, 13% vit C, 114% folate.

Sun-Dried Tomato Pesto: In bowl, soak ⅓ cup (75 mL) dry-packed sun-dried tomatoes in ⅓ cup (75 mL) boiling water until softened, about 10 minutes. Drain, reserving 2 tbsp (30 mL) liquid. In food processor, finely chop tomatoes; reserved liquid; 3 tbsp (45 mL) toasted pine nuts; 2 tbsp (30 mL) tomato paste; 1 clove garlic; ¼ tsp (1 mL) pepper; and pinch salt. With motor running, add ¼ cup (60 mL) extra-virgin olive oil in thin steady stream until puréed. Pulse in 3 tbsp (45 mL) grated Parmesan cheese.

Makes ¾ cup (175 mL).

•Fresh garlic is much stronger than cooked garlic. The flavour gets sweeter the longer and more slowly the garlic is cooked, but you have to be careful not to burn it, as it turns bitter.

Bean and Grain Salad

Look for wheat berries in the health food section of most grocery stores, or at bulk or health food stores. If you want to use pearl (polished) wheat berries, reduce cooking time to 25 minutes.

½ cup (125 mL) **soft wheat berries**

1 can (19 oz/540 mL) **black beans,** drained and rinsed

1 cup (250 mL) halved **cherry tomatoes** or grape tomatoes

1 each **sweet red** and **yellow pepper,** diced

2 **green onions,** thinly sliced

1 **avocado** (optional), peeled, pitted and cubed

½ cup (125 mL) crumbled **feta cheese**

3 cups (750 mL) torn **romaine lettuce**

1 cup (250 mL) shredded **kale leaves** (see Best Tips, page 186)

CORIANDER CHILI DRESSING:

2 tbsp (30 mL) chopped **fresh coriander**

2 tbsp (30 mL) **extra-virgin olive oil**

2 tbsp (30 mL) **canola oil** or vegetable oil

2 tbsp (30 mL) **cider vinegar**

1 tbsp (15 mL) minced **shallot**

1 small clove **garlic,** minced

1 tsp (5 mL) minced **hot red pepper** or hot green pepper

Pinch each **salt** and **pepper**

Bring large saucepan of salted water to boil. Add wheat berries; reduce heat to medium-low, cover and simmer until tender, 45 to 60 minutes. Drain and transfer to large bowl; let cool for 15 minutes.

Coriander Chili Dressing: Whisk together coriander, olive and canola oils, vinegar, shallot, garlic, hot pepper, salt and pepper.

To wheat berries, add black beans, tomatoes, red and yellow peppers, onions, avocado (if using), and feta cheese; toss with dressing to coat.

Divide lettuce and kale among plates; top with wheat berry mixture.

Makes 4 servings.

PER SERVING: about 379 cal, 14 g pro, 19 g total fat (5 g sat. fat), 44 g carb, 13 g fibre, 17 mg chol, 655 mg sodium. % RDI: 17% calcium, 27% iron, 53% vit A, 250% vit C, 66% folate.

super foods for dinner

Fresh Salmon Burgers

Enjoy these moist, tasty fish burgers with Mango Salsa (below). If you can find them, use less expensive salmon tail pieces and remove any bones with tweezers. You can make and refrigerate the patties up to 24 hours ahead.

1 lb (500 g) **salmon pieces** or fillets, skinned

1 small **onion,** grated

¼ cup (60 mL) **light mayonnaise**

2 tbsp (30 mL) **dry bread crumbs**

1 tbsp (15 mL) minced **fresh parsley** or coriander

½ tsp (2 mL) **salt**

¼ tsp (1 mL) **pepper**

¼ tsp (1 mL) **lemon juice**

Dash **hot pepper sauce**

4 **hamburger buns**

Cut salmon into chunks. In food processor, pulse together salmon, onion, mayonnaise, bread crumbs, parsley, salt, pepper, lemon juice and hot pepper sauce until finely chopped. Shape into four ¾-inch (2 cm) thick patties.

Place patties on greased grill over medium-high heat; close lid and grill, turning once, until digital thermometer inserted sideways into centre reads 158°F (70°C), about 10 minutes. Sandwich in buns.

Makes 4 servings.

PER SERVING (WITHOUT MANGO SALSA): about 423 cal, 25 g pro, 19 g total fat (3 g sat. fat), 36 g carb, 2 g fibre, 61 mg chol, 804 mg sodium. % RDI: 10% calcium, 19% iron, 3% vit A, 8% vit C, 43% folate.

Mango Salsa: Toss together ½ cup (125 mL) diced peeled ripe mango; 1 jalapeño pepper, diced; 2 tbsp (30 mL) diced sweet red pepper; 2 tsp (10 mL) lime juice; and pinch each salt and granulated sugar.

Makes about ⅔ cup (150 mL).

best tips:

• Kale is a super dark leafy green. It's rich in vitamins (especially vitamin C), minerals, beta-carotene, iron and calcium. It's also a strong antioxidant, and fights colds, flus and cancer.

• Both red Russian and dinosaur kale are good to eat raw, but be sure to remove any thick woody stems first.

• Smaller kale leaves are more tender. Try combining them with romaine lettuce in a salad, as we have on page 185, to lighten the flavour and add nutrients.

Strawberry Peach Sundaes

You can control the amount of fat in these sundaes by using a lower-fat frozen yogurt. If fresh peaches aren't in season, use frozen peach slices.

4 cups (1 L) **vanilla frozen yogurt**

4 whole **strawberries**

STRAWBERRY PEACH SAUCE:

2 cups (500 mL) sliced peeled **peaches** or nectarines

¼ cup (60 mL) **granulated sugar**

Pinch **cinnamon**

1 cup (250 mL) sliced **strawberries**

Strawberry Peach Sauce: In saucepan, bring peaches, sugar and cinnamon to boil over medium heat. Reduce heat and simmer, stirring gently once or twice, until peaches are tender, about 10 minutes. Add sliced strawberries; let cool.

In 4 parfait glasses or bowls, alternately layer sauce and frozen yogurt. Garnish each with 1 whole strawberry.

Makes 4 servings.

PER SERVING: about 407 cal, 9 g pro, 11 g total fat (7 g sat. fat), 71 g carb, 3 g fibre, 19 mg chol, 116 mg sodium. % RDI: 26% calcium, 4% iron, 8% vit A, 50% vit C, 9% folate.

VARIATIONS

Blueberry Raspberry Parfaits: Replace peaches with blueberries and sliced strawberries with raspberries. Garnish with blueberries or raspberries.

Sweet Cherry Berry Parfaits: Replace peaches with pitted sweet cherries. If desired, replace sliced strawberries with raspberries or blueberries. Garnish with cherries or berries.

Lightened-Up Eggplant Parmigiana With Marinara Sauce

½ cup (125 mL) **dry bread crumbs**

2 tbsp (30 mL) grated **Parmesan cheese** (approx)

½ tsp (2 mL) **dried oregano**

½ cup (125 mL) **all-purpose flour**

2 **eggs,** lightly beaten

1 **eggplant** (about 1 lb/500 g)

2 tbsp (30 mL) **extra-virgin olive oil**

Marinara Sauce (below)

Thinly sliced **fresh basil**

In shallow dish, combine bread crumbs, cheese and oregano. Place flour in second shallow dish and eggs in third. Cut eggplant into ½-inch (1 cm) thick rounds; coat lightly in flour. Coat in eggs, then crumb mixture.

Place on greased foil-lined baking sheet; drizzle with oil. Bake in 400°F (200°C) oven, turning once, until soft inside and crispy and golden outside, 15 to 18 minutes. Serve with Marinara Sauce. Sprinkle with basil and more Parmesan cheese.

Makes 4 servings.

PER SERVING: about 325 cal, 10 g pro, 15 g total fat (3 g sat. fat), 40 g carb, 6 g fibre, 96 mg chol, 582 mg sodium. % RDI: 14% calcium, 29% iron, 7% vit A, 48% vit C, 39% folate.

Marinara Sauce: In saucepan, heat 1 tbsp (15 mL) olive oil over medium heat; fry 1 clove garlic until golden, about 2 minutes. Let cool slightly. Add 1 can (28 oz/796 mL) whole tomatoes, breaking up with spoon; 1 tsp (5 mL) balsamic vinegar; ¼ tsp (1 mL) each salt, hot pepper flakes and granulated sugar; and 1 sprig (or 3 to 4 leaves) fresh basil. Bring to boil; reduce heat and simmer for 30 minutes. Let cool slightly; discard basil. Transfer to food processor and process until smooth. Reheat to serve.

Makes 1⅓ cups (325 mL).

best meatless mains

Squash and Chickpea Curry Whether you make it on the stove top or in a slow cooker, this vegetarian dish is great with hot couscous or rice.

1 tbsp (15 mL) **vegetable oil**

1 **onion,** diced

2 cloves **garlic,** minced

1 tbsp (15 mL) minced **gingerroot**

3 tbsp (45 mL) **mild curry paste**

2 cups (500 mL) cubed peeled **butternut squash**

2 cups (500 mL) diced peeled **potato**

1 can (19 oz/540 mL) **chickpeas,** drained and rinsed

1 can (400 mL) **light coconut milk**

1 cup (250 mL) **vegetable broth**

¼ cup (60 mL) **natural cashew butter** or peanut butter

¼ tsp (1 mL) **salt**

2 cups (500 mL) packed shredded **Swiss chard**

1 cup (250 mL) **frozen peas**

2 tbsp (30 mL) chopped **fresh coriander**

In Dutch oven, heat oil over medium heat; fry onion, garlic and ginger, stirring occasionally, until softened, about 7 minutes. Add curry paste; cook, stirring, until fragrant, about 1 minute.

Add squash, potato and chickpeas; stir to coat. Add coconut milk, broth, cashew butter and salt; bring to boil. Cover and simmer, stirring occasionally, until vegetables are tender, about 30 minutes.

Gently stir in Swiss chard and peas; cook, stirring, until Swiss chard is wilted, about 5 minutes. Sprinkle with coriander.

Makes 6 to 8 servings.

PER EACH OF 8 SERVINGS: about 217 cal, 6 g pro, 8 g total fat (3 g sat. fat), 32 g carb, 5 g fibre, 0 mg chol, 543 mg sodium. % RDI: 4% calcium, 11% iron, 50% vit A, 23% vit C, 25% folate.

VARIATION

Slow Cooker Squash and Chickpea Curry: In slow cooker, combine squash, potato and chickpeas. In large skillet, heat oil over medium heat; fry onion, garlic and ginger, stirring occasionally, until onion is golden, about 7 minutes. Add curry paste; cook, stirring, until fragrant, about 1 minute. Add to slow cooker. Add coconut milk and broth to slow cooker; stir in cashew butter and salt. Cover and cook on low until vegetables are tender, about 4 hours. Stir in Swiss chard and peas. Cover and cook on high until Swiss chard is wilted, about 15 minutes. Sprinkle with coriander.

Bulgur and Mushroom Burgers

Top the burgers with Fresh Herb Mayonnaise (below), lettuce and tomato slices and serve on whole wheat kaiser rolls.

¾ cup (175 mL) **bulgur**

1 **egg,** beaten

1 cup (250 mL) **fresh whole wheat bread crumbs**

¼ cup (60 mL) minced **fresh parsley**

2 tbsp (30 mL) **extra-virgin olive oil**

1 small **onion,** finely chopped

2 cloves **garlic,** minced

2 cups (500 mL) finely chopped **mushrooms** (8 oz/250 g)

¼ cup (60 mL) **dry white wine** or vegetable broth

½ tsp (2 mL) **salt**

¼ tsp (1 mL) **pepper**

¼ tsp (1 mL) crumbled **dried thyme**

Place bulgur in heatproof bowl; cover with 1 cup (250 mL) boiling water. Let stand until liquid is absorbed, about 20 minutes. Drain; mix in egg, bread crumbs and parsley.

Meanwhile, in skillet, heat oil over medium heat; fry onion and garlic until softened, about 3 minutes. Stir in mushrooms, wine, salt, pepper and thyme; cook over medium-high heat, stirring occasionally, until liquid is evaporated and mushrooms begin to brown, about 8 minutes.

Scrape mushroom mixture over bulgur mixture; stir to combine. Shape into four ¾-inch (2 cm) thick patties. Place on greased grill over medium heat; close lid and grill, turning once, until heated through and crispy outside, about 15 minutes.

Makes 4 servings.

PER SERVING: about 220 cal, 7 g pro, 9 g total fat (1 g sat. fat), 30 g carb, 5 g fibre, 47 mg chol, 370 mg sodium. % RDI: 4% calcium, 19% iron, 4% vit A, 12% vit C, 20% folate.

Fresh Herb Mayonnaise: Mix together 3 tbsp (45 mL) light mayonnaise; 1 tbsp (15 mL) each minced fresh basil, parsley and chives; 1 tbsp (15 mL) extra-virgin olive oil; 1 small clove garlic, minced; 1 tsp (5 mL) lemon juice; 1 tsp (5 mL) Dijon mustard; and dash hot pepper sauce.

Makes ⅓ cup (75 mL).

best tips:

- Finely chopped mushrooms are essential for this vegetarian burger, as are fresh bread crumbs, so a food processor is the ideal effort-saving appliance.
- Since you're buying whole wheat buns to serve the burgers on, buy extras and process into fresh crumbs.
- You can make these patties and refrigerate them up to 24 hours ahead of time.

Oven-Poached Salmon Salad With Mustard Vinaigrette

4 **skinless centre-cut salmon fillets** (about 6 oz/ 175 g each)

¼ tsp (1 mL) each **salt** and **pepper**

1 tbsp (15 mL) drained **capers**

1 **lemon,** thinly sliced

4 sprigs **fresh thyme**

1 lb (500 g) **new potatoes,** scrubbed and halved

1 lb (500 g) **green beans**

1 cup (250 mL) **grape tomatoes**

6 cups (1.5 L) torn **romaine lettuce**

4 **hard-cooked eggs** (see Best Tips, page 45)**,** peeled and quartered

MUSTARD VINAIGRETTE:

3 tbsp (45 mL) **extra-virgin olive oil**

1 tbsp (15 mL) **white wine vinegar**

2 tsp (10 mL) **lemon juice**

2 tsp (10 mL) **Dijon mustard**

1 **shallot** or green onion (white part only), minced

1 tsp (5 mL) minced **fresh thyme**

¼ tsp (1 mL) each **salt** and **pepper**

Pinch **granulated sugar**

Mustard Vinaigrette: In large bowl, whisk together oil, vinegar, lemon juice, mustard, shallot, thyme, salt, pepper and sugar; set aside.

Place salmon in centre of large piece of parchment paper. Sprinkle with salt and pepper; top with capers, lemon and thyme. Fold paper over salmon so edges meet; double-fold all edges and pinch to seal packet. Roast on baking sheet in 450°F (230°C) oven until fish flakes easily when tested, about 15 minutes.

Meanwhile, in saucepan of boiling salted water, cook potatoes until almost fork-tender, about 8 minutes.

Add beans; cook until tender-crisp, 3 to 4 minutes. Drain and rinse under cold water; pat dry. Add to vinaigrette along with tomatoes; toss to coat.

Arrange lettuce on plates. Top with potato mixture, eggs and salmon; drizzle with any remaining vinaigrette.

Makes 4 servings.

PER SERVING: about 575 cal, 41 g pro, 32 g total fat (6 g sat. fat), 32 g carb, 7 g fibre, 270 mg chol, 978 mg sodium, 1,344 mg potassium. % RDI: 12% calcium, 25% iron, 59% vit A, 88% vit C, 96% folate.

best satisfying salads

Vegetarian Chef's Salad

6 cups (1.5 L) torn **iceberg lettuce** (about half head)

2 cups (500 mL) torn **radicchio** (about half head)

4 **radishes,** thinly sliced

¾ cup (175 mL) sliced **English cucumber**

½ cup (125 mL) **alfalfa sprouts** (about half 35 g pkg)

⅓ cup (75 mL) thinly sliced **sweet onion**

½ cup (125 mL) rinsed drained canned **chickpeas**

3 **hard-cooked eggs** (see Best Tips, page 45), quartered

1 large **tomato,** cut into 12 wedges

Half **avocado,** peeled and sliced

2 oz (60 g) each **Swiss** and **Cheddar cheese,** julienned

DRESSING:

¼ cup (60 mL) **light mayonnaise**

1 tbsp (15 mL) minced **dill pickle**

1 tbsp (15 mL) **extra-virgin olive oil**

2 tsp (10 mL) **chili sauce**

1½ tsp (7 mL) **lemon juice**

½ tsp (2 mL) drained **capers,** minced

½ tsp (2 mL) **Dijon mustard**

Pinch each **salt** and **pepper**

Dressing: Stir together mayonnaise, pickle, oil, chili sauce, lemon juice, capers, mustard, salt and pepper.

In large bowl, toss together lettuce, radicchio, radishes, cucumber, sprouts, onion and half of the dressing; arrange on 4 large plates. Top with chickpeas, eggs, tomato, avocado and Swiss and Cheddar cheeses; spoon remaining dressing over top.

Makes 4 servings.

PER SERVING: about 349 cal, 16 g pro, 25 g total fat (9 g sat. fat), 17 g carb, 5 g fibre, 173 mg chol, 430 mg sodium. % RDI: 25% calcium, 14% iron, 20% vit A, 32% vit C, 60% folate.

Crunchy Crouton, Steak and Arugula Salad

You can use leftover Family-Size T-Bone Steaks (page 61) or 12 oz (375 g) deli roast beef for this fresh, elegant salad.

12 oz (375 g) **cooked steak**

2 bunches **arugula**

3 tbsp (45 mL) **wine vinegar**

3 tbsp (45 mL) **extra-virgin olive oil**

¼ tsp (1 mL) **granulated sugar**

¼ tsp (1 mL) each **salt** and **pepper**

2 cups (500 mL) **cherry tomatoes** or grape tomatoes, halved

½ cup (125 mL) shaved **Parmesan cheese** (2 oz/60 g)

CROUTONS:

4 slices (1 inch/2.5 cm thick) **sourdough bread**

2 tbsp (30 mL) **extra-virgin olive oil**

2 cloves **garlic,** minced

¼ tsp (1 mL) **salt**

Croutons: Cut bread into 1-inch (2.5 cm) cubes to make 4 cups (1 L). Toss together bread, oil, garlic and salt. Spread on large rimmed baking sheet; toast in 425°F (220°C) oven, stirring once, until golden, about 10 minutes.

Thinly slice steak across the grain on angle. Trim stems from arugula; tear into bite-size pieces to make about 6 cups (1.5 L).

In large bowl, whisk together vinegar, oil, sugar, salt and pepper. Add arugula, tomatoes and croutons; toss to coat. Serve topped with steak and Parmesan cheese.

Makes 4 servings.

PER SERVING: about 487 cal, 35 g pro, 27 g total fat (6 g sat. fat), 25 g carb, 2 g fibre, 62 mg chol, 881 mg sodium. % RDI: 30% calcium, 36% iron, 26% vit A, 42% vit C, 55% folate.

best tips: To easily shave Parmesan or other hard cheeses, such as Asiago or romano, use a vegetable peeler.

Roasted Sweet Potato Wedges

4 **sweet potatoes** (3 lb/1.5 kg)
2 tbsp (30 mL) **vegetable oil**
½ tsp (2 mL) each **salt** and **pepper**

Scrub sweet potatoes; cut each lengthwise into 8 wedges. Toss together potatoes, oil, salt and pepper.

Roast on large rimmed baking sheet in 400°F (200°C) oven, turning once, until tender, about 30 minutes.

Makes 8 servings.

PER SERVING: about 185 cal, 3 g pro, 1 g total fat (trace sat. fat), 41 g carb, 5 g fibre, 0 mg chol, 160 mg sodium. % RDI: 4% calcium, 6% iron, 371% vit A, 70% vit C, 17% folate.

best light family meal

Parmesan Chicken Strips With Tomato Dipping Sauce

You can use a food processor to crush the melba toasts.

16 rectangular **melba toasts**

4 **boneless skinless chicken breasts**

1 **egg**

2 tbsp (30 mL) grated **Parmesan cheese**

1 tsp (5 mL) **dried oregano**

¼ tsp (1 mL) each **salt** and **pepper**

1 tbsp (15 mL) **vegetable oil**

TOMATO DIPPING SAUCE:

1 can (14 oz/398 mL) **whole tomatoes**

¼ cup (60 mL) **tomato paste**

2 **green onions,** chopped

1 tsp (5 mL) **dried basil**

¼ tsp (1 mL) each **salt** and **pepper**

Tomato Dipping Sauce: In saucepan, mash tomatoes. Add tomato paste, green onions, basil, salt and pepper; bring to boil. Reduce heat to medium-low; simmer, stirring, until thick enough to mound on spoon, about 20 minutes.

Meanwhile, in resealable bag with saucepan or rolling pin, crush toasts. Cut chicken lengthwise into 1-inch (2.5 cm) thick strips. In shallow dish, beat egg. In separate shallow dish, stir together melba toast crumbs, Parmesan cheese, oregano, salt and pepper. Dip chicken strips into egg, letting excess drip off; dip into crumb mixture, turning to coat. Bake on greased baking sheets in 425°F (220°C) oven, turning once, until golden, crisp, and no longer pink inside, about 15 minutes. Serve with Tomato Dipping Sauce.

Makes 4 servings.

PER SERVING: about 326 cal, 37 g pro, 9 g total fat (2 g sat. fat), 24 g carb, 3 g fibre, 126 mg chol, 761 mg sodium. % RDI: 11% calcium, 20% iron, 13% vit A, 38% vit C, 21% folate.

best tips:

Protein-rich foods, such as chicken, help boost your levels of bacteria-fighting antibodies, which aid in the fight against infections.

Chunky Greek Salad on a Stick
When you're ready to eat, just pull the skewer from this fun hands-on appetizer.

1 piece (4 inches/10 cm) **English cucumber**

Quarter each **sweet green** and **red pepper** and **small red onion**

16 **cherry tomatoes** or grape tomatoes

8 pitted **black olives**

8 leaves **romaine lettuce heart**

2 tbsp (30 mL) crumbled **feta cheese**

DRESSING:

3 tbsp (45 mL) **extra-virgin olive oil**

2 tsp (10 mL) **lemon juice**

1 tsp (5 mL) **red wine vinegar**

½ tsp (2 mL) **dried oregano**

¼ tsp (1 mL) each **salt** and **pepper**

Cut cucumber lengthwise into quarters; cut crosswise into quarters to make 16 pieces. Cut green and red pepper into 8 chunks each. Cut onion into sixteen 1-inch (2.5 cm) pieces.

Onto each of eight 8-inch (20 cm) wooden skewers, thread 1 tomato and 1 piece each cucumber, onion and sweet pepper; repeat once on same skewers. End each with olive.

Dressing: Whisk together oil, lemon juice, vinegar, oregano, salt and pepper.

Serve 1 skewer in each romaine leaf; drizzle with dressing and sprinkle with feta cheese.

Makes 8 servings.

PER SERVING: about 72 cal, 1 g pro, 7 g total fat (1 g sat. fat), 3 g carb, 1 g fibre, 2 mg chol, 177 mg sodium. % RDI: 2% calcium, 3% iron, 7% vit A, 33% vit C, 10% folate.

Quick Strawberry Shortcake

2 cups (500 mL) sliced hulled **strawberries**

2 tsp (10 mL) **granulated sugar**

Four wedges (each about 2 inches/5 cm wide) prepared **angel food cake**

1 cup (250 mL) **vanilla yogurt**

In bowl, stir strawberries with sugar; let stand until juicy, about 15 minutes.

Top each wedge of cake with ½ cup (125 mL) of the strawberries and ¼ cup (60 mL) of the yogurt.

Makes 4 servings.

PER SERVING: about 215 cal, 6 g pro, 2 g total fat (1 g sat. fat), 46 g carb, 2 g fibre, 3 mg chol, 411 mg sodium. % RDI: 15% calcium, 4% iron, 2% vit A, 72% vit C, 17% folate.

best tips: Angel food cake is great for the quick shortcake above, but you could use the berry mixture to top slices of vanilla or chocolate cake, scones or pound cake instead.

Brown Sugar Meringues With Citrus Curd

Brown sugar lends a delicate caramel taste to this melt-in-your-mouth dairy-free, gluten-free and nut-free dessert. Both the meringues and the curd can be made up to 2 days ahead. Keep the meringues in an airtight container and the curd in the refrigerator.

2 tsp (10 mL) **cornstarch**

1 tsp (5 mL) **vanilla**

3 **egg whites**

¼ tsp (1 mL) **cream of tartar**

½ cup (125 mL) **granulated sugar**

¼ cup (60 mL) packed **brown sugar**

4 **blood oranges**

CITRUS CURD:

2 **egg yolks**

2 **eggs**

⅓ cup (75 mL) **granulated sugar**

¼ cup (60 mL) each **orange** and **lemon juice**

Line rimless baking sheet with parchment paper. Using 3-inch (8 cm) round cookie cutter as guide, draw 8 circles on paper; turn paper over. Set aside.

In small bowl, stir together cornstarch, vanilla and ½ tsp (2 mL) water until cornstarch is dissolved; set aside.

In bowl, beat egg whites with cream of tartar until soft peaks form; beat in granulated and brown sugars, 2 tbsp (30 mL) at a time, until stiff glossy peaks form. Beat in cornstarch mixture. Spoon onto circles on paper, shaping with back of spoon into nests.

Bake in 250°F (120°C) oven until light golden but still soft inside, about 1 hour. Let cool on pan on rack.

Citrus Curd: Meanwhile, in heatproof bowl over saucepan of simmering water, whisk together egg yolks, eggs, sugar, and orange and lemon juices; cook, stirring, until thick enough to mound on spoon, about 8 minutes. Strain through fine sieve into bowl. Place plastic wrap directly on surface; refrigerate until cold, about 30 minutes.

Cut peel and pith from blood oranges; cut segments away from membranes. Spoon citrus curd into hollow of each meringue; top with orange segments.

Makes 8 servings.

PER SERVING: about 185 cal, 4 g pro, 3 g total fat (1 g sat. fat), 37 g carb, 1 g fibre, 97 mg chol, 41 mg sodium. % RDI: 4% calcium, 4% iron, 5% vit A, 63% vit C, 16% folate.

guilt-free desserts

Yogurt and Fresh Fruit Parfait

⅓ cup (75 mL) **granulated sugar**

2 tbsp (30 mL) **cornstarch**

2 tsp (10 mL) grated **lemon rind**

1½ tsp (7 mL) **unflavoured gelatin**

1 cup (250 mL) **2% milk**

1 cup (250 mL) **low-fat plain yogurt**

1 tsp (5 mL) **vanilla**

2 cups (500 mL) **fresh berries,** such as blueberries
   or raspberries

In small saucepan, stir together sugar, cornstarch, lemon rind and gelatin; stir in milk. Cook, stirring, over medium heat until thickened and smooth, about 8 minutes.

Remove from heat and gradually stir in yogurt; stir in vanilla. Refrigerate, stirring occasionally, until chilled, about 1 hour.

Beat yogurt mixture until smooth and light, about 1 minute. In 4 parfait glasses, alternately layer yogurt mixture and berries.

Makes 4 servings.

PER SERVING: about 194 cal, 7 g pro, 2 g total fat (1 g sat. fat), 38 g carb, 2 g fibre, 9 mg chol, 71 mg sodium, 293 mg potassium. % RDI: 17% calcium, 2% iron, 4% vit A, 15% vit C, 5% folate.

best tips: Replace berries with 2 cups (500 mL) sliced strawberries or peaches. Or use thawed frozen berries. Vanilla yogurt can replace the plain yogurt.

Lean-but-Luscious Chocolate Brownies

Surprise! The secret ingredient here is baby food plums, which give the brownies their luscious texture. Dust with icing sugar for an attractive and low-fat finish.

½ cup (125 mL) **all-purpose flour**

½ cup (125 mL) **unsweetened cocoa powder**

½ tsp (2 mL) **baking powder**

¼ tsp (1 mL) **salt**

⅔ cup (150 mL) **granulated sugar**

¼ cup (60 mL) **butter,** melted

1 **egg**

2 tbsp (30 mL) **milk**

½ tsp (2 mL) **vanilla**

1 jar (4½ oz/128 mL) **baby food strained plums**

Sift together flour, cocoa, baking powder and salt; set aside.

In bowl, beat sugar with butter until combined but not smooth; beat in egg, milk and vanilla. Stir in flour mixture alternately with plums, making 2 additions of dry ingredients and 1 of plums. Spread in greased 8-inch (2 L) square cake pan, smoothing top.

Bake in 350°F (180°C) oven until cake tester inserted in centre comes out with a few moist crumbs clinging, about 20 minutes. Let cool in pan on rack.

Makes 16 large brownies.

PER BROWNIE: about 90 cal, 1 g pro, 4 g total fat (2 g sat. fat), 15 g carb, 1 g fibre, 19 mg chol, 71 mg sodium, 87 mg potassium. % RDI: 1% calcium, 5% iron, 3% vit A, 5% folate.

best tips: To make ahead, refrigerate brownies in airtight container for up to 3 days or wrap individually in plastic wrap and freeze for up to 1 week.

party fare

Puff Pastry Sausage Rolls
These ever-popular appetizers are so tasty and easy to make that you'll never want the store-bought variety again. Serve hot or at room temperature, or make them ahead and rewarm in 325°F (160°C) oven.

¼ cup (60 mL) **fresh bread crumbs**

2 **eggs**

8 oz (250 g) **sweet Italian sausage,** casings removed

¼ cup (60 mL) minced **fresh parsley**

¼ cup (60) minced **onion**

2 cloves **garlic,** minced

Half pkg (450 g pkg) frozen **all-butter puff pastry,** thawed and chilled

1 tbsp (15 mL) **Dijon mustard**

Toast bread crumbs on rimmed baking sheet in 350°F (180°C) oven until golden, about 10 minutes. Let cool.

In bowl, beat 1 of the eggs until frothy; stir in sausage, bread crumbs, parsley, onion and garlic.

On lightly floured surface, unroll pastry; cut crosswise into three 10- x 3½-inch (25 x 9 cm) strips. Brush with mustard; spoon about one-third of the sausage mixture lengthwise down centre of each. Fold long sides over to cover filling and slightly overlap; press edge to seal.

Arrange rolls, seam side down, on parchment paper–lined pan. Cover and freeze until firm, about 15 minutes. Cut each roll crosswise into 8 pieces; space about 1 inch (2.5 cm) apart.

Whisk remaining egg with 1 tbsp (15 mL) water; brush over rolls. Bake in 425°F (220°C) oven until puffed and golden, about 20 minutes.

Makes 24 pieces.

PER PIECE: about 72 cal, 3 g pro, 5 g total fat (2 g sat. fat), 4 g carb, trace fibre, 24 mg chol, 109 mg sodium. % RDI: 1% calcium, 4% iron, 2% vit A, 2% vit C, 2% folate.

open house

Mixed Olives and Chorizo

This make-ahead appetizer can be refrigerated in an airtight container for up to 3 days. Rewarm along with a splash of red wine, if desired.

4 oz (125 g) **smoked chorizo** or other smoked sausage

Half small **navel orange**

2 tbsp (30 mL) **extra-virgin olive oil**

1 cup (250 mL) **oil-cured black olives**

1 cup (250 mL) **brined black olives** (such as Kalamata)

1 cup (250 mL) large **green olives**

2 cloves **garlic,** thinly sliced

1 tsp (5 mL) **hot pepper flakes**

1 tbsp (15 mL) **fresh sage leaves,** thinly sliced

Slice chorizo thinly. Cut orange in half; thinly slice into half-moon shapes; set aside.

In large skillet, heat oil over medium heat; cook chorizo for 1 minute. Add oil-cured and brined black olives, green olives, garlic and hot pepper flakes; cook, stirring occasionally, until heated through and fragrant, about 3 minutes.

Stir in sage and orange; cook until orange starts to break down, about 2 minutes. Remove from heat; cover and let stand for 10 minutes. Serve warm.

Makes 4 cups (1 L).

PER 2 TBSP (30 ML): about 61 cal, 1 g pro, 6 g total fat (1 g sat. fat), 2 g carb, 1 g fibre, 3 mg chol, 393 mg sodium, 27 mg potassium. % RDI: 1% calcium, 1% iron, 1% vit A, 3% vit C.

Baked Brie With Caramelized Pears

1 round (8 oz/250 g) **Brie cheese**

1 tbsp (15 mL) **sliced hazelnuts** or slivered almonds, toasted

CARAMELIZED PEAR:

2 tsp (10 mL) **butter**

1 **shallot,** thinly sliced

1 **pear,** thinly sliced

Pinch each **salt** and **pepper**

¼ cup (60 mL) **pear juice** or apple juice

1 tbsp (15 mL) **brandy** or pear juice

2 tsp (10 mL) chopped **fresh thyme** (or ½ tsp/2 mL dried)

1 tsp (5 mL) packed **brown sugar**

Caramelized Pear: In nonstick skillet, melt butter over medium heat; fry shallot, pear, salt and pepper until shallot is softened, about 5 minutes.

Add pear juice, brandy, thyme and sugar; bring to boil. Boil, stirring occasionally, until no liquid remains and pear is softened, about 5 minutes.

Place Brie on foil-lined pie plate or in small cake pan; top with pear mixture. Bake in 350°F (180°C) oven until cheese is softened, about 10 minutes. Let stand for 5 minutes. Sprinkle with hazelnuts.

Makes 8 to 10 servings.

PER EACH OF 10 SERVINGS: about 111 cal, 5 g pro, 8 g total fat (5 g sat. fat), 4 g carb, 1 g fibre, 27 mg chol, 166 mg sodium. % RDI: 5% calcium, 2% iron, 6% vit A, 5% vit C, 8% folate.

Cajun Crab Cakes

What's a double-duty appetizer? One you can make ahead and reheat or bake at party time, or serve as part of a main course alongside a salad. Freeze a batch of these crab cakes ahead, then thaw in the refrigerator and reheat on a baking sheet in 400°F (200°C) oven until hot, about 8 minutes.

2 pkg (each 7 oz/200 g) frozen **crabmeat,** thawed

1⅓ cups (325 mL) crushed **unsalted soda crackers** (about 35)

1 cup (250 mL) **light mayonnaise**

¼ cup (60 mL) each finely diced **carrot** and **sweet green pepper**

¼ cup (60 mL) grated **radishes**

¼ cup (60 mL) finely chopped **green onions**

1 tbsp (15 mL) **Cajun seasoning**

1 tbsp (15 mL) **Dijon mustard**

1 tsp (5 mL) **hot pepper sauce**

¼ tsp (1 mL) each **salt** and **pepper**

½ cup (125 mL) **light sour cream**

2 tbsp (30 mL) chopped **fresh chives** or green onions

2 tbsp (30 mL) **vegetable oil**

Place crabmeat in sieve; pick through to remove any cartilage. Press firmly to remove liquid. Transfer to large bowl; stir in crackers, mayonnaise, carrot, green pepper, radishes, green onions, Cajun seasoning, mustard, hot pepper sauce, salt and pepper until combined.

Press heaping tablespoonfuls (15 mL) into ½-inch (1 cm) thick patties. In small bowl, stir sour cream with chives. Set aside.

In nonstick skillet, heat 1 tbsp (15 mL) of the oil over medium-high heat. Fry crab cakes, in batches and adding more oil as necessary, until golden, 3 minutes per side. Serve with sour cream mixture.

Makes about 32 pieces.

PER PIECE: about 65 cal, 4 g pro, 4 g total fat (trace sat. fat), 4 g carb, trace fibre, 9 mg chol, 199 mg sodium. % RDI: 2% calcium, 4% iron, 4% vit A, 3% vit C, 3% folate.

double-duty appetizers

Brie, Apple and Walnut Phyllo Triangles

A perfect fusion of Brie, apple and walnuts hides inside crisp, buttery phyllo pastry. Since they freeze beautifully, you may want to make several batches to have on hand.

8 sheets **phyllo pastry**

⅓ cup (75 mL) **butter,** melted

FILLING:

1 tbsp (15 mL) **butter**

2 **shallots** (or 1 small onion), finely chopped

½ cup (125 mL) finely diced (unpeeled) **green apple**

¼ tsp (1 mL) each **salt** and **pepper**

½ cup (125 mL) chopped **walnuts**

8 oz (250 g) **Brie cheese,** diced

2 tbsp (30 mL) chopped **fresh parsley**

Filling: In skillet, melt butter over medium heat; cook shallots, apple, salt and pepper until shallots are softened, about 4 minutes. Let cool.

In bowl, stir together walnuts, Brie and parsley; add apple mixture, stirring to combine.

Place 1 sheet of the phyllo pastry on work surface, keeping remainder covered with damp tea towel. Cut lengthwise into five 2½-inch (6 cm) wide strips.

Brush each strip lightly with some of the butter. Spoon 1 tsp (5 mL) of the filling about ½ inch (1 cm) from end of each strip. Fold 1 corner of phyllo over filling so bottom edge meets side edge to form triangle. Continue folding triangle sideways and upward to end of strip. Fold end flap over to stick. Repeat with remaining phyllo and filling.

Brush both sides of phyllo triangles lightly with butter. Bake in single layer on rimmed baking sheet in 375°F (190°C) oven until golden, about 18 minutes.

Makes 40 pieces.

PER PIECE: about 61 cal, 2 g pro, 5 g total fat (2 g sat. fat), 3 g carb, trace fibre, 11 mg chol, 93 mg sodium. % RDI: 1% calcium, 2% iron, 3% vit A, 3% folate.

best tips: To make ahead, layer assembled and unbaked phyllo triangles in airtight container and freeze for up to 2 weeks. Brush with melted butter; bake from frozen.

Saucy Barbecue Meatballs

⅔ cup (150 mL) **fresh bread crumbs**

½ cup (125 mL) **water**

1 **egg**

1 clove **garlic,** minced

¼ cup (60 mL) chopped **fresh parsley**

2 tsp (10 mL) **Dijon mustard**

1 tsp (5 mL) **Worcestershire sauce**

½ tsp (2 mL) each **salt** and **pepper**

1 lb (500 g) **lean ground beef**

SAUCE:

1 **onion,** finely chopped

1 clove **garlic,** minced

1 can (28 oz/796 mL) **ground tomatoes**

¼ cup (60 mL) packed **brown sugar**

¼ cup (60 mL) **cider vinegar**

1 tbsp (15 mL) **Dijon mustard**

1 tbsp (15 mL) **Worcestershire sauce**

Dash **hot pepper sauce**

In bowl, stir bread crumbs with water; let stand until water is absorbed, about 5 minutes. Beat in egg, garlic, parsley, mustard, Worcestershire sauce, salt and pepper; mix in beef. Roll by rounded tablespoonfuls (15 mL) into balls.

Brush large nonstick skillet with vegetable oil; heat over medium-high heat. Brown meatballs, in batches, about 5 minutes. Transfer to bowl.

Sauce: Drain any fat from pan; cook onion and garlic over medium heat, stirring often, for 3 minutes. Add tomatoes, brown sugar, vinegar, mustard, Worcestershire sauce and hot pepper sauce; simmer, stirring occasionally, until slightly thickened, about 25 minutes.

Return meatballs and any accumulated juices to pan; simmer, turning meatballs occasionally, until no longer pink inside and sauce is thickened, about 20 minutes.

Makes about 32 pieces.

PER PIECE: about 52 cal, 4 g pro, 2 g total fat (1 g sat. fat), 5 g carb, 1 g fibre, 14 mg chol, 104 mg sodium, 140 mg potassium. % RDI: 2% calcium, 6% iron, 2% vit A, 5% vit C, 3% folate.

best tips:

• Freeze a batch or two of meatballs in sauce to have on hand for any occasion. Thaw before reheating.

• Serve and keep warm in a slow cooker and accompany with toothpicks for skewering.

Beef Koftas With Pitas and Minted Yogurt

There's no such thing as a dry kofta if you add moist ingredients to lean beef. Choose whole wheat or white pitas, with or without pockets, or omit pitas and serve koftas on skewers with minted yogurt for dipping.

1 cup (250 mL) lightly packed **fresh parsley leaves**

3 **green onions,** coarsely chopped

2 tsp (10 mL) **dried mint**

½ tsp (2 mL) each **ground cumin** and **paprika**

½ tsp (2 mL) **salt**

¼ tsp (1 mL) **pepper**

1 **egg**

1 lb (500 g) **lean ground beef**

4 **pitas**

½ cup (125 mL) **Balkan-style plain yogurt**

2 tbsp (30 mL) minced **fresh parsley**

In food processor, purée together parsley leaves, green onions, half of the mint, the cumin, paprika, salt and pepper. Transfer to large bowl; beat in egg. Add beef and 2 tbsp (30 mL) water; mix well. Shape by heaping 2 tbsp (30 mL) into small sausages; thread each lengthwise onto metal or soaked wooden skewer.

Place skewers on greased grill over medium heat or under broiler; close lid and grill, turning once, until no longer pink inside and instant-read thermometer inserted into several koftas registers 160°F (71°C), about 12 minutes on grill, 7 minutes under broiler.

Meanwhile, grill or broil pitas, turning once, until crisp, about 3 minutes; cut into quarters. Stir together yogurt, remaining mint and minced parsley. Serve koftas with pita quarters and minted yogurt.

Makes 16 pieces.

PER PIECE: about 98 cal, 8 g pro, 4 g total fat (1 g sat. fat), 9 g carb, 1 g fibre, 27 mg chol, 178 mg sodium. % RDI: 3% calcium, 10% iron, 4% vit A, 11% vit C, 9% folate.

best finger foods

Creamy Cheddar Cheese Ball
While you could use another type of Cheddar, the extra-old orange-coloured variety provides ultimate flavour and looks appealing. Instead of Port, you can use bourbon, whisky or whipping cream.

2 cups (500 mL) shredded **extra-old Cheddar cheese**
  (about 8 oz/250 g)
1 pkg (8 oz/250 g) **cream cheese,** softened
2 tbsp (30 mL) **tawny Port** or white Port
1 tsp (5 mL) **dry mustard**
¼ tsp (1 mL) **cayenne pepper**

In food processor, purée together Cheddar cheese, cream cheese, Port, dry mustard and cayenne pepper until smooth.

Scrape into plastic wrap–lined bowl; cover and refrigerate until firm, about 2 hours, or up to 5 days.

Turn out onto plate; peel off plastic.

Makes about 2 cups (500 mL).

PER 1 TBSP (15 mL): about 57 cal, 2 g pro, 5 g total fat (3 g sat. fat), trace carb, 0 g fibre, 16 mg chol, 67 mg sodium, 18 mg potassium. % RDI: 5% calcium, 1% iron, 5% vit A, 1% folate.

VARIATION
Grape Cheese Ball Truffles: Make Creamy Cheddar Cheese Ball but refrigerate just until firm but still pliable, about 30 minutes. Place 1 cup (250 mL) finely chopped toasted pecans or walnuts in shallow dish. For each truffle, scoop about 1 tbsp (15 mL) cheese ball mixture; mould around 1 seedless red or green grape to enclose. Roll in pecans. Cover and refrigerate on waxed paper–lined tray until firm, about 2 hours.

Makes about 32 pieces.

Curried Chicken Salad Cups

Phyllo pastry moulded into cup shapes makes ideal appetizer-size vessels for fillings. If your chutney is chunky, chop before topping cups.

2 sheets **phyllo pastry**

2 tbsp (30 mL) **butter,** melted

SALAD:

1 **boneless skinless chicken breast,** cooked and diced

1 rib **celery,** finely diced

1 **green onion,** minced

¼ cup (60 mL) **mayonnaise**

1 tsp (5 mL) **lemon juice**

½ tsp (2 mL) **mild curry paste**

¼ tsp (1 mL) each **salt** and **pepper**

GARNISH:

2 tbsp (30 mL) **mango chutney**

Place 1 sheet of the phyllo on work surface; brush lightly with butter. Top with remaining sheet; brush with butter. Cut lengthwise into 4 strips and crosswise into 6 strips to make 24 squares. Press each, buttered side down, into mini-muffin or tart tins.

Bake in 400°F (200°C) oven until cups are crisp and golden, 3 to 4 minutes. Let cool in pan on rack.

Salad: Stir together chicken, celery, green onion, mayonnaise, lemon juice, curry paste, salt and pepper. Spoon rounded 1 tsp (5 mL) into each prepared cup.

Garnish: Top each cup with ¼ tsp (1 mL) of the chutney.

Makes 24 pieces.

PER PIECE: about 42 cal, 2 g pro, 3 g total fat (1 g sat. fat), 2 g carb, trace fibre, 7 mg chol, 78 mg sodium. % RDI: 1% iron, 1% vit A, 1% folate.

best tips:

• You can make phyllo cups ahead and keep in an airtight container for up to 24 hours. Or freeze in single layer in airtight container for up to 1 month; recrisp in 350°F (180°C) oven for 3 minutes.

• This chicken salad can also be served on toasted sliced baguette or naan bread, or in Belgian endive spears.

Layered Mexican Dip

This classic appetizer is lightened with lots of fresh veggies and light sour cream. You can make and refrigerate it for up to 6 hours before the party begins. Serve with tortilla chips.

1 can (14 oz/398 mL) **refried beans**

1¼ cups (300 mL) **light sour cream**

½ tsp (2 mL) each **ground cumin** and **salt**

½ tsp (2 mL) **hot pepper sauce**

2 **avocados,** peeled and pitted

⅓ cup (75 mL) finely diced **red onion**

2 tbsp (30 mL) **lime juice**

2 cups (500 mL) shredded **Cheddar cheese**

2 **tomatoes,** chopped

⅓ cup (75 mL) sliced **green onions**

½ cup (125 mL) sliced pitted **black olives**

Stir together beans, ¼ cup (60 mL) of the sour cream, cumin, half each of the salt and hot pepper sauce; spread in 12-inch (30 cm) round serving dish that is at least 1½ inches (4 cm) deep.

Mash together avocados, onion, lime juice, remaining salt and hot pepper sauce, and ¼ cup (60 mL) of the remaining sour cream; spread over bean layer. Top with remaining sour cream.

Starting at outside, garnish with concentric rings of cheese, tomatoes, green onions and olives.

Makes 24 servings.

PER SERVING: about 105 cal, 5 g pro, 7 g total fat (3 g sat. fat), 7 g carb, 2 g fibre, 12 mg chol, 219 mg sodium. % RDI: 10% calcium, 6% iron, 5% vit A, 8% vit C, 14% folate.

Warm Roasted Red Pepper Pasta Salad

This summery salad is quick and easy to prepare, making it the perfect dish to take to a last-minute potluck or picnic. Use basil or sun-dried tomato pesto.

5 cups (1.25 L) **rotini** or other short pasta (1 lb/500 g)

1 cup (250 mL) drained **roasted red peppers**

1 tbsp (15 mL) **extra-virgin olive oil**

6 cloves **garlic,** slivered

4 **anchovy fillets,** chopped (or 2 tsp/10 mL anchovy paste)

¼ tsp (1 mL) each **salt** and **hot pepper flakes**

2 tbsp (30 mL) **pesto**

1 tbsp (15 mL) **wine vinegar**

In large pot of boiling salted water, cook pasta until al dente, 8 to 10 minutes. Reserving 1 cup (250 mL) of the cooking liquid, drain pasta and return to pot.

Meanwhile, in food processor, purée red peppers; set aside.

In large skillet, heat oil over medium heat; cook garlic, anchovies, salt and hot pepper flakes, stirring, until fragrant, about 1 minute. Stir in pesto, vinegar, reserved cooking liquid and pepper purée; add to pasta and toss to coat.

Makes 6 servings.

PER SERVING: about 337 cal, 11 g pro, 6 g total fat (1 g sat. fat), 59 g carb, 4 g fibre, 4 mg chol, 505 mg sodium. % RDI: 4% calcium, 15% iron, 10% vit A, 67% vit C, 50% folate.

best tips:

• This salad is just as nice served cold; add an extra ½ cup (125 mL) of the cooking liquid before cooling.

Super Chocolate Chunk Fudge Brownies

Sure to please every chocoholic, these brownies are so chocolaty you don't need icing.

¾ cup (175 mL) **granulated sugar**

⅓ cup (75 mL) **butter**

8 oz (250 g) **bittersweet chocolate,** chopped

2 **eggs**

1 tsp (5 mL) **vanilla**

¾ cup (175 mL) **all-purpose flour**

¼ tsp (1 mL) each **baking soda** and **salt**

4 oz (125 g) **white chocolate,** chopped

In saucepan over medium-high heat, bring sugar, butter and 2 tbsp (30 mL) water to boil, stirring occasionally. Remove from heat; stir in half of the bittersweet chocolate until melted. Let cool for 10 minutes. Whisk in eggs, 1 at a time; whisk in vanilla.

In separate bowl, whisk together flour, baking soda and salt; stir into chocolate mixture. Stir in remaining bittersweet chocolate and white chocolate. Pour into parchment paper–lined 9-inch (2.5 L) square cake pan.

Bake in 325°F (160°C) oven until cake tester inserted in centre comes out with a few moist crumbs clinging, about 30 minutes. Let cool in pan on rack.

Makes 24 bars.

PER BAR: about 146 cal, 2 g pro, 8 g total fat (5 g sat. fat), 17 g carb, 1 g fibre, 23 mg chol, 44 mg sodium. % RDI: 2% calcium, 5% iron, 3% vit A, 5% folate.

best tips:

Customize your brownies by stirring 1 cup (250 mL) chopped walnuts into the batter, or replacing white chocolate with chopped milk chocolate.

No-Bake Lime Cheesecake Squares

You can make this dessert in just a few minutes, but people will think you spent much longer.

1 tbsp (15 mL) each finely slivered **lemon** and **lime rind**

1½ cups (375 mL) **chocolate cookie crumbs**

⅓ cup (75 mL) **butter,** melted

1½ pkg (each 8 oz/250 g) **cream cheese,** softened

⅔ cup (150 mL) **sweetened condensed milk**

½ cup (125 mL) **whipping cream**

2 tsp (10 mL) finely grated **lime rind**

¼ cup (60 mL) **lime juice** (about 2 limes)

1 tbsp (15 mL) **granulated sugar**

Line 8-inch (2 L) square cake pan with parchment paper, leaving 1-inch (2.5 cm) overhang on 2 opposite sides.

Refrigerate lemon and lime slivers in bowl of ice water. Stir cookie crumbs with butter; press evenly into prepared pan. Refrigerate until firm, about 30 minutes.

In large bowl, beat cream cheese until smooth; beat in condensed milk, ¼ cup (60 mL) of the cream, grated lime rind and juice, and sugar until smooth. Scrape over base; smooth top. Cover and refrigerate until set, about 4 hours, or up to 2 days.

Using paper overhang as handles, transfer cheesecake from pan to cutting board. Using hot knife and wiping blade clean after each cut, cut into 16 squares.

Whip remaining cream; spoon or pipe about 1 tsp (5 mL) onto each square. Drain lemon and lime slivers and pat dry; arrange on whipped cream.

Makes 16 squares.

PER SQUARE: about 230 cal, 4 g pro, 17 g total fat (10 g sat. fat), 16 g carb, trace fibre, 52 mg chol, 208 mg sodium. % RDI: 6% calcium, 7% iron, 16% vit A, 5% vit C, 2% folate.

more potluck pleasers

Potato Salad With Buttermilk Dressing

1½ lb (750 g) **new potatoes** (about 7)

½ cup (125 mL) sliced **radishes**

2 **green onions,** sliced

1 **sweet yellow pepper,** diced

DRESSING:

½ cup (125 mL) **buttermilk**

¼ cup (60 mL) **plain yogurt**

2 tbsp (30 mL) chopped **fresh dill**

1 tbsp (15 mL) **wine vinegar**

1 tbsp (15 mL) **vegetable oil** or olive oil

½ tsp (2 mL) **Dijon mustard**

¼ tsp (1 mL) each **salt** and **pepper**

Scrub and halve potatoes lengthwise. In large pot of boiling salted water, cover and cook potatoes until fork-tender, about 15 minutes.

Dressing: In large bowl, whisk together buttermilk, yogurt, dill, vinegar, oil, mustard, salt and pepper.

Drain potatoes; let cool until no longer steaming, 5 to 10 minutes. Cut potatoes into bite-size pieces; gently stir into dressing along with radishes, onions and yellow pepper.

Makes 4 to 6 servings.

PER EACH OF 6 SERVINGS: about 129 cal, 4 g pro, 3 g total fat (1 g sat. fat), 23 g carb, 2 g fibre, 3 mg chol, 357 mg sodium, 501 mg potassium. % RDI: 6% calcium, 8% iron, 2% vit A, 85% vit C, 10% folate.

Honey Garlic Meatballs

Roasting meatballs is a smart technique because it requires no extra fat and doesn't leave you with an oil-spattered stove. Serve over noodles or rice.

1 **egg**

1 small **onion,** grated

Quarter **sweet red pepper,** finely diced

¼ cup (60 mL) **dry bread crumbs**

2 tsp (10 mL) **soy sauce**

2 tsp (10 mL) **Worcestershire sauce**

¼ tsp (1 mL) **pepper**

1 lb (500 g) **lean ground beef**

1 cup (250 mL) **beef broth**

4 cloves **garlic,** minced

4 tsp (20 mL) **liquid honey**

1 tbsp (15 mL) **cornstarch**

Dash **hot pepper sauce**

1 **green onion,** chopped

In bowl, whisk together egg, onion, red pepper, bread crumbs, soy sauce, Worcestershire sauce and pepper; mix in beef. Roll by rounded 1 tbsp (15 mL) into balls; bake on greased rimmed baking sheet in 450°F (230°C) oven until instant-read thermometer inserted into several meatballs registers 160°F (71°C), 10 to 12 minutes.

Meanwhile, in large skillet, whisk together broth, garlic, honey, cornstarch and hot pepper sauce; cook, whisking, over medium heat until thickened, about 2 minutes.

Add meatballs and any accumulated juices to pan, stirring to coat. Serve sprinkled with onion.

Makes 4 servings.

PER SERVING: about 296 cal, 25 g pro, 14 g total fat (5 g sat. fat), 16 g carb, 1 g fibre, 104 mg chol, 515 mg sodium. % RDI: 4% calcium, 21% iron, 5% vit A, 23% vit C, 10% folate.

best tips:

You can freeze these meatballs for up to 1 month. Just freeze them in single layer on parchment paper–lined baking sheet until firm. Then transfer to resealable bags, press out air and seal. Thaw before making the sauce.

Roasted Beet and Arugula Salad With Walnut Dressing

If beets have the greens still on, cut them off, leaving 1 inch (2.5 cm) attached to beets. Chop greens to add to soups or use smaller leaves in salads. Sprinkle salad with crumbled goat cheese or blue cheese, if desired.

1½ lb (750 g) **beets** (6 to 8), trimmed

4 cloves **garlic,** sliced

1 sprig **fresh rosemary** (or 1 tsp/5 mL dried)

3 tbsp (45 mL) **extra-virgin olive oil**

½ tsp (2 mL) each **salt** and **pepper**

8 cups (2 L) **arugula,** trimmed

1 cup (250 mL) toasted **walnuts,** coarsely chopped

WALNUT VINAIGRETTE:

⅓ cup (75 mL) **walnut oil** or extra-virgin olive oil

1 small **shallot,** minced

3 tbsp (45 mL) **cider vinegar**

½ tsp (2 mL) **dry mustard**

¼ tsp (1 mL) each **salt** and **pepper**

Pinch **granulated sugar**

Place beets on 20-inch (50 cm) piece of foil. Sprinkle with garlic, rosemary, oil, salt and pepper; fold and seal edges to form packet. Roast on baking sheet in 400°F (200°C) oven until fork-tender, about 1½ hours. Let cool enough to handle.

Peel and trim beets; cut into 1-inch (2.5 cm) thick wedges.

Walnut Vinaigrette: In large bowl, whisk together oil, shallot, vinegar, mustard, salt, pepper and sugar. Transfer 2 tbsp (30 mL) to separate bowl; add beets and toss to coat.

Add arugula to remaining vinaigrette; toss to coat. Top with beets; sprinkle with walnuts.

Makes 8 servings.

PER SERVING: about 254 cal, 3 g pro, 24 g total fat (2 g sat. fat), 10 g carb, 2 g fibre, 0 mg chol, 266 mg sodium. % RDI: 3% calcium, 8% iron, 1% vit A, 5% vit C, 30% folate.

Oven-Poached Salmon

This classic, beautiful buffet dish is delicious hot or cold. Cutting the fish before cooking gives the pieces nice, clean edges. To serve, garnish with more sliced lemon, and parsley and thyme sprigs.

¼ cup (60 mL) **dry white vermouth**

2 tbsp (30 mL) chopped **fresh thyme** (or 1 tsp/5 mL dried)

2 sides **salmon** (about 2 lb/1 kg each)

½ tsp (2 mL) **salt**

1 **lemon,** thinly sliced

12 sprigs **fresh thyme** or parsley

In small saucepan, heat vermouth with chopped fresh thyme over medium heat; let cool for 10 minutes. Strain through sieve.

Cut two 40-inch (1 m) long pieces of foil; place 1 piece on each of 2 rimless baking sheets. Grease foil. Cutting just to skin, cut each side of salmon into 6 portions; place, skin side down, on each pan. Sprinkle with salt; divide lemon slices and thyme sprigs over each. Drizzle with vermouth mixture. Seal in foil to form packet.

Roast in top and bottom thirds of 400°F (200°C) oven, rotating and switching pans halfway through, until fish flakes easily when tested, about 25 minutes. Discard thyme sprigs; scrape off white protein. (To serve cold, let cool for 30 minutes. Discard lemon; refrigerate until cold. Cover and refrigerate for up to 24 hours.)

Makes 12 servings.

PER SERVING: about 218 cal, 23 g pro, 13 g total fat (3 g sat. fat), 1 g carb, trace fibre, 66 mg chol, 160 mg sodium. % RDI: 2% calcium, 3% iron, 2% vit A, 17% vit C, 16% folate.

best tips:

There are dozens of varieties of vinegars. Here are some general tips on how to use three common types.

• **Balsamic vinegar** is rich, flavourful and not too acidic. It's great in sauces and salad dressings. Or reduce it slightly to drizzle over chicken, steak, or rich fish or shellfish, such as salmon or sea scallops.

• **Wine vinegars** are lighter, with higher acidity. They add subtle fruit flavor to dressings. Use red to deglaze pans and in marinades. Add white when caramelizing onions to bring out their natural sweetness.

New Potato Salad

30 mini **new red potatoes** (1½ lb/750 g), scrubbed
½ cup (125 mL) diced **sweet red pepper**
½ cup (125 mL) diced **celery**
½ cup (125 mL) thinly sliced **green olives**
¼ cup (60 mL) sliced **green onions**

DRESSING:

2 tbsp (30 mL) **white wine vinegar**
2 tsp (10 mL) **grainy mustard**
1 clove **garlic,** minced
½ tsp (2 mL) **salt**
¼ tsp (1 mL) **pepper**
¼ cup (60 mL) **extra-virgin olive oil**

In saucepan of boiling salted water, cover and cook potatoes just until fork-tender, about 10 minutes; drain and let cool.

Dressing: Meanwhile, in large bowl, whisk together wine vinegar, mustard, garlic, salt and pepper; gradually whisk in oil until blended.

Quarter or halve potatoes; add to dressing along with red pepper, celery, olives and green onions. Gently toss to coat.

Makes 4 to 6 servings.

PER EACH OF 6 SERVINGS: about 187 cal, 3 g pro, 11 g total fat (2 g sat. fat), 20 g carb, 3 g fibre, 0 mg chol, 623 mg sodium, 533 mg potassium. % RDI: 3% calcium, 8% iron, 6% vit A, 65% vit C, 10% folate.

• **Cider vinegar,** made by fermenting apple cider, is crisp and highly acidic with a faintly sweet apple flavour. Add it to coleslaw to cut the richness of the mayo. It's also great in glazes for pork or chicken.

True Canadian Cheese Fondue

For a Canadian version of the Swiss classic, we used easy-to-find Canadian cheeses with robust flavours. Extra-old Cheddar cheese melts well and adds a little bite to the Oka.

2 cups (500 mL) **dry white wine**

1 clove **garlic,** minced

1⅓ lb (670 g) **Oka cheese,** shredded (5½ cups/1.375 L)

12 oz (375 g) **extra-old Cheddar cheese,** shredded (3 cups/750 mL)

2 tbsp (30 mL) **cornstarch**

1½ tsp (7 mL) **Dijon mustard**

1 tsp (5 mL) **Worcestershire sauce**

¼ tsp (1 mL) **pepper**

Pinch each **grated nutmeg** and **cayenne pepper**

1 tbsp (15 mL) **whisky**

2 **baguettes,** cut in 1-inch (2.5 cm) cubes

1 each **apple** and **pear,** cubed

Pour all but 2 tbsp (30 mL) of the wine into fondue pot; add garlic and bring to simmer over medium heat on stove top.

Stir in Oka and Cheddar cheeses, 1 handful at a time, until melted. Dissolve cornstarch in remaining wine; stir in mustard, Worcestershire sauce, pepper, nutmeg and cayenne. Add to fondue pot and bring to simmer, stirring; simmer for 1 minute. Stir in whisky.

Place over medium-low heat of fondue burner on table, adjusting heat as necessary to maintain low simmer and stirring often. Serve with bread, apple and pear cubes to skewer and dip into cheese mixture.

Makes 6 servings.

PER SERVING: about 968 cal, 50 g pro, 54 g total fat (32 g sat. fat), 65 g carb, 4 g fibre, 199 mg chol, 1,598 mg sodium. % RDI: 112% calcium, 28% iron, 60% vit A, 5% vit C, 59% folate.

Peameal Bacon Sliders

A classic Canadian staple becomes an instant hit in bite-size form. Mini-buns are available in many grocery stores and bakeries. Or cut a loaf of focaccia in half horizontally, then cut into 1½-inch (4 cm) squares.

1 **sweet onion,** such as Vidalia

2 tbsp (30 mL) **butter**

½ tsp (2 mL) each **salt** and **pepper**

½ cup (125 mL) **sodium-reduced chicken broth**

¼ cup (60 mL) **maple syrup**

¼ cup (60 mL) **grainy mustard**

2 tbsp (30 mL) **olive oil**

2 lb (1 kg) **peameal bacon,** cut in ¼-inch (5 mm) thick slices

24 **mini-buns** or small dinner rolls

24 **gherkins,** cornichons, small pickled peppers or cocktail onions

Cut onion into ¼-inch (5 mm) thick rings. In skillet, melt butter over medium heat; cook onion with half each of the salt and pepper until softened, about 8 minutes.

Add chicken broth; cook, stirring, until no liquid remains, about 8 minutes. Set aside and keep warm.

In large bowl, stir together maple syrup, mustard, and remaining salt and pepper; set aside.

In nonstick skillet, heat half of the oil over medium-high heat; cook bacon, in batches and adding more oil as necessary, turning once, until golden, about 4 minutes. Cut each slice into 4 pieces. Add to maple mixture; toss to coat.

Cut buns in half; broil, cut side up, on baking sheet until golden and toasted, about 1 minute.

In saucepan, warm bacon mixture over medium heat, 1 to 3 minutes. Stack 4 pieces bacon on each bun bottom; top with onions, then bun top. Secure with toothpick-skewered gherkin.

Makes 24 pieces.

PER PIECE: about 207 cal, 11 g pro, 7 g total fat (2 g sat. fat), 26 g carb, 1 g fibre, 21 mg chol, 981 mg sodium, 194 mg potassium. % RDI: 4% calcium, 10% iron, 1% vit A, 2% vit C, 12% folate.

Maple Apple and Blueberry Crisp

6 cups (1.5 L) sliced peeled **apples**

1 pkg (300 g) frozen **blueberries**

¼ cup (60 mL) **granulated sugar**

2 tbsp (30 mL) **all-purpose flour**

1 tbsp (15 mL) **lemon juice**

¼ tsp (1 mL) **cinnamon**

TOPPING:

½ cup (125 mL) packed **brown sugar**

½ cup (125 mL) **all-purpose flour**

½ cup (125 mL) **rolled oats**

½ tsp (2 mL) **cinnamon**

⅓ cup (75 mL) **maple syrup**

2 tbsp (30 mL) **butter,** melted

Toss together apples, blueberries, granulated sugar, flour, lemon juice and cinnamon; spread in 8-inch (2 L) square baking dish.

Topping: In bowl, stir together brown sugar, flour, rolled oats and cinnamon. Pour in maple syrup and butter; toss until moistened. Sprinkle over fruit. Bake in 350°F (180°C) oven until golden and fruit is fork-tender, about 1 hour. Let cool in pan on rack for 15 minutes.

Makes 6 servings.

PER SERVING: about 340 cal, 3 g pro, 5 g total fat (3 g sat. fat), 74 g carb, 5 g fibre, 10 mg chol, 48 mg sodium. % RDI: 5% calcium, 12% iron, 4% vit A, 8% vit C, 4% folate.

best tips: For this dessert, the best apples are locally grown ones that hold their shape when cooked. Try Crispin, Cortland, Spartan, Russet, Jonagold and Northern Spy.

Rainbow Trout en Papillote

For a fun, casual presentation, serve the fish in its package, letting people open their own at the table. Serve with light, tasty Green Onion Couscous (below).

8 **rainbow trout fillets** or Arctic char fillets
   (each about 6 oz/175 g)

48 thin slices **lemon** (about 4 lemons)

¼ cup (60 mL) **extra-virgin olive oil**

4 cloves **garlic,** thinly sliced

16 sprigs **fresh thyme**

¼ cup (60 mL) drained **capers**

1 tsp (5 mL) each **salt** and **pepper**

Cut eight 15-inch (38 cm) squares parchment paper; fold each crosswise in half then open out. Top each with 1 fish fillet, skin side down; top with lemon slices. Drizzle with oil; top with garlic, thyme and capers. Sprinkle each with salt and pepper. Fold paper over so edges meet; double-fold edges and pinch to seal packets.

Bake on large baking sheet in 400°F (200°C) oven until fish flakes easily when tested, 10 to 15 minutes. Transfer fish to plate; pour sauce from packet over top.

Makes 8 servings.

PER SERVING: about 274 cal, 29 g pro, 15 g total fat (3 g sat. fat), 7 g carb, 3 g fibre, 80 mg chol, 468 mg sodium. % RDI: 13% calcium, 9% iron, 11% vit A, 77% vit C, 15% folate.

Green Onion Couscous: In saucepan, bring 2½ cups (625 mL) water and ½ tsp (2 mL) salt to boil. Stir in 2 cups (500 mL) couscous and 4 green onions, chopped. Remove from heat; cover and let stand until liquid is absorbed, about 5 minutes. Fluff with fork.

Makes 8 servings.

An Especially Good Green Salad

4 cups (1 L) torn **fresh spinach**

4 cups (1 L) torn **Boston lettuce**

½ cup (125 mL) sliced **red onion**

½ cup (125 mL) **pecan pieces**, toasted

3 **oranges**

DRESSING:

1 tsp (5 mL) finely grated **orange rind**

2 tbsp (30 mL) **orange juice**

1 tbsp (15 mL) **liquid honey**

1 tbsp (15 mL) **white wine vinegar**

1 tbsp (15 mL) **Dijon mustard**

½ tsp (2 mL) **poppy seeds**

¼ tsp (1 mL) each **salt** and **pepper**

2 tbsp (30 mL) **vegetable oil** or olive oil

In salad bowl, combine spinach, lettuce, onion and pecans. Cut peel and pith off oranges; slice oranges crosswise and add to bowl.

Dressing: Whisk together orange rind and juice, honey, vinegar, mustard, poppy seeds, salt and pepper; gradually whisk in oil. Toss with salad to coat.

Makes 8 servings.

PER SERVING: about 128 cal, 3 g pro, 9 g total fat (1 g sat. fat), 13 g carb, 3 g fibre, 0 mg chol, 121 mg sodium. % RDI: 6% calcium, 9% iron, 23% vit A, 65% vit C, 44% folate.

Lemony Grilled Zucchini Ribbons

¼ cup (60 mL) each **vegetable oil** and **lemon juice**

2 cloves **garlic,** minced

½ tsp (2 mL) each **salt** and **pepper**

Four 9-inch (23 cm) long **zucchini,** cut lengthwise in ¼-inch (5 mm) thick strips

Stir together oil, lemon juice, garlic, salt and pepper. Brush zucchini with lemon mixture. Bake on large greased foil-lined baking sheet in 400°F (200°C) oven, turning once, until tender and lightly browned, 10 to 15 minutes.

Makes 8 servings.

PER SERVING: about 76 cal, 1 g pro, 7 g total fat (trace sat. fat), 4 g carb, 1 g fibre, 0 mg chol, 148 mg sodium. % RDI: 1% calcium, 2% iron, 2% vit A, 8% vit C, 6% folate.

best tips:

• To bake both the trout and zucchini at the same time, bake in top and bottom thirds of oven, switching and rotating pans halfway through.

• Toast large amounts of nuts on baking sheet in 350°F (180°C) oven until golden, 6 to 10 minutes. Toast small amounts in dry skillet over medium heat, shaking pan often, for 3 to 8 minutes.

Chocolate Pâté

8 oz (227 g) **bittersweet chocolate,** chopped

¼ cup (60 mL) **unsalted butter**

¼ cup (60 mL) **icing sugar**

4 **egg yolks**

½ cup (125 mL) **whipping cream**

FIG TOPPING:

¾ cup (175 mL) **granulated sugar**

⅓ cup (75 mL) **water**

¼ cup (60 mL) **orange-flavoured liqueur**

3 tbsp (45 mL) **frozen orange juice concentrate**

4 **fresh green figs,** quartered

1½ tsp (7 mL) **lemon juice**

16 **fresh raspberries** (optional)

Line 5¾- x 3¼-inch (625 mL) loaf pan with plastic wrap; set aside.

In saucepan, melt together chocolate, butter and sugar over medium-low heat until smooth. Whisk in egg yolks, 1 at a time; cook, stirring, until thickened and glossy, about 3 minutes. Transfer to large bowl; let cool to room temperature.

In separate bowl, whip cream; fold one-quarter into chocolate. Fold in remaining whipped cream. Spoon into prepared loaf pan. Cover and refrigerate until firm, about 8 hours, or up to 2 days.

To unmould, gently pull on plastic wrap to loosen top edge of pâté from pan; unmould onto cutting board. Cut into 8 slices.

Fig Topping: Meanwhile, in saucepan, bring sugar, water, orange liqueur and orange juice concentrate to boil; boil for 5 minutes. Let cool slightly, about 2 minutes. Stir in figs and lemon juice. Spoon onto 8 dessert plates; top each with slice of pâté. Sprinkle plate with raspberries, if using.

Makes 8 servings.

PER SERVING: about 432 cal, 4 g pro, 25 g total fat (14 g sat. fat), 48 g carb, 4 g fibre, 136 mg chol, 11 mg sodium, 127 mg potassium. % RDI: 4% calcium, 12% iron, 14% vit A, 17% vit C, 10% folate.

Baked Potato Skins

This beloved pub grub dish is welcome at any get-together. Setting the skins out with fresh toppings alongside lets everyone personalize his or her own.

6 large **baking potatoes** (about 4 lb/2 kg)

¼ tsp (1 mL) each **salt** and **pepper**

1 cup (250 mL) shredded **Cheddar cheese,** or Swiss or Asiago cheese

TOPPINGS:

8 slices **bacon,** cooked and crumbled

4 **plum tomatoes,** chopped

3 **green onions,** chopped

½ cup (125 mL) chopped **oil-packed sun-dried tomatoes**

½ cup (125 mL) **pesto**

½ cup (125 mL) **light sour cream**

Scrub potatoes; prick several times with fork. Bake in 450°F (230°C) oven until tender, about 1 hour. Let stand until cool enough to handle.

Cut lengthwise in half; scoop out flesh, leaving ½-inch (1 cm) thick walls (reserve flesh for another use, such as soup or mashed potatoes).

Cut each potato half in half lengthwise. Arrange, cut side up, on rimmed baking sheet; sprinkle with salt and pepper, then cheese. Bake in 450°F (230°C) oven until cheese is melted, about 10 minutes.

Toppings: Place bacon, plum tomatoes, onions, sun-dried tomatoes, pesto and sour cream in separate small bowls for guests to sprinkle onto potato skins.

Makes 8 servings.

PER SERVING: about 312 cal, 11 g pro, 16 g total fat (7 g sat. fat), 33 g carb, 5 g fibre, 28 mg chol, 454 mg sodium. % RDI: 18% calcium, 24% iron, 11% vit A, 45% vit C, 13% folate.

game day dishes

Green Onion Parmesan Dip

4 **green onions,** minced
½ cup (125 mL) grated **Parmesan cheese**
⅓ cup (75 mL) **light sour cream**
⅓ cup (75 mL) **light mayonnaise**
¼ cup (60 mL) **fresh parsley leaves**
2 tsp (10 mL) **white wine vinegar**
¼ tsp (1 mL) each **salt** and **pepper**

In bowl, combine green onions with Parmesan cheese.

In food processor, purée together sour cream, mayonnaise, parsley, vinegar, salt and pepper until smooth, about 2 minutes. Stir into onion mixture.

Makes about 1 cup (250 mL).

PER 1 TBSP (15 mL): about 37 cal, 2 g pro, 3 g total fat (1 g sat. fat), 1 g carb, trace fibre, 5 mg chol, 123 mg sodium, 35 mg potassium. % RDI: 4% calcium, 1% iron, 2% vit A, 3% vit C, 2% folate.

Stuffed Jalapeño Peppers

10 **jalapeño peppers**
½ cup (125 mL) shredded **Cheddar cheese**
¼ cup (60 mL) **cream cheese,** softened
¼ cup (60 mL) **salsa**
¾ cup (175 mL) **fresh bread crumbs**
2 tbsp (30 mL) chopped **fresh parsley**
2 tbsp (30 mL) **butter,** melted

Wearing rubber gloves to protect hands, cut peppers in half lengthwise, leaving stem intact. Scrape out seeds and membranes.

In bowl, combine Cheddar cheese, cream cheese and salsa; blend in ¼ cup (60 mL) of the bread crumbs. Spoon filling into each pepper half.

Toss together remaining bread crumbs, parsley and butter. Top each jalapeño with bread crumb mixture.

Bake in 375°F (190°C) oven until topping is golden and crisp, about 20 minutes.

Makes 20 pieces.

PER PIECE: about 39 cal, 1 g pro, 3 g total fat (2 g sat. fat), 2 g carb, trace fibre, 9 mg chol, 63 mg sodium, 35 mg potassium. % RDI: 2% calcium, 1% iron, 4% vit A, 5% vit C, 2% folate.

Chili Chicken Wings

If you're grill-less, roast wings on foil-lined baking sheet in 400°F (200°C) oven, turning once, for about 45 minutes.

3 lb (1.5 kg) **chicken wings**

CHILI SPICE MIX:

1½ tbsp (22 mL) **chili powder**

1 tbsp (15 mL) **paprika**

1 tbsp (15 mL) packed **brown sugar**

1½ tsp (7 mL) **ground cumin**

½ tsp (2 mL) **garlic powder**

¼ tsp (1 mL) each **salt** and **pepper**

ANCHO CHILI TOMATO SAUCE:

1 tbsp (15 mL) **vegetable oil**

¼ cup (60 mL) minced **onion**

2 cloves **garlic,** minced

¾ cup (175 mL) **ketchup** or chili sauce

2 tbsp (30 mL) **fancy molasses**

1 tbsp (15 mL) **cider vinegar**

2 tsp (10 mL) **ancho chili powder** or chili powder

1 tsp (5 mL) **dry mustard**

1 tsp (5 mL) **hot pepper sauce**

Chili Spice Mix: Mix together chili powder, paprika, sugar, cumin, garlic powder, salt and pepper.

Straighten each chicken wing; push skewer through length from base to tip. Rub all over with chili spice mix. Cover and let stand for 30 minutes, or refrigerate for up to 24 hours, turning occasionally.

Ancho Chili Tomato Sauce: Meanwhile, in saucepan, heat oil over medium heat; fry onion and garlic, stirring occasionally, until softened, about 3 minutes.

Stir in ketchup, molasses, vinegar, ancho chili powder, mustard and hot pepper sauce; reduce heat and simmer, stirring occasionally, until bubbly, about 5 minutes. Let cool.

Place wings on greased grill over medium heat; close lid and grill, turning once, for 10 minutes. Baste with sauce; grill, basting and turning occasionally, until crisp and juices run clear when chicken is pierced, 15 to 25 minutes.

Makes about 30 pieces.

PER PIECE: about 93 cal, 7 g pro, 5 g total fat (1 g sat. fat), 4 g carb, trace fibre, 21 mg chol, 137 mg sodium. % RDI: 1% calcium, 5% iron, 6% vit A, 3% vit C, 1% folate.

Cornmeal-Coated Wings with Blue Cheese Dip

A miniature version of Southern fried chicken, these breaded wings bake up crunchy and golden. Along with the blue cheese dip, serve some raw celery or carrot sticks.

3 lb (1.5 kg) **chicken wings**

⅔ cup (150 mL) **buttermilk**

1 **egg**

1 tsp (5 mL) **salt**

1 tsp (5 mL) **hot pepper sauce**

½ cup (125 mL) **cornmeal**

½ cup (125 mL) **all-purpose flour**

1½ tsp (7 mL) each **chili powder** and **ground cumin**

BLUE CHEESE DIP:

1 cup (250 mL) crumbled **blue cheese** (about 4 oz/125 g)

½ cup (125 mL) **buttermilk**

1 **green onion,** thinly sliced

¼ tsp (1 mL) **pepper**

Remove tips from wings and reserve for stock if desired; separate wings at joint. In baking dish, whisk together buttermilk, egg, salt and hot pepper sauce; add wings, tossing to coat. Cover and refrigerate for 4 hours or up to 24 hours.

Blue Cheese Dip: Mash blue cheese with buttermilk until fairly smooth. Stir in green onion and pepper.

In large resealable bag, shake together cornmeal, flour, chili powder and cumin. Remove wings from buttermilk mixture, letting excess drip off. In batches, shake in cornmeal mixture to coat; shake off any excess. Arrange on rack on foil-lined rimmed baking sheet.

Roast in 400°F (200°C) oven, turning once, until crisp and juices run clear when wings are pierced, about 45 minutes. Serve with blue cheese dip.

Makes 6 servings.

PER SERVING: about 428 cal, 29 g pro, 25 g total fat (9 g sat. fat), 20 g carb, 2 g fibre, 118 mg chol, 631 mg sodium. % RDI: 17% calcium, 16% iron, 12% vit A, 3% vit C, 27% folate.

sports night

Herbed Crab Dip
Serve this make-ahead dip with crackers and raw veggies for scooping.

1 pkg (7 oz/200 g) frozen **crabmeat,** thawed

2 tbsp (30 mL) **extra-virgin olive oil**

¼ cup (60 mL) minced **shallots** or onion

4 cloves **garlic,** minced

½ tsp (2 mL) **salt**

¼ tsp (1 mL) **pepper**

¼ tsp (1 mL) **mace** or nutmeg

⅓ cup (75 mL) **dry white wine** or dry white vermouth

1 tbsp (15 mL) **lemon juice**

½ tsp (2 mL) crumbled **dried tarragon** or dillweed

¾ cup (175 mL) **light cream cheese,** cubed and softened

¼ cup (60 mL) **light sour cream**

¼ cup (60 mL) each minced **fresh parsley** and **chives**

¼ cup (60 mL) diced roasted or fresh **sweet red pepper**

Place crabmeat in sieve; pick through to remove any cartilage. Press firmly to remove liquid.

In saucepan, heat oil over medium-low heat; fry shallots, garlic, salt, pepper and mace, without browning, until softened and fragrant, about 4 minutes.

Add wine, lemon juice and tarragon; boil over medium heat until reduced by half, about 3 minutes. Let cool.

In food processor or in bowl with fork, blend cream cheese with sour cream until smooth; stir in shallot mixture, crabmeat, parsley, chives and red pepper. Scrape into serving dish.

Makes 2 cups (500 mL).

PER 1 TBSP (15 mL): about 30 cal, 2 g pro, 2 g total fat (1 g sat. fat), 1 g carb, 0 g fibre, 6 mg chol, 120 mg sodium. % RDI: 1% calcium, 1% iron, 2% vit A, 5% vit C, 1% folate.

VARIATION
Herbed Smoked Salmon Dip: Omit salt. Use 8 oz (250 g) smoked salmon, finely chopped, instead of crabmeat.

Meat-Lover Nachos

8 oz (250 g) **lean Italian sausage**

8 oz (250 g) **lean ground beef**

2 cloves **garlic,** minced

2 tsp (10 mL) **Cajun seasoning** or chili powder

2 tbsp (30 mL) coarsely chopped pickled or
   fresh **jalapeño peppers**

1 **tomato,** chopped

3 **green onions,** chopped

2 tbsp (30 mL) chopped **fresh coriander**

1 tbsp (15 mL) **lime juice**

1 bag (345 g) **tortilla chips**

1 cup (250 mL) shredded **old Cheddar cheese**

Squeeze sausage from casings into large skillet; add beef and sauté over medium-high heat, breaking up with spoon, until no longer pink, about 5 minutes. Drain off fat.

Add garlic and Cajun seasoning; sauté until garlic is softened, about 2 minutes. Add jalapeño peppers, tomato, green onions, coriander and lime juice; stir to combine.

Arrange tortilla chips in single layer on large rimmed baking sheet. Sprinkle with sausage mixture and cheese. Bake in 375°F (190°C) oven until cheese is melted, 6 to 10 minutes.

Makes 10 servings.

PER SERVING: about 308 cal, 13 g pro, 18 g total fat (6 g sat. fat), 24 g carb, 3 g fibre, 32 mg chol, 439 mg sodium. % RDI: 13% calcium, 11% iron, 8% vit A, 10% vit C, 4% folate.

Warm Cherry Tomato Crostini
Olive oil and garlic enhance the bright, sweet flavours of juicy cherry tomatoes.

4 cups (1 L) **cherry tomatoes** or grape tomatoes, halved

¼ cup (60 mL) **extra-virgin olive oil**

2 cloves **garlic,** minced

½ tsp (2 mL) **salt**

¼ tsp (1 mL) **pepper**

¼ cup (60 mL) thinly shredded **fresh basil**

CROSTINI:

24 slices (½ inch/1 cm thick) **baguette**

¼ cup (60 mL) **extra-virgin olive oil**

2 cloves **garlic**

In foil pan, toss together tomatoes, oil, garlic, salt and pepper. Place on grill over medium-high heat; close lid and cook, stirring occasionally, until softened and juicy, about 10 minutes. Stir in basil.

Crostini: Meanwhile, brush 1 side of each baguette slice with oil. Grill over medium-high heat until toasted and golden, about 3 minutes.

Cut garlic cloves in half; rub cut sides over toasted side of slices. Top with tomato mixture.

Makes 24 pieces.

PER PIECE: about 65 cal, 1 g pro, 5 g total fat (1 g sat. fat), 5 g carb, 1 g fibre, 0 mg chol, 93 mg sodium. % RDI: 1% calcium, 2% iron, 2% vit A, 5% vit C, 4% folate.

last-minute dinner guests

Romaine Salad With Lemon Thyme Vinaigrette

Toss this refreshingly lemony salad with crunchy additions such as croutons, sliced mushrooms, radishes, cucumbers or shaved fennel.

⅓ cup (75 mL) **vegetable oil** or olive oil

3 tbsp (45 mL) **lemon juice**

2 tsp (10 mL) chopped **fresh thyme** (or ¼ tsp/1 mL dried)

1 tsp (5 mL) **Dijon mustard**

½ tsp (2 mL) **salt**

¼ tsp (1 mL) each **granulated sugar** and **pepper**

1 head **romaine lettuce**

Whisk together oil, lemon juice, thyme, mustard, salt, sugar and pepper.

Tear lettuce into bite-size pieces to make 12 cups (3 L). In large bowl, toss lettuce with dressing.

Makes 8 servings.

PER SERVING: about 96 cal, 1 g pro, 9 g total fat (1 g sat. fat), 3 g carb, 1 g fibre, 0 mg chol, 160 mg sodium. % RDI: 3% calcium, 7% iron, 22% vit A, 37% vit C, 52% folate.

best tips:

• Dijon mustard's clean, sharp taste and medium-high heat suits many dishes. Its flavour is a balance of spicy mustard seeds, wine and salt. Creamy Dijon contains ground seeds; grainy contains whole seeds.

• Use Dijon mustard to add an instant flavour boost to salad dressings, marinades, rubs, hot and cold sauces, meatloaf and your favourite burger recipe.

• Dijon mustard matches perfectly with beef, pork, chicken and lamb. It's also ideal with meaty salmon.

Beer and Bacon-Steamed Mussels

Serve with crusty bread to sop up the juices. Choose your favourite microbrew (wheat beer is best) for steaming and drinking. This recipe doubles easily.

4 lb (2 kg) **mussels**

2 tbsp (30 mL) **butter**

2 thick slices **bacon,** chopped

2 ribs **celery,** diced

1 small **onion,** diced

1 **bay leaf**

Half **lemon**

2 bottles (each 341 mL) **beer**

¼ cup (60 mL) each minced **celery leaves** and **fresh parsley**

Rinse mussels, pulling off any beards. Discard any mussels that do not close when tapped. Set aside.

In large Dutch oven, melt butter over medium heat; cook bacon, celery, onion and bay leaf, stirring occasionally, until vegetables are softened, about 5 minutes.

Squeeze juice from lemon into pan; add remaining lemon. Add beer and bring to boil.

Add mussels; reduce heat, cover and simmer until mussels open, about 10 minutes. Discard any that do not open. Discard lemon and bay leaf. Stir in celery leaves and parsley.

Makes 4 to 6 servings.

PER EACH OF 6 SERVINGS: about 96 cal, 6 g pro, 6 g total fat (2 g sat. fat), 6 g carb, 1 g fibre, 20 mg chol, 180 mg sodium, 206 mg potassium. % RDI: 2% calcium, 12% iron, 6% vit A, 10% vit C, 10% folate.

Frozen Grand Marnier Orange Soufflés

For a change, omit Candied Kumquats, chocolate and cream. Substitute 1 jar (375 mL) Seville orange marmalade, melted and strained. Use ½ cup (125 mL) in soufflés as directed and remainder as garnish.

3 **egg yolks**

⅓ cup (75 mL) **granulated sugar**

3 tbsp (45 mL) **orange-flavoured liqueur**
  (such as Grand Marnier)

⅓ cup (75 mL) **pasteurized egg whites**

¾ cup (175 mL) **whipping cream**

CANDIED KUMQUATS:

1 cup (250 mL) **granulated sugar**

3 cups (750 mL) **kumquats,** halved

GARNISH:

¼ cup (60 mL) **whipping cream**

2 oz (60 g) **bittersweet chocolate,** finely chopped

1 cup (250 mL) **Candied Kumquats** (with syrup),
  recipe above

Candied Kumquats: In saucepan, bring sugar and 1 cup (250 mL) water to boil, stirring until dissolved. Add kumquats; reduce heat and simmer, stirring, until tender and slightly wrinkled, about 12 minutes. Set aside.

Line bottoms of four 1-cup (250 mL) ramekins with parchment paper rounds. Cut four 13- x 5-inch (33 x 12 cm) strips of parchment paper; fold in half lengthwise and line insides of ramekins. Set aside.

In large heatproof bowl, whisk together egg yolks, ¼ cup (60 mL) of the sugar and liqueur. Place over saucepan of simmering water; whisk until pale yellow and batter falls in ribbons when whisk is lifted, about 4 minutes. Let cool.

Seed and coarsely chop ½ cup (125 mL) of the candied kumquats. Set aside.

Beat egg whites until soft peaks form; beat in remaining sugar, 1 tbsp (15 mL) at a time, until stiff peaks form. Whip cream. Fold one-third into egg yolk mixture; fold in remaining cream. Fold in one-third of the egg whites; fold in remaining egg whites. Fold in chopped candied kumquats. Spoon about ¾ cup (175 mL) into each ramekin; smooth tops. Cover and freeze until firm, about 8 hours, or up to 2 days.

Garnish: In saucepan, heat cream until bubbles form around edge; stir with chocolate in heatproof bowl until smooth. Run knife around each soufflé to loosen; pull from dish. Remove paper base. Set soufflé on chilled plate; remove paper. Drizzle with chocolate; garnish with candied kumquats.

Makes 4 servings.

PER SERVING: about 567 cal, 8 g pro, 34 g total fat (19 g sat. fat), 63 g carb, 6 g fibre, 229 mg chol, 69 mg sodium. % RDI: 10% calcium, 14% iron, 30% vit A, 35% vit C, 13% folate.

best fancy dinner party

Lobster Risotto
If you have seafood stock on hand, all the better. Or use half clam juice and half vegetable broth, or all sodium-reduced chicken broth.

3⅓ cups (825 mL) **vegetable broth**

1 **cooked lobster** (1¼ lb/625 g), shelled
  (see Best Tips, below)

2 tbsp (30 mL) **butter**

1 tbsp (15 mL) **extra-virgin olive oil**

2 **shallots,** minced

1 clove **garlic,** minced

¼ tsp (1 mL) each **salt** and white or black **pepper**

Pinch **dried thyme**

1 cup (250 mL) **arborio rice**

⅓ cup (75 mL) **dry white wine**

2 tsp (10 mL) minced **fresh parsley**

½ tsp (2 mL) grated **lemon rind**

In saucepan, heat broth until steaming; keep warm. Chop lobster meat into bite-size pieces; set aside.

In separate saucepan, melt 1 tbsp (15 mL) of the butter and oil over medium heat; cook shallots, garlic, salt, pepper and thyme, stirring occasionally, until softened, 2 to 3 minutes.

Add rice, stirring to coat. Add wine; cook, stirring, until no liquid remains.

Add 3 cups (750 mL) of the broth, ½ cup (125 mL) at a time, stirring after each addition until completely absorbed before adding more broth, about 17 minutes total.

Add remaining broth and butter, parsley, lemon rind and chopped lobster meat, stirring until rice is creamy and tender, liquid is completely absorbed and lobster is heated through, about 3 minutes.

Makes 4 servings.

PER SERVING: about 346 cal, 17 g pro, 11 g total fat (5 g sat. fat), 41 g carb, 1 g fibre, 49 mg chol, 894 mg sodium. % RDI: 4% calcium, 5% iron, 7% vit A, 2% vit C, 22% folate.

best tips:

To shell lobster, halve lengthwise. Twist off claws at joint at body; separate into claw and arm sections. Break off small part of claw and remove meat. Crack large part of claw at widest part; lift out meat. Crack arm; pick out meat and set aside. Discard claw shells. Remove meat from tail.

Beef Tenderloin With Cabernet Shallot Sauce This may make more than you need, but any leftovers are just as delicious the next day.

4 lb (2 kg) **beef tenderloin premium oven roast**

2 tbsp (30 mL) **black peppercorns,** coarsely crushed

1 tsp (5 mL) **sea salt**

2 tbsp (30 mL) **olive oil**

CABERNET SHALLOT SAUCE:

¼ cup (60 mL) **butter**

2 cups (500 mL) sliced **shallots**

4 cloves **garlic,** minced

1 tbsp (15 mL) minced **fresh thyme**

1 tsp (5 mL) **granulated sugar**

1 **bay leaf**

2 cups (500 mL) **beef broth**

¾ cup (175 mL) **dry red wine**

¼ cup (60 mL) **brandy**

1 tbsp (15 mL) **cornstarch**

Sprinkle tenderloin with peppercorns and salt, pressing to adhere. In roasting pan, heat oil over medium-high heat; sear tenderloin all over.

Roast in 375°F (190°C) oven until meat thermometer inserted in centre registers 140°F (60°C) for rare or 150°F (65°C) for medium-rare, about 55 minutes. Transfer to cutting board. Tent with foil; let stand for 15 minutes before carving.

Cabernet Shallot Sauce: Meanwhile, in saucepan, melt half of the butter over medium heat; cook shallots, stirring occasionally, until softened, about 10 minutes. Stir in garlic, thyme, sugar and bay leaf; cook until shallots are golden and caramelized, about 12 minutes.

Add beef broth, wine and brandy; bring to boil. Reduce heat and simmer until sauce is reduced to about 2 cups (500 mL), about 30 minutes. Whisk cornstarch with 1 tbsp (15 mL) water; whisk into sauce and boil until thickened and smooth. Discard bay leaf. Add roasting pan juices to sauce. Bring to boil; whisk in remaining butter. Serve with roast.

Makes 8 servings.

PER SERVING: about 450 cal, 51 g pro, 21 g total fat (9 g sat. fat), 9 g carb, 1 g fibre, 137 mg chol, 705 mg sodium, 884 mg potassium. % RDI: 4% calcium, 54% iron, 8% vit A, 3% vit C, 9% folate.

Chunky Chili con Carne

Chili without beans is as traditional as the popular bean-and-beef combo. Feel free to add pinto or red kidney beans (one 19-oz/540 mL can, drained and rinsed) if you like. Top each serving with Herbed Sour Cream (below) for a fresh hit of creamy flavour.

2 lb (1 kg) **stewing beef cubes**

1 tbsp (15 mL) **vegetable oil**

2 **onions,** chopped

2 cloves **garlic,** slivered

2 tbsp (30 mL) **chili powder**

2 tsp (10 mL) **ground cumin**

1 tsp (5 mL) each **cinnamon** and **dried oregano**

1 tsp (5 mL) **granulated sugar**

¼ tsp (1 mL) **salt**

1 can (28 oz/796 mL) **whole tomatoes**

1 cup (250 mL) **beef broth**

2 tbsp (30 mL) **red wine vinegar**

2 tbsp (30 mL) **tomato paste**

Cut beef into bite-size pieces. In Dutch oven, heat half of the oil over medium-high heat; brown beef, in batches and adding remaining oil as needed.

Reduce heat to medium. Add onions, garlic, chili powder, cumin, cinnamon, oregano, sugar and salt; cook, stirring often, until softened, about 5 minutes.

Add tomatoes, broth, vinegar and tomato paste, mashing tomatoes with back of spoon; bring to boil. Reduce heat to low; cover and simmer for 1 hour, stirring occasionally.

Uncover and simmer, stirring occasionally, until thickened, about 1¼ hours.

Makes 8 servings.

PER SERVING: about 255 cal, 27 g pro, 12 g total fat (4 g sat. fat), 10 g carb, 2 g fibre, 63 mg chol, 408 mg sodium. % RDI: 6% calcium, 26% iron, 13% vit A, 30% vit C, 8% folate.

Herbed Sour Cream: Stir together 1 cup (250 mL) sour cream; ¼ cup (60 mL) finely chopped chives or green onion; and pinch each salt and cayenne pepper.

Makes about 1 cup (250 mL).

feeding a crowd

Corn Muffins with Green Onions

Corn kernels and creamed corn add crunch and moistness to these muffins. You can substitute buttermilk for the milk-and-vinegar combination if you have it on hand.

½ cup (125 mL) **milk**

1½ tsp (7 mL) **vinegar**

1 cup (250 mL) **cornmeal**

1 cup (250 mL) **all-purpose flour**

½ tsp (2 mL) **baking soda**

½ tsp (2 mL) each **salt** and **pepper**

1 can (14 oz/398 mL) **creamed corn**

¼ cup (60 mL) **vegetable oil**

2 **eggs**

¼ tsp (1 mL) **hot pepper sauce**

1 cup (250 mL) shredded **Cheddar cheese**

½ cup (125 mL) frozen **corn kernels**

3 **green onions,** thinly sliced

¼ cup (60 mL) minced **fresh parsley**

Stir milk with vinegar; let stand for 5 minutes.

In large bowl, whisk together cornmeal, flour, baking soda, salt and pepper. Whisk together creamed corn, milk mixture, oil, eggs and hot pepper sauce; pour over cornmeal mixture. Sprinkle with cheese, frozen corn, green onions and parsley; stir just until dry ingredients are moistened.

Spoon into greased or paper-lined muffin cups. Bake in 400°F (200°C) oven until cake tester inserted in centre comes out clean, about 20 minutes. Let cool in pan on rack.

Makes 12 muffins.

PER MUFFIN: about 207 cal, 7 g pro, 9 g total fat (3 g sat. fat), 26 g carb, 2 g fibre, 41 mg chol, 329 mg sodium. % RDI: 8% calcium, 8% iron, 6% vit A, 7% vit C, 21% folate.

best
tips:

These muffins can be refrigerated in an airtight container for up to 2 days, or wrapped individually and frozen in an airtight container for up to 2 weeks.

Light Caesar Salad

For ease, you can shake this dressing together in a sealed jar or container. You can also make it ahead and refrigerate it for up to 3 days.

¼ cup (60 mL) grated **Parmesan cheese**

¼ cup (60 mL) **light mayonnaise**

2 tbsp (30 mL) **white wine vinegar**

1 tbsp (15 mL) **extra-virgin olive oil**

1 tbsp (15 mL) **water**

1 tbsp (15 mL) **Dijon mustard**

1 tsp (5 mL) **Worcestershire sauce**

1 clove **garlic,** minced

Pinch each **salt** and **pepper**

8 cups (2 L) torn **romaine lettuce** (1 small head)

1 cup (250 mL) **croutons**

2 tbsp (30 mL) crumbled cooked **bacon**

Whisk together Parmesan cheese, mayonnaise, vinegar, oil, water, mustard, Worcestershire sauce, garlic, salt and pepper until smooth.

In large bowl, toss lettuce with dressing to coat. Sprinkle with croutons and bacon.

Makes 4 servings.

PER SERVING: about 171 cal, 7 g pro, 12 g total fat (3 g sat. fat), 11 g carb, 2 g fibre, 12 mg chol, 392 mg sodium. % RDI: 13% calcium, 13% iron, 30% vit A, 45% vit C, 74% folate.

eggs and brunch

Maple-Baked Oatmeal

Especially during the cold months, enjoy a warm, hearty bowl served with milk and maple syrup. Instead of almonds, you can use dried cranberries, dried blueberries or raisins – or keep it au naturel.

1½ cups (375 mL) **large-flake rolled oats**

¼ cup (60 mL) **sliced almonds**

2 tbsp (30 mL) packed **maple sugar** or brown sugar

2 tbsp (30 mL) **maple syrup**

Pinch **salt**

3 cups (750 mL) **milk**

Cinnamon

In greased 8-inch (2 L) square baking dish, combine oats, almonds, maple sugar, maple syrup and salt; stir in milk.

Bake in 350°F (180°C) oven until oats are softened and milk is absorbed, about 40 minutes. Sprinkle with cinnamon to taste. Serve hot.

Makes 4 servings.

PER SERVING: about 309 cal, 13 g pro, 9 g total fat (3 g sat. fat), 46 g carb, 4 g fibre, 14 mg chol, 97 mg sodium. % RDI: 24% calcium, 16% iron, 9% vit A, 2% vit C, 10% folate.

easy everyday breakfast

French Toast With Blueberry Maple Syrup

Use your favourite bread for French toast. Instead of white bread, try multigrain, cinnamon raisin or challah (egg bread).

3 **eggs**
⅓ cup (75 mL) **milk**
½ tsp (2 mL) **cinnamon**
2 tbsp (30 mL) **butter**
8 slices **white bread**
Blueberry Maple Syrup (below)

In shallow dish, whisk together eggs, milk and cinnamon. In nonstick skillet, melt half of the butter over medium heat until bubbly.

Dip each bread slice into egg mixture, turning to coat and soak up liquid. Cook in skillet, in batches, adding remaining butter as necessary and turning halfway through, until golden, 4 to 6 minutes. Serve with Blueberry Maple Syrup.

Makes 4 servings.

PER SERVING: about 259 cal, 10 g pro, 12 g total fat (5 g sat. fat), 28 g carb, 1 g fibre, 178 mg chol, 401 mg sodium. % RDI: 10% calcium, 16% iron, 14% vit A, 24% folate.

Blueberry Maple Syrup: In small saucepan, bring 2 cups (500 mL) fresh blueberries or thawed frozen blueberries and 1 cup (250 mL) maple syrup to boil; reduce heat and simmer until berries break up, about 5 minutes. Stir in 2 tsp (10 mL) lemon juice; press through fine sieve or cheesecloth-lined sieve. Serve warm or refrigerate for up to 2 weeks.

Makes about 1½ cups (375 mL).

best tips: Available year-round, frozen wild blueberries retain all the flavour and nutrition of fresh. They offer great value and, because they're already washed, they're also convenient. Keep a bag in your freezer and use in smoothies, sauces, desserts, cereals and in Blueberry Maple Syrup (above).

All-Day-Breakfast in a Bun

1 tbsp (15 mL) **butter**

8 slices **peameal bacon** or back bacon

6 **eggs**

¼ cup (60 mL) **milk**

2 **green onions,** thinly sliced

¼ tsp (1 mL) each **salt** and **pepper**

4 thin slices **Havarti cheese** or Cheddar cheese

8 thin slices **tomato**

4 leaves **leaf lettuce** (optional)

4 **whole wheat kaiser rolls** or ciabatta buns,
    halved and toasted

In large nonstick skillet, melt 1 tsp (5 mL) of the butter over medium heat; cook bacon, turning once, about 4 minutes. Transfer to plate; keep warm.

Meanwhile, whisk together eggs, milk, green onions, salt and pepper. In same skillet, melt remaining butter over medium heat; pour in egg mixture and cook, lifting edges with spatula to allow uncooked eggs to flow underneath, until set, about 8 minutes. Cut into quarters.

Sandwich 2 slices bacon, 1 slice cheese, omelette quarter, 2 slices tomato, and 1 leaf lettuce (if using) in each bun.

Makes 4 servings.

PER SERVING: about 543 cal, 44 g pro, 25 g total fat (9 g sat. fat), 37 g carb, 5 g fibre, 360 mg chol, 2,324 mg sodium. % RDI: 16% calcium, 26% iron, 20% vit A, 12% vit C, 30% folate.

Hot Chocolate
This drink is so rich and authentic that it will be apparent it's not from a mix. The fuller fat the milk, the richer the flavour.

6 oz (175 g) **semisweet chocolate,** finely chopped
½ cup (125 mL) **water**
3 cups (750 mL) **milk**

In heatproof bowl over saucepan of hot (not boiling) water, melt chocolate with water, stirring until smooth.

Meanwhile, in saucepan, heat milk until steaming and small bubbles appear around edge. Using immersion blender or whisk, blend in chocolate. Pour into mugs.

Makes 4 servings.

PER SERVING: about 312 cal, 8 g pro, 15 g total fat (9 g sat. fat), 37 g carb, 3 g fibre, 16 mg chol, 77 mg sodium. % RDI: 21% calcium, 9% iron, 9% vit A, 8% folate.

Hot Chocolate Toppings and Garnishes: Try one of the following to dress up your steaming mug of chocolate.

- Whipped cream
- Regular or mini-marshmallows
- Grated chocolate
- Candy canes
- Cinnamon sticks
- Maple sugar or maple syrup
- Peppermint patties
- Skewered fresh raspberries
- Orange zest curls

make time for breakfast

Glazed Apple Cinnamon Puff

This baked pancake is somewhere between a soufflé and a crêpe. You can slice and lift it out of the pan, but for a dramatic presentation, invert it whole onto a serving plate. (Be careful – it's hot!)

⅓ cup (75 mL) **butter,** melted

3 **eggs**

¾ cup (175 mL) **all-purpose flour**

¾ cup (175 mL) **milk**

1 tbsp (15 mL) **granulated sugar**

Pinch **salt**

3 large **apples,** peeled and cut into ½-inch (1 cm) thick slices

¼ cup (60 mL) packed **brown sugar**

¼ tsp (1 mL) **cinnamon** or ground nutmeg

In blender or food processor, blend 2 tbsp (30 mL) of the butter, the eggs, flour, milk, sugar and salt until smooth. Set batter aside.

In 10-inch (25 cm) cast-iron or heavy ovenproof skillet, heat remaining butter over medium heat; cook apples, brown sugar and cinnamon, stirring occasionally, until golden and tender, about 15 minutes.

Pour batter over apple mixture. Bake in 425°F (220°C) oven until puffed and edge is browned, about 20 minutes.

If desired, invert onto serving plate, scraping any remaining apples and syrup onto puff. Serve immediately.

Makes 6 servings.

PER SERVING: about 284 cal, 6 g pro, 14 g total fat (8 g sat. fat), 36 g carb, 2 g fibre, 123 mg chol, 119 mg sodium. % RDI: 6% calcium, 9% iron, 14% vit A, 5% vit C, 20% folate.

Grilled Peameal Bacon

¼ cup (60 mL) **maple syrup**
2 tbsp (30 mL) **Dijon mustard**
Pinch **pepper**
1 lb (500 g) chunk **peameal bacon**

Stir together maple syrup, Dijon mustard and pepper; set half aside for serving.

Cut bacon into 8 generous ¼-inch (5 mm) thick slices. Brush 1 side of each with half of the remaining mustard mixture.

In batches, place bacon slices, mustard side down, on grill, greased nonstick grill pan or in skillet over medium-high heat. Brush slices with remaining mustard mixture; grill until bottom is golden, 3 to 5 minutes.

Turn and grill until browned, about 3 minutes. Serve with reserved mustard mixture.

Makes 4 servings.

PER SERVING: about 234 cal, 24 g pro, 9 g total fat (3 g sat. fat), 14 g carb, 0 g fibre, 56 mg chol, 1,593 mg sodium. % RDI: 3% calcium, 9% iron, 2% folate.

best tips:

• Back bacon is known as "Canadian bacon" south of the border. It comes from the tender pork loin and is cured, smoked and fully cooked.

• Peameal bacon is also from the loin but is cured in brine (or sweet pickled) and is uncooked. Peameal bacon is characterized by its cornmeal crust.

• Both back and peameal bacon are available in slices or chunks. They are leaner than side bacon (about 35 g less fat per 100 g) and therefore shrink less during cooking.

Hit-the-Road Mix

You can store this mix (minus the pineapple) in an airtight container for up to 1 month. Add the pineapple up to 24 hours before eating.

1 cup (250 mL) **corn and bran cereal squares**

1 cup (250 mL) **multigrain cereal circles,** such as Cheerios

1 cup (250 mL) **raisins,** dried cherries or dried cranberries

¾ cup (175 mL) chopped **dried pineapple chunks**

⅓ cup (75 mL) **roasted sunflower seeds** or pepitas (hulled pumpkin seeds)

¼ cup (60 mL) flaked or shredded **sweetened coconut**

¼ cup (60 mL) **roasted unsalted cashews**

¼ cup (60 mL) **unsalted peanuts**

Mix together corn squares, multigrain circles, raisins, pineapple, sunflower seeds, coconut, cashews and peanuts.

Makes about 5 cups (1.25 L).

PER ½ CUP (125 ML): about 179 cal, 4 g pro, 7 g total fat (1 g sat. fat), 31 g carb, 3 g fibre, 0 mg chol, 61 mg sodium, 334 mg potassium. % RDI: 4% calcium, 14% iron, 32% vit C, 10% folate.

grab-and-go family breakfast

Breakfast in a Cookie

2 **eggs**

½ cup (125 mL) **liquid honey**

¼ cup (60 mL) **butter,** melted, or vegetable oil

1 cup (250 mL) shredded **carrots**

1 cup (250 mL) coarsely chopped **walnuts**

½ cup (125 mL) **raisins** or dried cranberries

½ cup (125 mL) chopped **dried apricots**

½ cup (125 mL) chopped **dried dates**

1 cup (250 mL) **all-purpose flour**

1 cup (250 mL) **quick-cooking rolled oats** (not instant)

¾ tsp (4 mL) each **cinnamon** and **nutmeg**

½ tsp (2 mL) **baking soda**

¼ tsp (1 mL) **salt**

1½ cups (375 mL) **oat cereal circles,** such as Cheerios

In large bowl, whisk together eggs, honey and butter until smooth; stir in carrots, walnuts, raisins, apricots and dates.

Whisk together flour, rolled oats, cinnamon, nutmeg, baking soda and salt; stir in oat cereal. Stir into fruit mixture until no streaks of dry ingredients remain.

Drop dough by heaping tablespoonfuls (15 mL), about 1 inch (2.5 cm) apart, onto 2 parchment paper–lined baking sheets. Bake in top and bottom thirds of 350°F (180°C) oven, switching and rotating pans halfway through, until firm to the touch, about 15 minutes. Transfer to racks; let cool.

Makes about 48 cookies.

PER COOKIE: about 72 cal, 2 g pro, 3 g total fat (1 g sat. fat), 11 g carb, 1 g fibre, 10 mg chol, 43 mg sodium, 73 mg potassium. % RDI: 1% calcium, 4% iron, 5% vit A, 5% folate.

best tips:

You can make these highly addictive cookies ahead and store them in an airtight container for up to 2 days. Or freeze them for up to 2 weeks – they don't take long to thaw.

Yogurt Berry Ice Pops

Switch up the flavours: replace mixed berries with frozen sliced peaches and the cranberry cocktail with mango juice.

2 cups (500 mL) **frozen mixed berries**

1½ cups (375 mL) **Balkan-style plain yogurt**

⅓ cup (75 mL) **cranberry cocktail**

2 tbsp (30 mL) **liquid honey**

In blender, purée together berries, yogurt, cranberry cocktail and honey until smooth. Pour into ice-pop moulds; freeze until firm, about 4 hours.

Makes about 6 pops.

PER POP: about 124 cal, 3 g pro, 4 g total fat (2 g sat. fat), 20 g carb, 3 g fibre, 11 mg chol, 35 mg sodium, 133 mg potassium. % RDI: 9% calcium, 4% iron, 3% vit A, 20% vit C, 1% folate.

Grab-and-Go Breakfast Burritos

If you're enjoying these on the run, wrap each roll in waxed or parchment paper.

3 **eggs**

1 **green onion,** thinly sliced

Pinch each **salt** and **pepper**

1 tbsp (15 mL) **butter**

2 small **whole wheat tortillas** (6 inches/15 cm)

2 thin slices **Black Forest ham**

Half **avocado,** peeled, pitted and sliced

¼ cup (60 mL) shredded **Cheddar cheese**

2 tbsp (30 mL) **salsa**

Whisk together eggs, green onion, salt and pepper. In large nonstick skillet, melt butter over medium heat; cook egg mixture, stirring, just until softly set, about 3 minutes.

On each tortilla, arrange 1 slice ham and half of the avocado. Divide egg between tortillas; top with half each of the cheese and salsa. Roll up tortillas.

Makes 2 servings.

PER SERVING: about 421 cal, 20 g pro, 28 g total fat (11 g sat. fat), 23 g carb, 6 g fibre, 316 mg chol, 746 mg sodium, 474 mg potassium. % RDI: 16% calcium, 15% iron, 21% vit A, 10% vit C, 44% folate.

Egg and Bacon Bread This golden rolled loaf is layered with eggs, bacon and cheese. It's ideal for feeding a crowd.

8 oz (250 g) **bacon**

¼ cup (60 mL) **grainy mustard** or Dijon mustard

1 clove **garlic,** minced

¼ tsp (1 mL) **pepper**

¼ tsp (1 mL) **hot pepper sauce**

Pinch **salt**

1 lb (500 g) **pizza dough**

4 **hard-cooked eggs** (see Best Tips, page 45), chopped

1½ cups (375 mL) shredded **extra-old Cheddar cheese**

1 **egg,** lightly beaten

In skillet, cook bacon over medium-high heat, turning once, until crisp, about 6 minutes. Drain on paper towel–lined plate; chop or crumble.

Stir together mustard, garlic, pepper, hot pepper sauce and salt.

On floured surface, roll out dough to 14- x 12-inch (35 x 30 cm) rectangle. Brush with mustard mixture, leaving ½-inch (1 cm) border; sprinkle bacon, hard-cooked eggs and 1 cup (250 mL) of the cheese over mustard. Starting at 1 long side, roll up jelly roll–style; pinch seam to seal. Place, seam side down, in greased 10-inch (3 L) Bundt pan. Cover with greased plastic wrap; let rise until doubled in bulk, about 30 minutes.

Brush loaf with beaten egg. With serrated knife, cut slashes in top; sprinkle with remaining cheese. Bake in 375°F (190°C) oven until golden and loaf pulls away from sides of pan, about 45 minutes. Let cool in pan on rack for 10 minutes.

Turn out onto serving plate; let cool for 20 minutes before slicing.

Makes 12 to 16 servings.

PER EACH OF 16 SERVINGS: about 168 cal, 8 g pro, 9 g total fat (4 g sat. fat), 14 g carb, trace fibre, 335 mg sodium. % RDI: 9% calcium, 7% iron, 7% vit A, 8% folate.

weekend brunch

Grapefruit, Avocado and Watercress Salad

Tangy citrus dressing enlivens peppery watercress in this brunch salad.

3 **ruby red grapefruits**

¼ cup (60 mL) **vegetable oil**

½ tsp (2 mL) **granulated sugar**

¼ tsp (1 mL) each **salt** and **pepper**

1 large bunch **watercress,** coarse stems removed

2 cups (500 mL) torn **radicchio**

1 **avocado,** peeled, pitted and sliced

2 tbsp (30 mL) thinly sliced **green onion**

With vegetable peeler, peel rind from 1 of the grapefruits. With knife, cut enough rind, avoiding pith, into long paper-thin strips to make ¼ cup (60 mL); set aside.

Peel remaining grapefruit; cut pith off all grapefruits. Working over sieve set over measuring cup, cut between grapefruit membranes and pulp to release sections; set aside. Squeeze membranes to make ½ cup (125 mL) juice.

In small saucepan, cover reserved rind with water and bring to boil. Reduce heat and simmer until tender, about 1 minute; drain and add to grapefruit juice along with oil, sugar, salt and pepper.

In large bowl, toss watercress with radicchio. Top with grapefruit sections and avocado; drizzle with dressing. Sprinkle with onion.

Makes 4 to 6 servings.

PER EACH OF 6 SERVINGS: about 180 cal, 2 g pro, 14 g total fat (1 g sat. fat), 14 g carb, 5 g fibre, 0 mg chol, 110 mg sodium. % RDI: 4% calcium, 5% iron, 14% vit A, 105% vit C, 21% folate.

Slushy Limoncello Watermelon Lemonade

Quarter **watermelon**
4 cups (1 L) **ice cubes**
½ cup (125 mL) frozen **lemonade concentrate**
4 oz (120 mL) each **vodka** and **limoncello**
Fresh mint sprigs

Peel and cube watermelon to make 4 cups (1 L); freeze until solid.

In blender on low speed, blend together watermelon, ice, lemonade concentrate, vodka and limoncello until ice breaks down.

Blend on high speed until smooth and slushy. Pour into pitcher. Garnish each serving with mint.

Makes 6 servings.

PER SERVING: about 193 cal, 1 g pro, trace total fat (0 g sat. fat), 28 g carb, trace fibre, 0 mg chol, 5 mg sodium. % RDI: 1% calcium, 3% iron, 6% vit A, 20% vit C, 2% folate.

VARIATION
Nonalcoholic Slushy Watermelon Lemonade: Omit vodka and limoncello. Stir in 1 cup (250 mL) lemon-lime soda.

best tips:
Limoncello is the generic name for a sweet Italian lemon liqueur. It's a wonderful palate cleanser, after-dinner drink or flavouring for blender cocktails.

Cheddar and Bacon Cornmeal Waffles Benedict

Savoury waffles, bacon, cheese and eggs are an eggs Benedict–inspired breakfast that's sure to delight any lucky diner.

2 tsp (10 mL) **vegetable oil**

8 slices **bacon,** cooked

4 **poached eggs** (see Best Tips, page 56)

2 tbsp (30 mL) minced **fresh chives** or green onions

CHEDDAR SAUCE:

4 tsp (20 mL) **butter**

4 tsp (20 mL) **all-purpose flour**

¾ cup (175 mL) **milk**

⅔ cup (150 mL) shredded **old Cheddar cheese**

¼ tsp (1 mL) **paprika**

Pinch each **salt** and **cayenne pepper**

CORNMEAL WAFFLES:

⅔ cup (150 mL) **all-purpose flour**

⅓ cup (75 mL) **cornmeal**

1 tsp (5 mL) **baking powder**

½ tsp (2 mL) **baking soda**

½ tsp (2 mL) **granulated sugar**

¼ tsp (1 mL) each **salt** and **pepper**

2 **eggs**

1 cup (250 mL) **buttermilk**

2 tbsp (30 mL) **vegetable oil**

¼ cup (60 mL) minced **fresh chives** or green onions

¼ cup (60 mL) finely chopped **sweet red pepper**

Cheddar Sauce: In small saucepan, melt butter over medium heat; add flour, stirring until bubbly, about 2 minutes. Whisk in milk; cook, whisking, until thickened, about 2 minutes. Whisk in cheese, paprika, salt and cayenne pepper until melted and smooth. Cover and keep warm over low heat or pan of hot water.

Cornmeal Waffles: In large bowl, whisk together flour, cornmeal, baking powder, baking soda, sugar, salt and pepper. Whisk together eggs, buttermilk and oil; pour over dry ingredients. Sprinkle with chives and red pepper; whisk just until combined.

Heat waffle iron; brush with ½ tsp (2 mL) of the oil. Using about ½ cup (125 mL) batter per waffle, or enough to spread to edges, pour onto waffle iron. Close lid and cook until crisp, golden and steam stops, about 4 minutes. Repeat with remaining batter and oil.

Place waffles in single layer on wire rack on rimmed baking sheet. Keep warm in 200°F (100°C) oven.

To serve, top each waffle with 2 slices bacon and 1 poached egg. Pour cheese sauce over top; sprinkle with chives.

Makes 4 servings.

PER SERVING: about 534 cal, 25 g pro, 32 g total fat (12 g sat. fat), 35 g carb, 2 g fibre, 327 mg chol, 892 mg sodium. % RDI: 31% calcium, 19% iron, 30% vit A, 30% vit C, 38% folate.

Watermelon Fruit Salad

1 **grapefruit**

8 oz (250 g) **watermelon**

½ cup (125 mL) **fresh raspberries** or quartered fresh
   strawberries

1 tbsp (15 mL) **granulated sugar**

1 tbsp (15 mL) thinly sliced **fresh mint**

Slice off grapefruit rind, avoiding pith; finely chop enough to
make 1 tsp (5 mL). Set aside.

Working over large bowl to catch juice, cut off rind and
outer membrane of grapefruit. Cut between membrane and
pulp to release sections into bowl, squeezing membranes to
extract all juice.

Cut watermelon into 1½-inch (4 cm) cubes to make
1½ cups (375 mL); add to grapefruit. Add raspberries, sugar
and mint; stir gently. Let stand for 15 minutes. Sprinkle with
reserved grapefruit rind.

Makes 4 servings.

PER SERVING: about 57 cal, 1 g pro, trace total fat (0 g sat. fat),
14 g carb, 2 g fibre, 0 mg chol, 1 mg sodium. % RDI: 2% calcium,
4% iron, 5% vit A, 50% vit C, 6% folate.

best tips:

Sweet, juicy watermelon is packed with antioxidants and vitamins A and C. It has an extremely high water content (about 92 per cent), giving its flesh a subtly crunchy texture and making it a favourite thirst-quencher. For best flavour, choose melons that have brightly coloured flesh with no white streaks. When choosing a whole watermelon, look for one that is heavy for its size with a relatively smooth rind that is neither overly shiny nor overly dull.

Strawberry Lemon Crush

Serve these colourful summer sippers in tall glasses and garnish with additional strawberries, mint sprigs or lemon wedges.

3 cups (750 mL) **cold water**

2 cups (500 mL) chopped **strawberries**

1 cup (250 mL) **granulated sugar**

1 cup (250 mL) **lemon juice**

16 **ice cubes**

In blender, purée together 1 cup (250 mL) of the water, the strawberries, sugar and lemon juice until blended and sugar is dissolved, about 1 minute. With motor running, gradually adding remaining water until mixture is smooth.

Divide ice between 4 glasses; pour in strawberry mixture.

Makes 4 servings.

PER SERVING: about 233 cal, 1 g pro, trace total fat (0 g sat. fat), 60 g carb, 2 g fibre, 0 mg chol, 19 mg sodium, 190 mg potassium. % RDI: 2% calcium, 3% iron, 107% vit C, 12% folate.

Rhubarb Coffee Cake

Studded with juicy pink rhubarb and topped with a crunchy nut streusel, this cake is perfect as part of a spring brunch, or as a snack or dessert. Choose fresh or thawed frozen rhubarb.

½ cup (125 mL) **butter,** softened

1 cup (250 mL) packed **brown sugar**

2 **eggs**

1 tsp (5 mL) **vanilla**

2 cups (500 mL) **all-purpose flour**

1 tsp (5 mL) **baking soda**

1 tsp (5 mL) **baking powder**

½ tsp (2 mL) **salt**

1 cup (250 mL) **buttermilk**

2 cups (500 mL) chopped **rhubarb**

TOPPING:

½ cup (125 mL) packed **brown sugar**

½ cup (125 mL) **all-purpose flour**

½ tsp (2 mL) **cinnamon**

¼ cup (60 mL) **butter,** softened

⅓ cup (75 mL) coarsely chopped **hazelnuts** or slivered almonds

Topping: In bowl, combine brown sugar, flour and cinnamon. Using fingers, rub in butter until crumbly. Stir in hazelnuts; set aside.

In large bowl, beat butter with brown sugar until light and fluffy; beat in eggs, 1 at a time. Beat in vanilla. Whisk together flour, baking soda, baking powder and salt. Add to butter mixture alternately with buttermilk, making 3 additions of flour mixture and 2 of buttermilk. Fold in chopped rhubarb. Scrape into greased 9-inch (2.5 L) springform pan.

Bake in 350°F (180°C) oven for 15 minutes; sprinkle evenly with topping. Continue baking until cake tester inserted in centre of cake comes out clean, about 1 hour. Let cool in pan on rack for 5 minutes. Remove side of pan. Serve warm or let cool temperature.

Makes 8 to 10 servings.

PER EACH OF 10 SERVINGS: about 419 cal, 6 g pro, 18 g total fat (10 g sat. fat), 59 g carb, 2 g fibre, 76 mg chol, 417 mg sodium, 298 mg potassium. % RDI: 11% calcium, 18% iron, 14% vit A, 3% vit C, 34% folate.

classic brunch menu

Classic Quiche Lorraine

This quiche is just as delicious if made a day ahead. Let baked quiche cool for 30 minutes, then refrigerate until cold. Cover and refrigerate for up to 24 hours, then uncover and reheat in 350°F (180°C) oven for about 20 minutes.

1½ cups (375 mL) **all-purpose flour**
¼ tsp (1 mL) **salt**
¼ cup (60 mL) cold **butter,** cubed
¼ cup (60 mL) cold **lard** or butter, cubed
1 **egg yolk**
1 tsp (5 mL) **vinegar**
Ice water

FILLING:

6 slices **bacon**
1 **onion,** finely chopped
½ tsp (2 mL) **pepper**
¼ tsp (1 mL) **salt**
4 **eggs**
½ cup (125 mL) **milk**
¼ cup (60 mL) 6% or 10% **cream**
2 tbsp (30 mL) **Dijon mustard**
¾ cup (175 mL) shredded **Gruyère cheese**

In large bowl, whisk flour with salt. Using pastry blender or 2 knives, cut in butter and lard until mixture resembles fine crumbs with a few larger pieces. In liquid measure, whisk egg yolk with vinegar; add enough ice water to make ⅓ cup (75 mL). Drizzle over dry ingredients, stirring briskly with fork until pastry clumps together. Press into disc. Wrap in plastic wrap; refrigerate until chilled, about 30 minutes.

On floured surface, roll out pastry to scant ¼-inch (5 mm) thickness. Fit into 9-inch (23 cm) fluted quiche pan or pie plate. Trim edge to leave 1-inch (2.5 cm) overhang; fold inside rim. Flute edge if using pie plate. Prick all over with fork. Refrigerate for 30 minutes.

Line pie shell with foil; fill with pie weights or dried beans. Bake in bottom third of 400°F (200°C) oven until rim is light golden, 20 minutes. Remove weights and foil; let cool on rack.

Filling: In large skillet, fry bacon over medium-high heat until crisp, about 5 minutes. Drain on paper towel–lined plate. Drain fat from pan; fry onion, pepper and salt over medium heat until softened, about 4 minutes.

In large bowl, whisk together eggs, milk and cream. Crumble bacon; add to egg mixture along with onion. Brush mustard over bottom of pastry shell; sprinkle with cheese. Pour in egg mixture.

Bake in centre of 375°F (190°C) oven until knife inserted in centre comes out clean, about 35 minutes. Let cool in pan on rack for 10 minutes.

Makes 8 servings.

PER SERVING: about 333 cal, 12 g pro, 22 g total fat (11 g sat. fat), 21 g carb, 1 g fibre, 161 mg chol, 407 mg sodium. % RDI: 15% calcium, 12% iron, 15% vit A, 2% vit C, 22% folate.

best tips:

Pie dough can be refrigerated for up to 3 days after you make it. Or enclose in heavy-duty foil or resealable freezer bag and freeze for up to 2 weeks. Let cold or thawed pastry stand at room temperature for 15 minutes before rolling.

Honey Poppy Seed Dressing This creamy, tangy and sweet dressing pairs nicely with a spinach and strawberry salad.

½ cup (125 mL) **Balkan-style plain yogurt**

2 tbsp (30 mL) **liquid honey**

4 tsp (20 mL) **lemon juice**

1 tsp (5 mL) **poppy seeds**

1 tsp (5 mL) **Dijon mustard**

¼ tsp (1 mL) **paprika**

Pinch **salt**

Whisk together yogurt, honey, lemon juice, poppy seeds, mustard, paprika and salt until smooth.

Makes ⅔ cup (150 mL).

PER 1 TBSP (15 mL): about 26 cal, 1 g pro, 1 g total fat (trace sat. fat), 4 g carb, 0 g fibre, 2 mg chol, 13 mg sodium. % RDI: 2% calcium, 1% iron, 1% vit A, 2% vit C.

best tips: This dressing makes enough for about 8 cups (2 L) torn greens. It can easily be doubled, and you can store any leftovers in the refrigerator for up to 5 days.

Sunrise Banana Split Parfait

It's easy to customize your parfait. Try adding granola or sliced almonds, a sprinkle of shaved dark chocolate or a drizzle of chocolate syrup; or use frozen yogurt instead of regular yogurt. However you prefer your parfait, it's a nice way to start or finish your day.

1 cup (250 mL) sliced **strawberries**

2 tsp (10 mL) **granulated sugar** or maple syrup

1 cup (250 mL) vanilla or plain **yogurt**

1 **banana,** sliced

2 tsp (10 mL) roasted **sunflower seeds**

Mash strawberries with sugar; let stand for 10 minutes. Divide half of the yogurt between 2 sundae cups or glasses; divide half of the strawberry mixture over top, then half of the banana. Repeat layers. Sprinkle with sunflower seeds.

Makes 2 servings.

PER SERVING: about 224 cal, 7 g pro, 4 g total fat (2 g sat. fat), 44 g carb, 3 g fibre, 7 mg chol, 72 mg sodium, 529 mg potassium. % RDI: 16% calcium, 5% iron, 3% vit A, 92% vit C, 24% folate.

breakfast for dinner

Baked Dill and Green Onion Omelette

8 **eggs**

4 **green onions,** chopped

½ cup (125 mL) chopped **fresh dill**

2 cloves **garlic,** minced

1 tbsp (15 mL) **all-purpose flour**

1 tsp (5 mL) **baking powder**

¼ tsp (1 mL) each **salt** and **pepper**

2 tsp (10 mL) **extra-virgin olive oil**

Whisk together eggs, green onions, dill, garlic, flour, baking powder, salt and pepper.

Heat 9- or 10-inch (23 or 25 cm) nonstick ovenproof skillet over medium-high heat; brush all over with oil. Pour in egg mixture. Bake in 350°F (180°C) oven until crusty and golden, about 20 minutes.

Run spatula or knife around edge; transfer to serving platter. Cut into wedges; serve warm or at room temperature.

Makes 4 servings.

PER SERVING: about 181 cal, 13 g pro, 12 g total fat (3 g sat. fat), 4 g carb, trace fibre, 372 mg chol, 333 mg sodium. % RDI: 9% calcium, 11% iron, 18% vit A, 5% vit C, 27% folate.

Herbed Home Fries

3 **baking potatoes** (2 lb/1 kg)

2 tbsp (30 mL) **butter**

1 **onion,** diced

1 tbsp (15 mL) chopped **fresh rosemary** or thyme

¾ tsp (4 mL) each **salt** and **pepper**

¾ tsp (4 mL) **paprika**

¼ cup (60 mL) whipping or 18% **cream**

In saucepan of boiling salted water, cover and cook potatoes just until tender, 20 to 25 minutes. Drain and let cool. Cover and refrigerate for 4 hours.

Peel and cut potatoes into ½-inch (1 cm) cubes. In large nonstick skillet, melt butter over medium heat; fry onion, stirring occasionally, until softened, 6 to 8 minutes.

Stir in potatoes, rosemary, salt, pepper and paprika; fry, without stirring, until lightly browned on bottom, about 4 minutes. With spatula, turn and stir home fries. Drizzle with cream; cook, without stirring, until lightly browned on bottom, about 5 minutes. Stir again; cook until most of the cream is absorbed and potatoes are crusty and browned, about 2 minutes.

Makes 4 servings.

PER SERVING: about 263 cal, 4 g pro, 11 g total fat (7 g sat. fat), 38 g carb, 3 g fibre, 37 mg chol, 911 mg sodium. % RDI: 3% calcium, 6% iron, 13% vit A, 42% vit C, 11% folate.

best tips: Since this recipe uses cold cooked potatoes, it's a great way to use up leftover baked potatoes. Or bake twice as many as you need, then use the extras for this recipe or Baked Potato Skins (recipe, page 239).

Buttermilk Pancakes

These fluffy cakes need only a drizzle of syrup and a few fresh berries scattered over top.

1½ cups (375 mL) **all-purpose flour**

3 tbsp (45 mL) **granulated sugar**

1 tsp (5 mL) each **baking powder** and **baking soda**

¼ tsp (1 mL) **salt**

1¾ cups (425 mL) **buttermilk**

1 **egg**

2 tbsp (30 mL) **butter,** melted

2 tsp (10 mL) **vanilla**

1 tbsp (15 mL) **canola oil** or melted butter

In large bowl, whisk together flour, sugar, baking powder, baking soda and salt. Whisk together buttermilk, egg, butter and vanilla; pour over dry ingredients and whisk until combined but still slightly lumpy.

Lightly brush large nonstick skillet or griddle with some of the oil; heat over medium-high heat. Using ¼ cup (60 mL) per pancake, pour in batter, spreading slightly. Cook until bubbles appear on top, about 3 minutes. Flip and cook until bottom is golden, about 1 minute. Transfer to rimmed baking sheet; cover and keep warm in 200°F (100°C) oven.

Makes about 14 pancakes.

PER PANCAKE: about 100 cal, 3 g pro, 3 g total fat (1 g sat. fat), 15 g carb, trace fibre, 20 mg chol, 196 mg sodium. % RDI: 4% calcium, 5% iron, 2% vit A, 9% folate.

all-day breakfast

Baked Beans With Apples

4 **apples,** peeled and diced

1 can (28 oz/796 mL) **crushed tomatoes**

1 large **onion,** diced

2 cloves **garlic,** minced

1 cup (250 mL) **apple cider**

3 tbsp (45 mL) **fancy molasses**

4 tsp (20 mL) **cider vinegar**

1 tbsp (15 mL) **dry mustard**

½ tsp (2 mL) **salt**

¼ tsp (1 mL) **pepper**

3 cans (each 19 oz/540 mL) **pinto beans** or navy beans, drained and rinsed

Peel and dice 2 of the apples; set aside.

In saucepan, bring tomatoes, onion, garlic, apple cider, molasses, vinegar, mustard, salt and pepper to boil; reduce heat and simmer for 10 minutes. Add beans and diced apples, stirring to coat. Scrape into 10-cup (2.5 L) casserole.

Peel and thinly slice remaining apples; overlap on top of beans. Bake in 300°F (150°C) oven until thickened, about 2 hours.

Makes 8 servings.

PER SERVING: about 310 cal, 15 g pro, 2 g total fat (trace sat. fat), 64 g carb, 6 g fibre, 0 mg chol, 898 mg sodium. % RDI: 11% calcium, 33% iron, 7% vit A, 22% vit C, 44% folate.

best tips: A great source of protein, vitamins, minerals and fibre, beans are something we should consider including more of in our diets. However, some delicious bean recipes can have a lot of sugar and saturated fat. This no-added-fat quick vegan version of baked beans uses a bit of molasses and the natural sweetness of apples, and has about half the fat and calories of traditional baked beans.

Corned Beef Hash Patties

These are fantastic with fried eggs (see Best Tips, below, for cooking tips). To make ahead, place cooked patties in single layer on baking sheet; cover and refrigerate for up to 8 hours. Uncover and reheat in 400°F (200°C) oven until hot, about 15 minutes.

2 **baking potatoes** (about 1 lb/500 g), peeled

12 oz (375 g) cooked **corned beef**

3 tbsp (45 mL) **butter**

1 **onion,** finely chopped

2 cloves **garlic,** minced

1 tsp (5 mL) **dried oregano**

¼ tsp (1 mL) each **salt** and **pepper**

2 tbsp (30 mL) minced **fresh parsley**

1 tbsp (15 mL) **Dijon mustard**

In saucepan of boiling salted water, cover and cook potatoes until slightly softened, about 10 minutes. Drain and let cool slightly; grate coarsely.

Meanwhile, cut corned beef into chunks; in food processor, pulse corned beef until finely chopped.

Meanwhile, in large nonstick skillet, melt 1 tbsp (15 mL) of the butter over medium heat; cook onion, garlic, oregano, salt and pepper until onion is softened, about 5 minutes. Add potatoes and corned beef; heat, stirring, until well combined, about 3 minutes. Remove from heat; mix in parsley and mustard. Let cool for 10 minutes.

Divide into 8 mounds; using hands, form into scant ½-inch (1 cm) thick patties. Wipe out skillet; heat half of the remaining butter over medium-high heat. Fry half of the patties, turning once, until crisp, about 6 minutes. Repeat with remaining patties and butter.

Makes about 8 patties.

PER PATTY: about 159 cal, 9 g pro, 9 g total fat (4 g sat. fat), 10 g carb, 1 g fibre, 55 mg chol, 736 mg sodium. % RDI: 2% calcium, 8% iron, 5% vit A, 8% vit C, 5% folate.

best tips:

• To make sunny-side-up eggs: In large nonstick skillet, melt 2 tsp (10 mL) butter over medium heat. Crack 4 eggs into skillet; cover and cook just until whites are set, 3 minutes.

• To make over-easy eggs: Cook as for sunny side up, but cook until whites are set, then turn over and cook just until white film forms over yolks, about 30 seconds.

• To make over-well eggs: Cook as for over-easy; but after turning, cook until yolk is completely set, about 1 minute.

Singapore Rice Crêpes With Scrambled Eggs and Curried Vegetables

Before rolling these up, garnish with crushed dry roasted peanuts, sliced hot peppers or hot pepper sauce. Or try garnishing with fresh lime juice and sprigs of fresh coriander, basil or mint to pique your taste buds.

1 cup (250 mL) **rice flour**

4 tsp (20 mL) **all-purpose flour**

¼ tsp (1 mL) **salt**

3 **eggs**

1½ cups (375 mL) **water**

1 tsp (5 mL) **vegetable oil**

CURRIED VEGETABLES:

1 tbsp (15 mL) **vegetable oil**

1 **onion,** thinly sliced

3 cloves **garlic,** minced

1 **carrot,** julienned (see Best Tips, page 120)

1 cup (250 mL) **snow peas,** julienned

4 tsp (20 mL) **mild curry paste**

2 cups (500 mL) **bean sprouts**

1 tbsp (15 mL) **soy sauce**

SCRAMBLED EGGS:

8 **eggs**

¼ tsp (1 mL) each **salt** and **pepper**

1 tbsp (15 mL) **butter**

Whisk together rice and all-purpose flours and salt. Whisk together eggs, water and oil; pour over flour mixture and stir until combined. Let stand for 30 minutes.

Heat greased 8-inch (20 cm) nonstick skillet over medium heat. Stirring batter each time, pour scant ¼ cup (60 mL) into pan for each crêpe, swirling to coat; cook until top is dry, 1 to 2 minutes. Stack on plate; cover with damp tea towel.

Curried Vegetables: In nonstick skillet, heat oil over medium heat; cook onion, stirring occasionally, until golden, about 8 minutes. Add garlic, carrot, snow peas and curry paste; cook, stirring occasionally, until vegetables are tender-crisp, about 5 minutes. Add bean sprouts and soy sauce; cook, stirring, just until sprouts are slightly wilted, about 1 minute.

Scrambled Eggs: Whisk together eggs, salt and pepper. In nonstick skillet, melt butter over medium heat; cook eggs, stirring, just until softly set but still moist, about 4 minutes.

Spoon some of the curried vegetables down centre of each crêpe; top with scrambled eggs. Roll up.

Makes 6 servings.

PER SERVING: about 331 cal, 15 g pro, 16 g total fat (5 g sat. fat), 31 g carb, 2 g fibre, 512 mg sodium. % RDI: 7% calcium, 17% iron, 50% vit A, 18% vit C, 26% folate.

eggs for dinner

Huevos Rancheros Cups

Serve one egg cup with a salad for a light Mexican-inspired meal. People with bigger appetites may want to have two egg cups.

8 small **whole wheat tortillas** (6 inches/15 cm)

1 tbsp (15 mL) **vegetable oil**

1 **onion,** chopped

4 cloves **garlic,** minced

1 **sweet green pepper** or red pepper, diced

1 tbsp (15 mL) **chili powder**

¼ tsp (1 mL) each **salt** and **pepper**

¼ tsp (1 mL) **hot pepper sauce**

2 cups (500 mL) **pasta sauce**

1 can (19 oz/540 mL) **black beans,** drained and rinsed

8 **poached eggs** (see Best Tips, page 56)

¼ cup (60 mL) chopped **fresh coriander** or parsley

Press each tortilla into greased 1¼-cup (300 mL) heatproof bowl or fluted tortilla pan, pleating tortilla to fit neatly. Bake on rimmed baking sheet in 400°F (200°C) oven until crisp, about 8 minutes. Let cool on rack.

Meanwhile, in saucepan, heat oil over medium heat; fry onion, garlic, green pepper, chili powder, salt, pepper and hot pepper sauce, stirring occasionally, until onion is softened, about 5 minutes. Add pasta sauce and beans; bring to boil. Reduce heat and simmer for 5 minutes.

Spoon bean mixture into tortilla cups; top with poached egg. Sprinkle with coriander.

Makes 6 to 8 servings.

PER EACH OF 8 SERVINGS: about 252 cal, 13 g pro, 9 g total fat (2 g sat. fat), 35 g carb, 7 g fibre, 186 mg chol, 767 mg sodium. % RDI: 7% calcium, 20% iron, 15% vit A, 30% vit C, 31% folate.

best tips:

To make tortillas more pliable and easier to handle when fitting into the moulds, heat them slightly. Either microwave them until warm, about 10 seconds, or wrap them in foil and heat in 350°F (180°C) oven for about 10 minutes.

All-Day Pizza

Topped with breakfast sausage, hash brown potatoes and baked eggs, this pizza is ideal for a lazy weekend brunch or weeknight family dinner.

1 lb (500 g) **pizza dough**

4 **eggs**

Pinch each **salt** and **pepper**

TOPPING:

4 **breakfast sausages** (about 4 oz/125 g)

¾ cup (175 mL) **pizza sauce** or pasta sauce

1½ cups (375 mL) shredded **mozzarella cheese**

½ cup (125 mL) frozen **hash brown potatoes,** thawed

Topping: In skillet, cook sausages over medium heat, turning occasionally, until browned and no longer pink inside, 8 to 10 minutes; drain on paper towel–lined plate. Cut into bite-size chunks.

Meanwhile, on lightly floured surface, roll out dough to 12-inch (30 cm) circle (for individual pizzas, divide dough into 4 balls; roll out each to 7-inch/18 cm circle). Place on large greased pizza pan. Spread with pizza sauce; sprinkle with cheese, potatoes and sausages.

Break eggs onto pizza toppings; sprinkle with salt and pepper. Bake in bottom third of 475°F (240°C) oven until crust is golden, cheese is bubbly and egg whites are firm, 15 to 18 minutes.

Makes 4 servings.

PER SERVING: about 618 cal, 27 g pro, 27 g total fat (12 g sat. fat), 65 g carb, 3 g fibre, 1,113 mg sodium. % RDI: 30% calcium, 29% iron, 22% vit A, 8% vit C, 30% folate.

VARIATIONS

Asparagus Egg Pizza: Omit topping. Brush rolled-out dough with 1 tbsp (15 mL) extra-virgin olive oil; sprinkle with 2 cloves garlic, minced. Top with 8 thin spears asparagus. Sprinkle with 1½ cups (375 mL) shredded Gruyère cheese. Break eggs onto pizza topping and bake as directed.

Artichoke, Red Pepper and Summer Sausage Pizza: Omit sausage, potatoes and eggs. Spread rolled-out dough with pizza sauce. Top with 6 slices summer sausage; 1 jar (170 mL) marinated artichoke hearts, drained and halved; and 1 cup (250 mL) sliced or chopped roasted red peppers. Sprinkle with cheese. Bake for about 12 minutes.

family, friends and fun

Pork Tenderloin With Creamy Cider-Herb Sauce

Apples with pork is a winning combination. The addition of Dijon mustard and fresh herbs elevates this dish, making it a real show-stopper.

2 **pork tenderloins** (about 2 lb/1 kg total)

¼ tsp (1 mL) each **salt** and **pepper**

1 tbsp (15 mL) **vegetable oil**

1 tbsp (15 mL) **butter**

½ cup (125 mL) finely diced **onion**

1 clove **garlic,** minced

½ cup (125 mL) **apple cider**

½ cup (125 mL) **sodium-reduced chicken broth**

¼ cup (60 mL) **whipping cream**

1 tsp (5 mL) **Dijon mustard**

1 tsp (5 mL) **cornstarch**

1 tbsp (15 mL) each minced **fresh thyme** and **parsley**

Sprinkle pork with salt and pepper. In large ovenproof skillet, heat oil over medium-high heat; sear pork all over, about 6 minutes.

Transfer to 400°F (200°C) oven; roast until juices run clear when pork is pierced and just a hint of pink remains inside, about 15 minutes. Transfer to cutting board and tent with foil; let stand for 5 minutes before slicing.

Meanwhile, in same skillet, melt butter over medium heat; cook onion, stirring occasionally, until softened, about 5 minutes. Add garlic; cook for 1 minute.

Add cider; bring to boil, scraping up any browned bits from bottom of pan. Stir in broth, cream and mustard; boil until reduced to 1 cup (250 mL), about 5 minutes.

Mix cornstarch with 2 tsp (10 mL) water; stir into sauce along with thyme and parsley. Cook, stirring, until slightly thickened, about 1 minute. Serve with pork.

Makes 4 to 6 servings.

PER EACH OF 6 SERVINGS: about 259 cal, 34 g pro, 11 g total fat (5 g sat. fat), 5 g carb, trace fibre, 100 mg chol, 242 mg sodium. % RDI: 2% calcium, 13% iron, 6% vit A, 3% vit C, 5% folate.

Shredded Brussels Sprout Salad

3 tbsp (45 mL) **light mayonnaise**

2 tbsp (30 mL) grated **Parmesan cheese**

1 tbsp (15 mL) **lemon juice**

1 tsp (5 mL) **Dijon mustard**

1 tsp (5 mL) **anchovy paste**

1 large clove **garlic,** minced

½ tsp (2 mL) **Worcestershire sauce**

Pinch **pepper**

4 cups (1 L) shredded **brussels sprouts** (about 16)

2 tbsp (30 mL) **extra-virgin olive oil**

2 tbsp (30 mL) diced **prosciutto** or bacon

In large bowl, whisk together mayonnaise, cheese, lemon juice, mustard, anchovy paste, garlic, Worcestershire sauce and pepper. Add brussels sprouts, tossing to coat.

In skillet, heat oil over medium heat; cook prosciutto until crisp. Add prosciutto and oil to sprouts mixture, tossing to combine. Let stand for 10 minutes to wilt slightly.

Makes 4 servings.

PER SERVING: about 160 cal, 5 g pro, 12 g total fat (2 g sat. fat), 10 g carb, 3 g fibre, 10 mg chol, 262 mg sodium. % RDI: 7% calcium, 11% iron, 9% vit A, 127% vit C, 25% folate.

Herbed Carrots

8 **carrots** (about 1½ lb/750 g)

¾ cup (175 mL) **sodium-reduced chicken broth**

1 tsp (5 mL) grated **lemon rind**

¼ tsp (1 mL) each **salt** and **pepper**

2 tbsp (30 mL) chopped **fresh oregano** or dill

2 tbsp (30 mL) **butter**

2 tbsp (30 mL) **lemon juice**

Peel and diagonally slice carrots, about ¾ inch (2 cm) thick.

In saucepan, bring broth, lemon rind, salt and pepper to boil. Add carrots; cover and cook over medium heat until almost tender, about 5 minutes.

Uncover and cook over medium-high heat, stirring often, until almost no liquid remains, about 3 minutes. Remove from heat. Stir in oregano, butter and lemon juice.

Makes 4 servings.

PER SERVING: about 110 cal, 2 g pro, 6 g total fat (4 g sat. fat), 14 g carb, 4 g fibre, 15 mg chol, 384 mg sodium. % RDI: 6% calcium, 6% iron, 260% vit A, 17% vit C, 11% folate.

VARIATION

Honey Almond Carrots: Substitute 2 tbsp (30 mL) liquid honey and ¼ tsp (1 mL) ground nutmeg for the lemon rind. Substitute ¼ cup (60 mL) sliced toasted almonds for the oregano and lemon juice.

Sublime Mac and Cheese

Before you bake it, this rich mix of sauce and pasta may appear soupy – but don't be alarmed. The macaroni will soak up much of the sauce and give you a perfectly creamy yet easy-to-cut dish.

4 cups (1 L) **elbow macaroni** (about 1 lb/500 g)

⅓ cup (75 mL) **butter**

⅓ cup (75 mL) **all-purpose flour**

4½ cups (1.125 L) 10% or 18% **cream**

3 cups (750 mL) shredded **old Cheddar cheese** (12 oz/375 g)

1½ tsp (7 mL) **dry mustard**

1 tsp (5 mL) **salt**

½ tsp (2 mL) **pepper**

¼ tsp (1 mL) **ground nutmeg**

1 cup (250 mL) full-fat (14%) **sour cream**

TOPPING:

2 cups (500 mL) **fresh bread crumbs**

1 cup (250 mL) shredded **old Cheddar cheese** (4 oz/125 g)

3 tbsp (45 mL) **butter,** melted

In large pot of boiling salted water, cook pasta until al dente, about 8 minutes. Drain.

Meanwhile, in large heavy saucepan, melt butter over medium heat; add flour and cook, stirring, for 2 minutes. Gradually whisk in cream; simmer, whisking, until thickened, about 8 minutes.

Add cheese, mustard, salt, pepper, and nutmeg, stirring until cheese is melted. Stir in sour cream, then pasta; spread in 12-cup (3 L) oval casserole or 13- x 9-inch (3 L) baking dish.

Topping: Toss together bread crumbs, cheese and butter; sprinkle over macaroni mixture. Bake in 350°F (180°C) oven until golden and bubbly, about 40 minutes.

Makes 10 to 12 servings.

PER EACH OF 12 SERVINGS: about 521 cal, 18 g pro, 33 g total fat (20 g sat. fat), 38 g carb, 2 g fibre, 101 mg chol, 682 mg sodium. % RDI: 37% calcium, 11% iron, 27% vit A, 2% vit C, 31% folate.

classic casseroles

Zucchini Meat Loaf Casserole

Vegetables and cheese turn meat loaf into a one-dish meal. Switch up the cheese and try shredded Cheddar, Gouda or Fontina in place of (or in combination with) the mozzarella. Slice any leftovers and sandwich in kaiser rolls.

2 **eggs**

1 cup (250 mL) **quick-cooking rolled oats** (not instant)

⅓ cup (75 mL) **tomato paste**

1 **onion,** grated

1 **carrot,** grated

1 clove **garlic,** minced

½ tsp (2 mL) **dried Italian herb seasoning**

½ tsp (2 mL) each **salt** and **pepper**

1½ lb (750 g) **extra-lean ground beef**

TOPPING:

1 **zucchini,** thinly sliced into rounds

1 cup (250 mL) thinly sliced **mushrooms**

½ cup (125 mL) **pasta sauce**

⅓ cup (75 mL) grated **Parmesan cheese**

¼ tsp (1 mL) each **salt** and **pepper**

1 cup (250 mL) shredded **mozzarella cheese**

2 tbsp (30 mL) chopped **fresh parsley**

In large bowl, lightly beat eggs; stir in oats, tomato paste, onion, carrot, garlic, Italian herb seasoning, salt and pepper. Mix in beef. Gently pat into 8-inch (2 L) square baking dish.

Topping: Combine zucchini, mushrooms, pasta sauce, Parmesan cheese, salt and pepper; spread over meat mixture. Sprinkle with mozzarella cheese.

Bake in 350°F (180°C) oven until instant-read thermometer inserted in centre registers 170°F (75°C), 1 to 1¼ hours. Sprinkle with parsley.

Makes 6 servings.

PER SERVING: about 403 cal, 34 g pro, 21 g total fat (9 g sat. fat), 19 g carb, 4 g fibre, 142 mg chol, 669 mg sodium. % RDI: 21% calcium, 31% iron, 45% vit A, 20% vit C, 17% folate.

Chicken Parmigiana Casserole
Artichoke hearts update this classic. If you make and freeze it ahead, add the artichokes after thawing to prevent the dish from getting watery.

¼ cup (60 mL) **vegetable oil** or olive oil

1 **onion,** chopped

1 **carrot,** diced

3 cloves **garlic,** minced

1 tsp (5 mL) **dried oregano**

½ tsp (2 mL) **salt**

½ tsp (2 mL) **pepper**

1 can (28 oz/796 mL) **whole tomatoes**

¼ cup (60 mL) **tomato paste**

1 can (14 oz/398 mL) **artichoke hearts,** drained and halved

1 cup (250 mL) shredded **mozzarella cheese**

CHICKEN:

6 **boneless skinless chicken breasts**

⅓ cup (75 mL) **all-purpose flour**

1 **egg**

¾ cup (175 mL) **dry bread crumbs**

¼ cup (60 mL) grated **Parmesan cheese**

½ tsp (2 mL) **dried oregano**

¼ tsp (1 mL) **cayenne pepper**

Pinch **salt**

In saucepan, heat 1 tbsp (15 mL) of the oil over medium heat; fry onion, carrot, garlic, oregano, salt and pepper, stirring occasionally, until softened, about 5 minutes.

Add tomatoes, mashing with fork; add tomato paste and bring to boil. Reduce heat and simmer until thick enough to mound on spoon, about 20 minutes.

Chicken: Meanwhile, between sheets of plastic wrap, pound chicken to ¼-inch (5 mm) thickness; cut in half crosswise.

Place flour in shallow dish. In separate shallow dish, whisk egg with 2 tbsp (30 mL) water. In third shallow dish, stir together bread crumbs, Parmesan cheese, oregano, cayenne pepper and salt. Dip chicken into flour, turning to coat; dip into egg mixture, then into bread crumb mixture to coat all over.

In large skillet, heat remaining oil over medium-high heat; fry chicken, in batches and turning once, until golden and no longer pink inside, 4 to 6 minutes.

Spread 1 cup (250 mL) of the sauce in 13- x 9-inch (3 L) baking dish. Place chicken on sauce, overlapping. Pour remaining sauce over top. Sprinkle artichokes, then mozzarella over casserole; bake in 375°F (190°C) oven until bubbly, about 20 minutes.

Makes 8 servings.

PER SERVING: about 343 cal, 32 g pro, 14 g total fat (4 g sat. fat), 22 g carb, 4 g fibre, 98 mg chol, 669 mg sodium. % RDI: 18% calcium, 19% iron, 37% vit A, 30% vit C, 17% folate.

best tips: If you're making this dish ahead of time, prepare up to and including pouring sauce over top; refrigerate until cold. Cover with plastic wrap and overwrap with heavy-duty foil; freeze for up to 2 weeks.

Thaw in refrigerator for 48 hours. Remove plastic wrap; re-cover with foil and bake in 375°F (190°C) oven for 30 minutes. Uncover; add artichokes and mozzarella; bake as directed.

Best-Ever Chocolate Chip Cookies

Canadian Living has published many chocolate chip cookie recipes, but founding food editor Carol Ferguson's recipe, with its big hit of vanilla, is the standout.

½ cup (125 mL) **butter,** softened

½ cup (125 mL) **shortening** or butter, softened

1 cup (250 mL) **granulated sugar**

½ cup (125 mL) packed **brown sugar**

2 **eggs**

1 tbsp (15 mL) **vanilla**

2 cups (500 mL) **all-purpose flour**

1 tsp (5 mL) **baking soda**

½ tsp (2 mL) **salt**

2 cups (500 mL) **semisweet chocolate chips**

1 cup (250 mL) chopped **walnuts** or pecans

In bowl, beat butter with shortening; gradually beat in granulated and brown sugars until smooth. Beat in eggs and vanilla. Whisk together flour, baking soda and salt; stir into butter mixture. Stir in chocolate chips and walnuts. Refrigerate for 30 minutes.

Drop by rounded tablespoonfuls (15 mL), about 2 inches (5 cm) apart, onto parchment paper–lined or greased rimless baking sheets. With fork, flatten cookies to ½-inch (1 cm) thickness.

Bake in 375°F (190°C) oven until edges are golden and centres are still slightly underbaked, about 15 minutes. Let cool on pans on racks for 5 minutes. Transfer to racks; let cool completely.

Makes about 48 cookies.

PER COOKIE: about 132 cal, 1 g pro, 8 g total fat (3 g sat. fat), 15 g carb, 1 g fibre, 14 mg chol, 72 mg sodium. % RDI: 1% calcium, 4% iron, 2% vit A, 4% folate.

VARIATIONS

Reverse Chocolate Chip Cookies: Substitute cocoa powder for ⅓ cup (75 mL) of the flour, sifting with flour before adding to batter; use white chocolate chips instead of semisweet chocolate chips. Bake as directed.

Chocolate Chip Ice-Cream Sandwiches: Sandwich 1 scoop ice cream between 2 cookies; press gently to push ice cream to edges. If desired, roll edges in sprinkles, chopped nuts or mini chocolate chips. Wrap each in plastic wrap and freeze in airtight container for up to 1 week.

best comfort foods

Chili Meat Loaf With Ratatouille Sauce

2 tsp (10 mL) **canola oil** or olive oil

1 **onion,** chopped

2 cloves **garlic,** minced

½ tsp (2 mL) each **salt** and **dried basil**

¼ tsp (1 mL) each **dried thyme** and **pepper**

1 **egg**

½ cup (125 mL) **dry bread crumbs**

⅓ cup (75 mL) **chili sauce** or salsa

2 tbsp (30 mL) chopped **fresh parsley**

1 tbsp (15 mL) **Dijon mustard**

1½ lb (750 g) **lean ground beef**

Ratatouille Sauce (below)

In nonstick skillet, heat oil over medium heat; cook onion, garlic, salt, basil, thyme and pepper, stirring occasionally, until onion is softened, about 5 minutes. Let cool.

In bowl, beat egg; mix in bread crumbs, chili sauce, parsley, mustard and onion mixture. Mix in beef.

Pack into 8- x 4-inch (1.5 L) loaf pan. Bake in 350°F (180°C) oven until instant-read thermometer registers 170°F (75°C), about 1 hour. Let stand for 5 minutes; drain off fat. Serve with Ratatouille Sauce.

Makes 6 servings.

PER SERVING: about 350 cal, 26 g pro, 18 g total fat (6 g sat. fat), 22 g carb, 4 g fibre, 89 mg chol, 900 mg sodium. % RDI: 8% calcium, 29% iron, 13% vit A, 58% vit C, 18% folate.

Ratatouille Sauce: In saucepan, heat 1 tbsp (15 mL) canola or olive oil over medium heat. Add 1 onion, chopped; 2 cloves garlic, minced; ½ tsp (2 mL) salt; and ¼ tsp (1 mL) each dried thyme, basil, crumbled rosemary and pepper. Cook, stirring occasionally, until onion is softened, about 3 minutes. Add 1 small zucchini, chopped; 2 cups (500 mL) chopped (unpeeled) eggplant; and ½ cup (125 mL) chopped sweet red pepper. Cook, stirring often, until softened, about 10 minutes. Add 1 can (19 oz/540 mL) whole tomatoes, breaking up with spoon. Add 1 tbsp (15 mL) wine vinegar; bring to boil. Reduce heat and simmer until thickened, about 10 minutes.

Makes 4 cups (1 L).

Bacon Mashed Potatoes

Paired with meat loaf, this is the ultimate comfort food. It's made all the more appealing with the addition of bacon and green onions. For an even richer version, replace milk with sour cream.

4 slices **bacon**

2 lb (1 kg) **potatoes** (about 5)

½ cup (125 mL) **milk**

2 tbsp (30 mL) **butter**

½ tsp (2 mL) **salt**

¼ tsp (1 mL) **pepper**

2 **green onions,** thinly sliced

In skillet, fry bacon over medium-high heat until crisp, about 5 minutes. Drain on paper towel-lined plate. Crumble or chop; set aside.

Meanwhile, peel and cut potatoes into quarters. In pot of boiling salted water, cover and cook potatoes until fork-tender, about 20 minutes. Drain well.

With potato masher, mash until smooth. Mash in milk, butter, salt and pepper. Fold in half each of the bacon and green onions. Sprinkle with remaining bacon and green onions.

Makes 4 servings.

PER SERVING: about 259 cal, 7 g pro, 9 g total fat (5 g sat. fat), 39 g carb, 3 g fibre, 25 mg chol, 923 mg sodium, 701 mg potassium. % RDI: 5% calcium, 6% iron, 7% vit A, 25% vit C, 10% folate.

Chicken Fingers With Peanut Apricot Sauce

4 **boneless skinless chicken breasts**

1 **egg**

1 tbsp (15 mL) **cold water**

1 cup (250 mL) **dry bread crumbs**

1 tbsp (15 mL) chopped **fresh coriander**
   (or ½ tsp/2 mL dried basil)

1 tsp (5 mL) **Cajun seasoning**

¼ tsp (1 mL) **salt**

PEANUT APRICOT SAUCE:

¼ cup (60 mL) **apple juice**

¼ cup (60 mL) **smooth peanut butter**

2 tbsp (30 mL) **apricot jam**

1 small clove **garlic,** minced

1½ tsp (7 mL) **cider vinegar**

Slice each chicken breast lengthwise into 4 strips. In shallow dish, whisk egg with cold water. In separate shallow dish, combine bread crumbs, coriander, Cajun seasoning and salt. Dip chicken strips into egg mixture, then bread crumb mixture, to coat all over.

Bake on greased rimmed baking sheet in 400°F (200°C) oven until golden and no longer pink inside, about 15 minutes.

Peanut Apricot Sauce: Meanwhile, in small saucepan over medium heat, combine apple juice, peanut butter, apricot jam, garlic and vinegar; simmer, stirring occasionally, for 3 minutes. Serve warm with chicken strips for dipping.

Makes 4 servings.

PER SERVING: about 350 cal, 38 g pro, 12 g total fat (3 g sat. fat), 22 g carb, 1 g fibre, 124 mg chol, 453 mg sodium. % RDI: 5% calcium, 14% iron, 5% vit A, 10% vit C, 13% folate.

best TV dinner

Roasted Garlic Mashed Potatoes

1 head **garlic**

½ tsp (2 mL) **extra-virgin olive oil**

2 lb (1 kg) **Yukon Gold potatoes** (about 4 or 5)

½ cup (125 mL) **buttermilk** (approx)

¼ tsp (1 mL) each **salt** and **pepper**

2 tbsp (30 mL) minced **fresh chives** or green onions

Trim off top of garlic to expose cloves. Place on square of foil and drizzle with oil; seal foil to form package. Roast in 375°F (190°C) oven until tender, about 45 minutes. Let cool.

Meanwhile, peel and quarter potatoes. In large pot of boiling salted water, cover and cook potatoes until tender, about 20 minutes. Drain well and return to pot.

Squeeze roasted garlic over potatoes. Mash in buttermilk, salt and pepper, adding more buttermilk, if desired. Stir in chives.

Makes 4 servings.

PER SERVING: about 174 cal, 5 g pro, 1 g total fat (trace sat. fat), 38 g carb, 3 g fibre, 1 mg chol, 185 mg sodium. % RDI: 6% calcium, 6% iron, 1% vit A, 25% vit C, 8% folate.

best tips: Roast extra heads of garlic, squeeze out roasted cloves and refrigerate them in an airtight container for up to 3 days. Add them to soups, pasta sauces, mayonnaise (to make a sandwich spread) or olive oil (to spread on toasted slices of baguette, or croûtes).

Corn and Zucchini Sauté

1 tbsp (15 mL) **vegetable oil,** olive oil or butter

3 **green onions,** sliced

1 **zucchini,** halved lengthwise and sliced

½ tsp (2 mL) **dried oregano**

¼ tsp (1 mL) each **salt** and **pepper**

2 cups (500 mL) frozen **corn kernels,** thawed

In large skillet, heat oil over medium-high heat; sauté green onions, zucchini, oregano, salt and pepper until onions are softened and zucchini is tender-crisp, about 3 minutes.

Stir in corn; sauté until hot, 2 to 4 minutes.

Makes 4 servings.

PER SERVING: about 104 cal, 3 g pro, 4 g total fat (trace sat. fat), 18 g carb, 2 g fibre, 0 mg chol, 150 mg sodium. % RDI: 2% calcium, 5% iron, 3% vit A, 10% vit C, 16% folate.

best tips:

When corn is in season, use freshly shucked kernels (from 2 or 3 cobs) and add ¼ cup (60 mL) vegetable broth or water to skillet. Sauté until liquid evaporates.

Nacho Wings With Guacamole and Crudités

Nothing is better than two pub-style favourites – nachos and wings – rolled into one. These wings are delicious hot, at room temperature and even cold.

3 lb (1.5 kg) **chicken wings**

⅔ cup (150 mL) **buttermilk**

1 **egg**

2 tsp (10 mL) **hot pepper sauce**

¼ tsp (1 mL) each **salt** and **pepper**

8 oz (250 g) **tortilla chips** (about 8 cups/2 L)

1½ tsp (7 mL) **dried oregano**

1½ tsp (7 mL) ancho or other **chili powder**

1 tsp (5 mL) **ground cumin**

6 cups (1.5 L) **vegetable crudités** (see Best Tips, page 316)

GUACAMOLE:

1 large ripe **avocado**

⅓ cup (75 mL) **light sour cream**

¼ cup (60 mL) finely chopped **red onion**

¼ cup (60 mL) chopped **fresh coriander**

1 tbsp (15 mL) **lime juice**

¼ tsp (1 mL) each **salt** and **pepper**

Remove tips from chicken wings (save for stock if desired); separate wings at joint.

In glass dish, whisk together buttermilk, egg, hot pepper sauce, salt and pepper; add wings, tossing to coat. Cover and refrigerate for 4 hours or up to 24 hours.

Guacamole: Meanwhile, scoop avocado flesh into bowl; mash until fairly smooth. Stir in sour cream, onion, coriander, lime juice, salt and pepper; cover and refrigerate for 1 hour.

In food processor, finely grind tortilla chips to make about 2 cups (500 mL) crumbs; transfer to bowl. Stir in oregano, chili powder and cumin.

Remove wings from buttermilk mixture. Press into crumb mixture to coat all over. Roast on rack on foil-lined rimmed baking sheet in 400°F (200°C) oven, turning once, until crisp and juices run clear when wings are pierced, about 45 minutes. Serve with guacamole and crudités.

Makes 6 to 8 servings.

PER EACH OF 8 SERVINGS: about 403 cal, 20 g pro, 26 g total fat (6 g sat. fat), 26 g carb, 5 g fibre, 71 mg chol, 364 mg sodium. % RDI: 11% calcium, 15% iron, 39% vit A, 33% vit C, 25% folate.

Sun-Dried Tomato and Artichoke Dip

Serve with a variety of crackers, pita chips and crudités. If you don't have a slow cooker, heat the dip on the stove top in a double boiler until blended and hot.

1 can (14 oz/398 mL) **artichoke hearts**

1 pkg (8 oz/250 g) **cream cheese,** cubed and softened

½ cup (125 mL) **sour cream**

½ cup (125 mL) **mayonnaise**

¼ cup (60 mL) grated **Parmesan cheese**

¼ cup (60 mL) chopped drained **oil-packed sun-dried tomatoes**

1 clove **garlic,** minced

¼ tsp (1 mL) **pepper**

2 tbsp (30 mL) chopped **green onions**

Drain artichoke hearts; pat dry and chop. In 6-cup (1.5 L) slow cooker, combine artichokes, cream cheese, sour cream, mayonnaise, Parmesan cheese, sun-dried tomatoes, garlic and pepper; stir to combine.

Cover and cook on low, stirring twice, until blended and hot, about 2 hours. Sprinkle with green onions.

Makes about 3 cups (750 mL).

PER 2 TBSP (30 ML): about 89 cal, 2 g pro, 8 g total fat (4 g sat. fat), 2 g carb, 1 g fibre, 16 mg chol, 88 mg sodium. % RDI: 3% calcium, 2% iron, 5% vit A, 3% vit C, 4% folate.

best tips: Crudités can be almost any raw vegetables you like. Try carrot and celery sticks; broccoli and cauliflower florets; sliced sweet peppers, cucumber or zucchini; grape or cherry tomatoes; and radishes.

Meat-and-Potato Lover's Shepherd's Pie

You can't go wrong with this updated classic, made richer with dried porcini mushrooms and pancetta. Ground beef balances the highly flavoured lamb, but you can use all beef or all lamb if you prefer.

1 pkg (14 g) **dried porcini mushrooms,** crumbled

2 tbsp (30 mL) **olive oil**

1 lb (500 g) **lean ground beef**

1 lb (500 g) **ground lamb**

2 oz (60 g) **pancetta** or bacon, diced

1 **onion,** diced

2 each ribs **celery** and **carrots,** diced

2 cloves **garlic,** minced

1 tsp (5 mL) crumbled **dried rosemary** or marjoram

1 tsp (5 mL) **dried thyme**

½ tsp (2 mL) **salt**

¼ tsp (1 mL) **pepper**

2 cups (500 mL) cremini or white **mushrooms,** quartered

¼ cup (60 mL) **dry red wine** or sodium-reduced beef broth

2 cups (500 mL) **sodium-reduced beef broth**

2 tbsp (30 mL) **tomato paste**

2 tsp (10 mL) **Worcestershire sauce**

3 tbsp (45 mL) **all-purpose flour**

TOPPING:

8 **Yukon Gold potatoes** (about 4 lb/2 kg), peeled and quartered

¼ cup (60 mL) **milk** or 10% cream

2 tbsp (30 mL) **butter**

½ tsp (2 mL) **Dijon mustard**

½ tsp (2 mL) **salt**

¼ tsp (1 mL) **pepper**

1 tbsp (15 mL) **olive oil** or butter

2 **leeks** (white and light green parts), thinly sliced

Soak dried porcini mushrooms in 1 cup (250 mL) boiling water until softened, about 30 minutes.

Meanwhile, in large shallow Dutch oven, heat half of the oil over medium-high heat; brown beef, lamb and pancetta until no longer pink, about 8 minutes. Drain in fine-mesh sieve.

Drain fat from pan. Heat remaining oil over medium heat; cook onion, celery, carrots, garlic, rosemary, thyme, salt and pepper until softened, about 6 minutes. Stir in cremini mushrooms; cook until golden, about 6 minutes.

Stir in wine, scraping up browned bits; boil until no liquid remains. Stir in broth, tomato paste, Worcestershire sauce, porcini mushrooms, soaking liquid and meat mixture. Bring to boil; reduce heat and simmer, uncovered, for 25 minutes.

Whisk flour with ¼ cup (60 mL) water; whisk into meat mixture and bring to boil. Boil until thickened, about 5 minutes. Scrape into 13- x 9-inch (3 L) baking dish.

Topping: Meanwhile, in large saucepan of boiling salted water, cover and cook potatoes until tender, about 20 minutes. Drain; return to pot. Return to heat, shaking pan until no liquid remains, about 1 minute. Mash with potato masher; mash in milk, butter, mustard, salt and pepper. Meanwhile, in saucepan, heat oil over medium-low heat; cook leeks until softened, about 6 minutes. Stir into potatoes; spread over meat mixture.

Bake in 375°F (190°C) oven until potatoes are golden and slightly crusty, 50 to 60 minutes.

Makes 12 servings.

PER SERVING: about 414 cal, 19 g pro, 14 g total fat (6 g sat. fat), 56 g carb, 7 g fibre, 48 mg chol, 507 mg sodium. % RDI: 5% calcium, 22% iron, 24% vit A, 20% vit C, 31% folate.

best tips: To make ahead, let assembled casserole cool for 30 minutes; refrigerate until cold. Cover and refrigerate for up to 24 hours. Reheat in 375°F (190°C) oven for 30 minutes.

Sausage Mushroom Calzone

You can make the sausage filling and refrigerate it in an airtight container for up to 3 days. Replace tomato sauce with tomato pasta sauce or pizza sauce if you prefer.

3 sweet or hot **Italian sausages**

1 **onion,** chopped

2 cloves **garlic,** minced

1½ cups (375 mL) sliced **mushrooms**

½ tsp (2 mL) each **dried oregano** and **basil**

¼ tsp (1 mL) each **salt** and **pepper**

1½ cups (375 mL) **tomato sauce**

½ cup (125 mL) diced **sweet green pepper**
 or sweet red pepper

1 lb (500 g) **pizza dough**

1½ cups (375 mL) shredded **provolone cheese** or
 mozzarella cheese

1 tbsp (15 mL) **all-purpose flour**

Remove casings from sausage. In nonstick skillet, sauté sausage over medium-high heat, breaking up with spoon, until no longer pink, about 5 minutes.

Spoon off fat from pan; sauté onion, garlic, mushrooms, oregano, basil, salt and pepper for 5 minutes. Stir in tomato sauce and green pepper; simmer for 5 minutes. Let cool.

On floured surface, roll out dough into four 8-inch (20 cm) rounds. Leaving ½-inch (1 cm) border uncovered, spoon about ¾ cup (175 mL) filling over half of each; sprinkle with cheese. Moisten border with water; fold dough over and pinch to seal.

Place on greased baking sheet; cut steam vents in tops. Dust with flour. Bake in 425°F (220°C) oven until golden, about 20 minutes.

Makes 4 servings.

PER SERVING: about 673 cal, 33 g pro, 29 g total fat (13 g sat. fat), 69 g carb, 4 g fibre, 69 mg chol, 2,087 mg sodium. % RDI: 36% calcium, 36% iron, 21% vit A, 37% vit C, 28% folate.

after-school snacks

Sunflower Seed Granola Bars

⅓ cup (75 mL) each **corn syrup, liquid honey** and
   vegetable oil
2 cups (500 mL) **large-flake rolled oats**
1½ cups (375 mL) unsalted hulled **sunflower seeds**
1 cup (250 mL) **rice crisp cereal**
1 cup (250 mL) **raisins** or sliced dried apricots
½ cup (125 mL) **sliced almonds**

Grease 13- x 9-inch (3.5 L) cake pan or line with parchment
paper. In saucepan, bring corn syrup, honey and oil to boil
over medium heat. Reduce heat and simmer until slightly
thickened, about 5 minutes. Remove from heat; let cool
slightly, about 1 minute.

Meanwhile, in large bowl, combine oats, sunflower seeds,
cereal, raisins and almonds. Pour syrup over top; stir to
coat evenly. Pack into prepared pan, pressing firmly with
back of spoon or greased spatula. Bake in 350°F (180°C)
oven until golden, about 25 minutes. Let cool in pan on rack.
Cut into bars.

Makes 24 bars.

PER BAR: about 167 cal, 4 g pro, 9 g total fat (1 g sat. fat), 20 g carb,
3 g fibre, 0 mg chol, 22 mg sodium. % RDI: 2% calcium, 9% iron,
1% vit C, 11% folate.

VARIATION
Peanut Butter Granola Bars: Reduce vegetable oil to
¼ cup (60 mL). Increase corn syrup to ½ cup (125 mL).
Replace sliced almonds with chopped peanuts. Add ½ cup
(125 mL) natural peanut butter to saucepan along with corn
syrup, honey and oil; heat over medium heat, stirring often,
until melted and smooth, about 2 minutes. Add to dry
ingredients and continue with recipe as directed.

Fruity Yogurt Smoothies

1 cup (250 mL) **frozen mixed berries**

Half **banana**

½ cup (125 mL) vanilla or plain **yogurt**

½ cup (125 mL) **orange juice**

In blender, purée together berries, banana, yogurt and orange juice until smooth.

Makes 2 servings.

PER SERVING: about 157 cal, 4 g pro, 1 g total fat (1 g sat. fat), 34 g carb, 2 g fibre, 3 mg chol, 36 mg sodium. % RDI: 9% calcium, 3% iron, 29% vit A, 92% vit C, 18% folate.

Peanut Butter Banana Wraps
Use bananas that are as straight as possible, because they are easier to roll, or cut to fit. You can replace the peanut butter with any nut butter.

4 small **tortillas** (6 inches/15 cm)

⅓ cup (75 mL) **natural peanut butter**

⅓ cup (75 mL) **chocolate chips**

4 small **bananas**

Spread tortillas with peanut butter; sprinkle with chocolate chips. Place banana at 1 edge of each tortilla; roll up. Wrap individually in foil; seal ends.

Bake on baking sheet in 425°F (220°C) oven until banana is tender, chocolate is melted and tortillas are light golden, about 20 minutes. Cut each wrap in half.

Makes 4 to 8 servings.

PER EACH OF 8 SERVINGS: about 192 cal, 5 g pro, 9 g total fat (2 g sat. fat), 27 g carb, 3 g fibre, 0 mg chol, 78 mg sodium, 224 mg potassium. % RDI: 2% calcium, 8% iron, 5% vit C, 18% folate.

best tips:

For a fun campfire-style snack, grill the Peanut Butter Banana Wraps (above). Double-wrap in foil; seal ends. Place on grill over medium heat; close lid and grill, turning twice, for 12 minutes.

Bite-Size Cake Doughnuts
It's easiest to shape, scoop and drop this thick cake-like batter into the hot oil using a mini ice-cream scoop.

3 cups (750 mL) **all-purpose flour**

1 tbsp (15 mL) **baking powder**

¾ tsp (4 mL) **salt**

½ tsp (2 mL) grated or ground **nutmeg**

½ cup (125 mL) **10% cream**

½ cup (125 mL) **whipping cream**

1 tsp (5 mL) **vanilla**

3 **eggs**

1 cup (250 mL) **granulated sugar**

Oil for deep-frying (canola, safflower or vegetable)

TOPPING:

1 cup (250 mL) **icing sugar**

½ tsp (2 mL) **cinnamon**

Whisk together flour, baking powder, salt and nutmeg. In separate bowl, whisk together 10% and whipping creams, and vanilla.

In large bowl, beat eggs with sugar until pale; gradually beat in cream mixture. Stir in flour mixture to make soft sticky dough. Cover and refrigerate for 1 hour.

Spray mini (1 tbsp/15 mL) ice-cream scoop or 1 tbsp (15 mL) measuring spoon with nonstick spray, or grease. In heavy fryer, wok or deep saucepan, heat 2 inches (5 cm) oil until deep-fry thermometer registers 350°F (180°C). Drop batter by tablespoonfuls (15 mL) into oil, 4 at a time; deep-fry, turning once, until golden, puffed and centre is cooked, 3 to 4 minutes. With slotted spoon, transfer to paper towel–lined plate; let drain. Transfer to rack; let cool.

Topping: In bowl, whisk icing sugar with cinnamon; toss doughnuts in cinnamon sugar mixture to coat.

Makes about 50 pieces.

PER PIECE: about 90 cal, 1 g pro, 4 g total fat (1 g sat. fat), 12 g carb, trace fibre, 15 mg chol, 58 mg sodium. % RDI: 1% calcium, 3% iron, 1% vit A, 8% folate.

Caramel Corn For a nut-free version, replace almonds with additional popped popcorn.

10 cups (2.5 L) popped **popcorn**

2 cups (500 mL) **whole unblanched almonds,** unsalted roasted peanuts or cashews

1¼ cups (300 mL) packed **brown sugar**

½ cup (125 mL) **butter**

¼ cup (60 mL) **corn syrup**

2 tsp (10 mL) **vanilla**

¼ tsp (1 mL) **baking soda**

Grease large rimmed baking sheet; mix popcorn with almonds on sheet. Set aside.

In saucepan, whisk together sugar, butter and corn syrup over medium-low heat until sugar is dissolved. Increase heat to high; boil, without stirring, until candy thermometer registers hard-ball stage of 255°F (124°C), or ½ tsp (2 mL) syrup dropped into very cold water forms rigid ball that is still a little pliable, about 4 minutes. Remove from heat; stir in vanilla and baking soda.

Drizzle over popcorn mixture, stirring gently until combined. Let cool completely.

Makes about 12 cups (3 L).

PER 1 CUP (250 mL): about 337 cal, 6 g pro, 20 g total fat (6 g sat. fat), 37 g carb, 3 g fibre, 21 mg chol, 43 mg sodium. % RDI: 8% calcium, 11%, iron, 7% vit A, 7% folate.

Barbecue Roast Almonds

2½ cups (625 mL) **whole blanched almonds**

2 tbsp (30 mL) **fancy molasses**

1 tbsp (15 mL) packed **brown sugar**

1 tbsp (15 mL) **chili powder**

1 tbsp (15 mL) **vegetable oil**

1½ tsp (7 mL) **cider vinegar**

½ tsp (2 mL) **ground cumin**

½ tsp (2 mL) **salt**

¼ tsp (1 mL) **garlic powder**

Pinch **cayenne pepper**

On parchment paper–lined rimmed baking sheet, toast almonds in 350°F (180°C) oven until fragrant but not browned, about 7 minutes.

Meanwhile, whisk together molasses, sugar, chili powder, oil, vinegar, cumin, salt, garlic powder and cayenne; drizzle over almonds, tossing to coat. Bake for 8 minutes, stirring halfway through.

Turn off oven; leave nuts in oven for 8 minutes. Let cool on pan on rack until crisp and dry; break pieces apart.

Makes about 3 cups (750 mL).

PER 1 TBSP (15 mL): about 50 cal, 2 g pro, 4 g total fat (trace sat. fat), 3 g carb, 1 g fibre, 0 mg chol, 28 mg sodium. % RDI: 2% calcium, 3%, iron, 1% vit A, 1% folate.

best tips:

• You'll need about ½ cup (125 mL) unpopped kernels to yield 10 cups (2.5 L) popped corn.

• You can store Caramel Corn in an airtight container for up to 1 week.

• If you're making Barbecue Roast Almonds ahead, store in an airtight container for up to 2 weeks. If almonds begin to soften, recrisp on baking sheet in 350°F (180°C) oven for about 5 minutes.

Quicky Quesadillas These fast, three-ingedient bites are sure to be popular because there are so many filling options to choose from.

4 large **tortillas** (10 inches/25 cm)
1 cup (250 mL) shredded Monterey Jack or Cheddar **cheese**
¼ cup (60 mL) chopped **pickled jalapeño peppers**

Lay each tortilla on work surface. Sprinkle ¼ cup (60 mL) of the cheese over half of each; top with one-quarter of the jalapeños. Fold uncovered half over filling.

Bake on greased rimmed baking sheet in 400°F (200°C) oven, turning once, until golden and cheese is melted, about 16 minutes. Cut each into 8 wedges.

Makes 32 pieces.

PER PIECE: about 37 cal, 2 g pro, 2 g total fat (1 g sat. fat), 4 g carb, trace fibre, 3 mg chol, 71 mg sodium. % RDI: 3% calcium, 2% iron, 1% vit A, 2% vit C, 1% folate.

VARIATIONS
Instead of (or in addition to) Monterey Jack or Cheddar cheese, try any of the following fillings.

Pesto Quesadillas: ¼ cup (60 mL) pesto or tapenade; and 1 cup (250 mL) crumbled goat cheese.

Mango Apple Quesadillas: ¼ cup (60 mL) mango chutney; 1 apple, thinly sliced; and 4 oz (125 g) Brie cheese, sliced.

Barbecue Chicken Quesadillas: ½ cup (125 mL) barbecue sauce; 1 cup (250 mL) chopped cooked chicken; and 1 cup (250 mL) shredded mozzarella cheese.

Spinach Quesadillas: 1 pkg (300 g) frozen spinach, thawed, squeezed dry and chopped; ¼ tsp (1 mL) dried dillweed; and ½ cup (125 mL) each shredded mozzarella and crumbled feta cheese.

Artichoke Prosciutto Quesadillas: 8 slices prosciutto or ham; 1 jar (6 oz/170 mL) marinated artichokes, drained and chopped; 1 cup (250 mL) shredded provolone cheese; and ¼ cup (60 mL) grated Parmesan cheese.

Creamy Rice Pudding

The hint of spice adds just the right amount of flavour to this ever-popular simple dessert. For added chew or crunch, sprinkle with raisins, dried cherries, chopped dried apricots or toasted sliced almonds. If you want to serve it cold, add ¼ cup (60 mL) more milk.

2 tbsp (30 mL) **butter**

½ cup (125 mL) **short-grain rice**

¼ tsp (1 mL) **ground cardamom** or cinnamon

¼ tsp (1 mL) **cinnamon**

2½ cups (625 mL) **milk**

2 tbsp (30 mL) **granulated sugar**

1 tsp (5 mL) grated **orange rind**

In small saucepan, melt butter over medium heat. Add rice, cardamom and cinnamon; stir to coat.

Stir in milk and sugar; bring to boil. Reduce heat, cover and simmer, stirring often, until most of the liquid is absorbed and rice is tender, about 25 minutes. Stir in orange rind. Serve warm.

Makes 4 servings.

PER SERVING: about 241 cal, 7 g pro, 9 g total fat (5 g sat. fat), 34 g carb, trace fibre, 30 mg chol, 135 mg sodium. % RDI: 17% calcium, 2% iron, 13% vit A, 2% vit C, 4% folate.

VARIATION
Coconut Rice Pudding: Reduce milk to ¾ cup (175 mL) and add 1 can (400 mL) coconut milk or light coconut milk. Sprinkle with toasted unsweetened desiccated coconut or chopped dried mango.

Easy Chocolate Cake

This all-purpose cake, made without butter or eggs, is so easy and moist that you'll make it again and again. It doesn't need a topping, but you can add your favourite icing, if you like, or dust with icing sugar.

3 cups (750 mL) **all-purpose flour**

2 cups (500 mL) **granulated sugar**

⅔ cup (150 mL) **cocoa powder**

2 tsp (10 mL) **baking soda**

½ tsp (2 mL) **salt**

2 cups (500 mL) cold brewed **coffee**

1 cup (250 mL) **vegetable oil**

2 tsp (10 mL) **vanilla**

3 tbsp (45 mL) **cider vinegar**

In large bowl, whisk together flour, sugar, cocoa powder, baking soda and salt. Whisk in coffee, oil and vanilla. Stir in vinegar.

Prepare pan(s) as directed below. Pour in batter; smooth top. Bake in 350°F (180°C) oven until cake tester inserted in centre comes out clean (see below for times).

Let cool for 10 to 20 minutes (see Best Tips, below). For sheet or layer cakes, invert onto rack and remove pan; peel off paper. For cupcakes, transfer to rack. Let cool completely.

Makes 12 to 16 servings.

PER EACH OF 16 SERVINGS: about 312 cal, 3 g pro, 14 g total fat (1 g sat. fat), 45 g carb, 2 g fibre, 0 mg chol, 231 mg sodium, 134 mg potassium. % RDI: 1% calcium, 12% iron, 22% folate.

One 13- x 9-inch (3.5 L) cake pan: Grease and line with parchment paper; bake for 30 to 35 minutes.

Two 8-inch (1.2 L) or 9-inch (1.5 L) round cake pans: Grease and line with parchment paper; bake for 20 to 25 minutes.

Two 8-inch (2 L) or 9-inch (2.5 L) square cake pans: Grease and line with parchment paper; bake for 20 to 25 minutes.

24 muffin cups for cupcakes: Grease or line with paper liners; bake for 18 to 20 minutes.

best tips:

• Set timer for 5 minutes less than the time in recipe. Check cake for signs of doneness (right). If it's not done, keep baking.

• A fully baked cake springs back when touched in the centre. It also draws away from the side of the pan, and a cake tester (a toothpick or skewer works well) inserted in the centre comes out clean. Also trust your sense of smell: the fresh aroma of butter and sugar wafting out of the oven can be the signal to check the cake.

Rum Butter Bananas and Ice Cream Vanilla is

always a hit, but try this topping over caramel or butterscotch ice cream or frozen yogurt for more flavour options.

¾ cup (175 mL) packed **brown sugar**

¼ cup (60 mL) **butter**

¼ cup (60 mL) **whipping cream**

2 tbsp (30 mL) **maple syrup**

2 large firm **bananas**

2 tbsp (30 mL) **amber rum,** or dark or spiced rum
   (or ½ tsp/2 mL rum extract)

3 cups (750 mL) **vanilla ice cream**

In heavy skillet, stir together sugar, butter, cream and maple syrup. Bring to boil over medium heat, stirring often until sugar is dissolved. Reduce heat and simmer for 1 minute.

Meanwhile, peel and cut bananas crosswise into thirds; cut each third lengthwise into quarters. Add to pan along with rum; stir until bananas are slightly softened, about 2 minutes. Serve over ice cream.

Makes 4 servings.

PER SERVING: about 604 cal, 5 g pro, 28 g total fat (17 g sat. fat), 86 g carb, 2 g fibre, 93 mg chol, 184 mg sodium, 619 mg potassium. % RDI: 17% calcium, 9% iron, 27% vit A, 8% vit C, 6% folate.

• When cakes emerge from the oven, their structure is set but still fragile. Let stand in pans on rack for 10 minutes (cupcakes and layer cakes) to 20 minutes (sheet cakes). Run knife around edge, then place rack over pan and invert cake onto rack. Peel off any paper. Let cool completely to firm up.

Mascarpone Berry Towers

Square Shanghai wonton wrappers, sometimes labelled large or white wonton wrappers, are available in the freezer or refrigerator sections of some large grocery stores and Asian food shops.

12 square **wonton wrappers** (about quarter 400 g pkg)

1 tbsp (15 mL) **butter,** melted

¼ cup (60 mL) **granulated sugar**

2 cups (500 mL) **fresh mixed berries,** or frozen mixed
   berries, thawed and undrained

2 tbsp (30 mL) **orange-flavoured liqueur** or orange juice

½ cup (125 mL) **whipping cream**

¼ cup (60 mL) **icing sugar**

½ tsp (2 mL) **vanilla**

½ cup (125 mL) **mascarpone cheese**

Arrange wonton wrappers in single layer on baking sheet. Brush with half of the butter; sprinkle with 1 tbsp (15 mL) of the granulated sugar. Turn and repeat. Bake in 350°F (180°C) oven, turning once, until crisp and golden, about 8 minutes. Transfer to rack; let cool.

Meanwhile, toss together berries, liqueur and remaining granulated sugar; let stand for 10 minutes.

Whip together cream, icing sugar and vanilla; fold into mascarpone in 2 additions.

For each serving, place scant 1 tsp (5 mL) cream mixture on centre of plate to secure tower. Place 1 wonton wrapper on cream mixture; top with about 1 tbsp (15 mL) cream mixture and heaping 1 tbsp (15 mL) berries. Repeat twice to make 3 layers.

Makes 4 servings.

PER SERVING: about 460 cal, 5 g pro, 28 g total fat (17 g sat. fat), 46 g carb, 3 g fibre, 91 mg chol, 186 mg sodium. % RDI: 6% calcium, 9% iron, 15% vit A, 27% vit C, 15% folate.

Chocolate Crispy Bars

These five-ingredient no-bake cookies are a snap. If you make them ahead, you can refrigerate them in an airtight container for up to 2 weeks or freeze for up to 1 month.

6 oz (175 g) **bittersweet chocolate,** chopped
⅓ cup (75 mL) **butter**
2½ cups (625 mL) **rice crisp cereal**
½ cup (125 mL) **salted roasted peanuts,** chopped
1 oz (30 g) **white chocolate,** melted

Line 9-inch (2.5 L) square cake pan with parchment paper.

In large heatproof bowl set over saucepan of hot (not boiling) water, melt bittersweet chocolate with butter; remove from heat.

Stir in cereal and half of the peanuts; press firmly into prepared pan. Press remaining peanuts firmly onto top. Drizzle with white chocolate.

Chill until barely firm, about 30 minutes. With serrated knife, cut into bars. Chill until hard; recut bars.

Makes 24 bars.

PER BAR: about 98 cal, 2 g pro, 7 g total fat (4 g sat. fat), 8 g carb, 1 g fibre, 8 mg chol, 73 mg sodium. % RDI: 1% calcium, 5% iron, 2% vit A, 3% folate.

Baked Apples With Dried Fruit
Serve these comforting, aromatic favourites with Maple Whipped Cream (below).

1 cup (250 mL) **apple cider**

¼ cup (60 mL) packed **brown sugar**

¼ tsp (1 mL) each **cinnamon** and **nutmeg**

1 tbsp (15 mL) **butter**

4 **baking apples** (such as Golden Delicious, Spartan or Idared)

½ cup (125 mL) mixed chopped **dried fruit** (such as apricots, figs, prunes, dates and/or whole raisins)

In small saucepan, bring cider, sugar, cinnamon and nutmeg to boil; stir in butter. Set aside.

Core each apple almost to bottom, leaving base intact. Pare off ¾-inch (2 cm) wide strip around core at top; trim base to level, if necessary.

Stuff dried fruit into each apple cavity. Place in 8-inch (2 L) square baking dish; pour cider mixture over top.

Cover and bake in 375°F (190°C) oven, basting twice, until tender, about 45 minutes. Uncover and bake until sauce is syrupy, about 20 minutes.

Makes 4 servings.

PER SERVING: about 220 cal, 1 g pro, 4 g total fat (2 g sat. fat), 51 g carb, 4 g fibre, 9 mg chol, 38 mg sodium. % RDI: 3% calcium, 9% iron, 4% vit A, 12% vit C, 1% folate.

Maple Whipped Cream: In bowl, whip ½ cup (125 mL) whipping cream with 2 tbsp (30 mL) maple syrup until soft peaks form; spoon onto apples.

Makes about ½ cup (125 mL).

best tips: Whipping cream whips best when it's cold. To make the fluffiest dollops, pour cream into a stainless-steel or copper bowl, then refrigerate it and the beaters for 10 to 20 minutes before whipping.

Canada's Best Carrot Cake With Cream Cheese Icing

This super-popular moist and tasty cake can be wrapped and refrigerated for up to 3 days, or wrapped and frozen for up to 1 month. Let thaw before icing.

2 cups (500 mL) **all-purpose flour**

2 tsp (10 mL) **baking powder**

2 tsp (10 mL) **cinnamon**

1 tsp (5 mL) **baking soda**

¾ tsp (4 mL) **salt**

½ tsp (2 mL) **nutmeg**

¾ cup (175 mL) **granulated sugar**

¾ cup (175 mL) packed **brown sugar**

3 **eggs**

¾ cup (175 mL) **vegetable oil**

1 tsp (5 mL) **vanilla**

2 cups (500 mL) grated **carrots**

1 can (14 oz/398 mL) **crushed pineapple,** drained

½ cup (125 mL) chopped **pecans**

ICING:

1 pkg (8 oz/250 g) **cream cheese,** softened

½ cup (125 mL) **butter,** softened

½ tsp (2 mL) **vanilla**

2 cups (500 mL) **icing sugar**

Grease and flour 13- x 9-inch (3.5 L) cake pan; set aside.

In large bowl, whisk together flour, baking powder, cinnamon, baking soda, salt and nutmeg. Beat together granulated and brown sugars, eggs, oil and vanilla until smooth; pour over flour mixture and stir just until moistened. Stir in carrots, pineapple and pecans. Spread in prepared pan.

Bake in 350°F (180°C) oven until cake tester inserted in centre comes out clean, about 40 minutes. Let cool in pan on rack for 20 minutes. Transfer to rack; let cool.

Icing: In bowl, beat cream cheese with butter until smooth; beat in vanilla. Beat in icing sugar, one-third at a time, until smooth. Spread over top of cake.

Makes 12 to 15 servings.

PER EACH OF 15 SERVINGS: about: 465 cal, 5 g pro, 27 g total fat (9 g sat. fat), 54 g carb, 2 g fibre, 72 mg chol, 357 mg sodium, 154 mg potassium. % RDI 6% calcium, 11% iron, 36% vit A, 2% vit C, 20% folate.

classic desserts

Crêpes Suzette

This classic French dessert needs only a garnish of orange segments. For ease, make the crêpes ahead and layer between waxed paper and wrap in plastic wrap; refrigerate for up to 3 days or freeze in airtight container for up to 1 month.

3 tbsp (45 mL) **granulated sugar**

2 tbsp (30 mL) **unsalted butter**

2 tsp (10 mL) grated **orange rind**

⅓ cup (75 mL) **orange juice**

3 tbsp (45 mL) **orange-flavoured liqueur**

CRÊPES:

½ cup (125 mL) **all-purpose flour**

¼ tsp (1 mL) **salt**

2 **eggs**

⅓ cup (75 mL) **milk**

⅓ cup (75 mL) **water** (approx)

2 tbsp (30 mL) **unsalted butter,** melted

Crêpes: In bowl, whisk flour with salt. Whisk together eggs, milk, water and 1 tbsp (15 mL) of the butter until slightly thickened, adding up to 2 tbsp (30 mL) more water if too thick. Pour over dry ingredients; whisk until smooth. Strain through fine sieve into clean bowl; cover and refrigerate for 1 hour. Stir before using.

Heat 8-inch (20 cm) crêpe pan or skillet over medium-low heat; brush lightly with some of the remaining butter. For each crêpe, pour scant ¼ cup (60 mL) batter into centre of pan, swirling to coat; pour out excess batter. Cook, turning once, until golden, about 2 minutes. Transfer to plate; round off edge of crêpe where batter was poured off.

In large skillet, melt sugar with butter over medium heat. Add orange rind and juice, and 1 tbsp (15 mL) of the orange liqueur; bring to boil. Reduce heat and simmer for 1 minute.

Add 1 crêpe to skillet, turning to coat. Using tongs, fold crêpe into quarters; move to side of skillet. Repeat with remaining crêpes, overlapping around edge of pan. Drizzle with remaining liqueur. Remove from heat and ignite pan. When flames subside, serve crêpes.

Makes 4 servings.

PER SERVING: about 290 cal, 6 g pro, 15 g total fat (8 g sat. fat), 30 g carb, 1 g fibre, 125 mg chol, 187 mg sodium. % RDI: 4% calcium, 8% iron, 15% vit A, 15% vit C, 22% folate.

best tips: Orange-flavoured liqueur options include Cointreau, Triple Sec and Grand Marnier. Or use brandy or cognac.

Chocolate Mousse

Demitasse cups or edible chocolate dessert cups hold just enough for a wonderful chocolate indulgence in a miniature format.

3 oz (90 g) **semisweet chocolate,** chopped
1 cup (250 mL) **whipping cream**
1 tsp (5 mL) **vanilla**

Place chocolate in large heatproof bowl. In saucepan, heat cream just until bubbles form around edge of pan. Pour over chocolate; whisk until smooth. Whisk in vanilla. Refrigerate until thickened and chilled, about 30 minutes.

Beat chocolate mixture until soft peaks form. Spoon into dessert dishes.

Makes 4 servings.

PER SERVING: about 297 cal, 2 g pro, 27 g total fat (17 g sat. fat), 15 g carb, 1 g fibre, 76 mg chol, 24 mg sodium. % RDI: 4% calcium, 5% iron, 19% vit A, 1% folate.

best tips:

Garnish each serving of mousse with fresh mint leaves, fresh berries, chopped toasted hazelnuts or peanuts, or dollops of whipped cream and chocolate shavings (or, during the festive season, crushed candy canes).

Butter Tart Squares

For a slightly thicker crust and filling layer, make these uniquely Canadian squares in an 8-inch (2 L) square cake pan.

1 cup (250 mL) **all-purpose flour**
¼ cup (60 mL) **granulated sugar**
½ cup (125 mL) **butter**

FILLING:
2 tbsp (30 mL) **butter,** melted
2 **eggs,** lightly beaten
1 cup (250 mL) packed **brown sugar**
2 tbsp (30 mL) **all-purpose flour**
½ tsp (2 mL) **baking powder**
½ tsp (2 mL) **vanilla**
Pinch **salt**
1 cup (250 mL) **raisins**
½ cup (125 mL) chopped **walnuts**

In bowl, mix flour with sugar; using pastry blender, cut in butter until crumbly. Press into 9-inch (2.5 L) square cake pan. Bake in 350°F (180°C) oven for 15 minutes.

Filling: In bowl, stir butter with eggs; stir in sugar, flour, baking powder, vanilla and salt. Stir in raisins and walnuts; pour over base.

Bake in 350°F (180°C) oven until top springs back when lightly touched, 20 to 25 minutes. Let cool in pan on rack. Cut into squares.

Makes 16 large squares.

PER SQUARE: about 221 cal, 3 g pro, 10 g total fat (5 g sat. fat), 31 g carb, 1 g fibre, 42 mg chol, 75 mg sodium, 151 mg potassium. % RDI: 3% calcium, 8% iron, 7% vit A, 12% folate.

Banana Buttermilk Cupcakes With Coconut Pecan Icing

Lighter in texture than banana bread, these cupcakes are a moist, tasty way to use up overly ripe, flavour-packed bananas.

½ cup (125 mL) **butter,** softened

¾ cup (175 mL) packed **brown sugar**

1 **egg**

¾ cup (175 mL) mashed ripe **banana**

1 tsp (5 mL) **vanilla**

1¼ cups (300 mL) **all-purpose flour**

½ tsp (2 mL) **baking powder**

½ tsp (2 mL) **baking soda**

¼ tsp (1 mL) **salt**

½ cup (125 mL) **buttermilk**

COCONUT PECAN ICING:

⅔ cup (150 mL) chopped **pecans**

⅔ cup (150 mL) **sweetened shredded coconut**

½ cup (125 mL) **granulated sugar**

½ cup (125 mL) **evaporated milk**

1 **egg yolk**

3 tbsp (45 mL) **butter**

½ tsp (2 mL) **vanilla**

In large bowl, beat butter with sugar until fluffy; beat in egg. Beat in banana and vanilla.

Whisk together flour, baking powder, baking soda and salt; stir into butter mixture alternately with buttermilk, making 3 additions of dry ingredients and 2 of buttermilk. Spoon into paper-lined or greased muffin cups.

Bake in 350°F (180°C) oven until cake tester inserted in centre comes out clean, 20 to 25 minutes. Transfer to rack; let cool.

Coconut Pecan Icing: Meanwhile, on separate baking sheets, toast pecans and coconut in 350°F (180°C) oven, stirring once, until golden, about 6 minutes for coconut, about 8 minutes for pecans. Transfer to same large bowl; let cool.

Meanwhile, in saucepan, whisk together sugar, milk and egg yolk; cook over medium heat, stirring constantly, until mixture is as thick as sweetened condensed milk, 8 to 10 minutes. Stir in butter and vanilla. Stir into pecan mixture until butter is melted. Let cool.

Spread icing over cupcakes.

Makes 12 cupcakes.

PER CUPCAKE: about 337 cal, 5 g pro, 19 g total fat (10 g sat. fat), 40 g carb, 2 g fibre, 65 mg chol, 229 mg sodium, 215 mg potassium. % RDI: 7% calcium, 10% iron, 11% vit A, 4% vit C, 16% folate.

best tips: Keep peeled ripe bananas in a resealable bag in the freezer; thaw and use in banana cakes, bread and other baked treats. Or blend from frozen for extra-frosty smoothies at any time.

Crispy Rice Pops

You'll need 24 lollipop sticks for these treats. For a bake sale, tie each with plastic wrap and secure with ribbon. These can also be made into 12 large pops.

¼ cup (60 mL) **butter**

1 bag (250 g) **mini-marshmallows** (about 6 cups/1.5 L)

1 tsp (5 mL) **vanilla**

6 cups (1.5 L) **rice crisp cereal** or puffed brown rice cereal

8 oz (250 g) **semisweet chocolate** or white chocolate, chopped

1 cup (250 mL) **candy sprinkles** or sweetened shredded coconut

In large saucepan, heat butter with marshmallows over medium heat, stirring, until melted, about 8 minutes. Stir in vanilla.

Stir in cereal until combined. Let cool enough to handle. Form into 24 balls. Push lollipop stick into each.

In heatproof bowl over saucepan of hot (not boiling) water, melt chocolate. Dip tops of cereal pops into chocolate; dip top of each pop into sprinkles. Refrigerate until set, about 30 minutes.

Makes 24 pops.

PER POP: about 155 cal, 1 g pro, 6 g total fat (3 g sat. fat), 27 g carb, trace fibre, 6 mg chol, 104 mg sodium. % RDI: 11% iron, 2% vit A, 2% folate.

best tips:

• If using coconut, you can tint it pretty colours: Place it in a resealable bag, add 2 or 3 drops desired food colouring, then seal bag and shake to distribute the colour.

• This sweet treat is simple, but it's worth splurging on great ingredients. Make sure you use good-quality chocolate for the best flavour and texture.

347

Most books require a large team of individuals to wrestle them from idea to finished product. But this book is a special case of collaboration between partners.

First, thanks go to the *Best Recipes Ever* team at CBC Television for their fresh take on *Canadian Living*'s extensive recipe collection. Thanks to Kary Osmond for her friendly, helpful presence, which reassures viewers that cooking is easy, fun and rewarding. Eternal gratitude goes to Kirstine Stewart, general manager of CBC Television, English services, and Julie Bristow, executive director of factual entertainment, who believed in the show from the very beginning. Kudos to Krista Look, executive producer, and Jennifer Dettman, executive in charge of production, factual entertainment, who head up the show and make it look so easy. The core behind-the-scenes team of Thérèse Attard, Portia Corman, Josie Malevich and Andrée Soulière, and the kitchen team, headed up by Flo Leung, are busy making magic long before (and long after) the cameras roll. Thanks also to Matthew Kimura, who snaps photos for the *Best Recipes Ever* website.

Next, thanks to the *Canadian Living* editorial team who pulled this book together. Project editor Tina Anson Mine coordinated the process from start to finish, and content editor Alison Kent gamely edited and wrote her way through reams of recipes. Content coordinator Pat Flynn dug through the archives to find all the copy and photos – always with a smile.

A round of grateful applause goes to art director Chris Bond for the cheerful, easy-to-navigate design of this book. Photography is a vital component of the design, and special thanks go to Jodi Pudge, who shot a series of photos especially for this project. Food stylist Lucie Richard and prop stylist Genevieve Wiseman worked with Jodi to make these mouth-watering images sing. Many other photographers and stylists also made their indelible mark on the book – for a complete list, see page 352.

The Canadian Living Test Kitchen team, past and present, deserves credit for the fabulous library of recipes they've created over the years. Currently, the kitchen features the talents of food director Annabelle Waugh, special publications food editor Alison Kent, senior food specialist Adell Shneer, and food specialists Soo Kim and Rheanna Kish. Thanks to all of them for creating accessible, tasty dishes that Canadians love to cook.

In the copy trenches, Austen Gilliland combed through every page of this book to make sure that all the t's were crossed and the i's were dotted. Indexer Gillian Watts created an index that makes it easy to find exactly what you're looking for. Thanks also to Info Access for the excellent (and sometimes split-second) delivery of nutrient analysis on every recipe.

Finally, big cheers to *Canadian Living* group publisher Lynn Chambers, Transcontinental Books publisher Jean Paré and *Canadian Living* editor-in-chief Susan Antonacci for their vision and guidance in making this book a reality. Thanks also to our friends at Random House Canada – especially Janet Joy Wilson, Duncan Shields and Adria Iwasutiak – for their encouragement on this project.

acknowledgments

Recipes

All recipes were developed by The Canadian Living Test Kitchen.

Photography

Michael Alberstat: pages 10, 64 and 122.

Hasnain Dattu: page 56.

Yvonne Duivenvoorden: pages 14, 18, 22, 24, 26, 30, 33, 34, 37, 38, 41, 42, 46, 60, 68, 76, 88, 92, 95, 104, 114, 118, 125, 126, 130, 134, 142, 152, 160, 164, 167, 168, 188, 198, 200, 206, 209, 214, 221, 222, 225, 230, 234, 238, 250, 263, 264, 272, 275, 278, 292, 310, 318, 320, 330 and 334.

Kevin Hewitt: pages 218 and 314.

Edward Pond: pages 100, 176, 184, 242, 246, 249, 276 and 302.

Jodi Pudge: pages 80, 84, 96, 110, 138, 146, 154, 172, 180, 192, 196, 210, 226, 254, 268, 280, 284, 288, 306, 316, 322, 326 and 338.

David Scott: pages 29, 50, 54, 72, 148, 150, 260, 298 and 300.

Stephen Sonne: page 4.

Food styling

Julie Aldis: pages 22, 26, 114, 142, 152, 225, 272 and 318.

Donna Bartolini: pages 34, 37, 56, 64, 130, 134, 198, 200, 214, 263, 310 and 320.

Carol Dudar: pages 10, 68 and 122.

Ruth Gangbar: page 218.

Lucie Richard: pages 24, 30, 33, 41, 42, 46, 50, 54, 72, 76, 80, 84, 88, 95, 96, 104, 110, 125, 138, 146, 148, 150, 154, 160, 172, 176, 180, 196, 210, 226, 230, 249, 254, 264, 268, 280, 284, 288, 292, 298, 300, 302, 306, 322, 326, 330, 334 and 338.

Claire Stancer: pages 92, 164, 188, 206, 209, 222, 234 and 250.

Claire Stubbs: pages 14, 29, 38, 60, 100, 118, 126, 167, 168, 184, 192, 221, 238, 242, 246, 275, 278 and 316.

Sandra Watson: pages 18 and 276.

Nicole Young: pages 260 and 314.

Prop styling

Laura Branson: pages 24, 104, 249, 302 and 334.

Catherine Doherty: pages 38, 92, 160, 188, 192 and 275.

Lynda Felton: page 316.

Marc-Philippe Gagné: pages 37, 221, 238 and 264.

Catherine MacFadyen: pages 34 and 292.

Lara McGraw: page 218.

Chareen Parsons: page 64.

Oksana Slavutych: pages 10, 14, 18, 22, 26, 29, 30, 33, 41, 42, 46, 50, 54, 56, 60, 68, 72, 76, 88, 95, 114, 118, 122, 125, 126, 130, 134, 142, 148, 150, 152, 164, 167, 168, 184, 198, 200, 206, 209, 214, 222, 225, 230, 234, 242, 246, 250, 260, 263, 272, 276, 278, 298, 300, 310, 318, 320 and 330.

Genevieve Wiseman: pages 80, 84, 96, 100, 110, 138, 146, 154, 172, 180, 196, 210, 226, 254, 268, 280, 284, 288, 306, 322, 326 and 338.

credits